MICHAEL PALIN
HIMALAYA

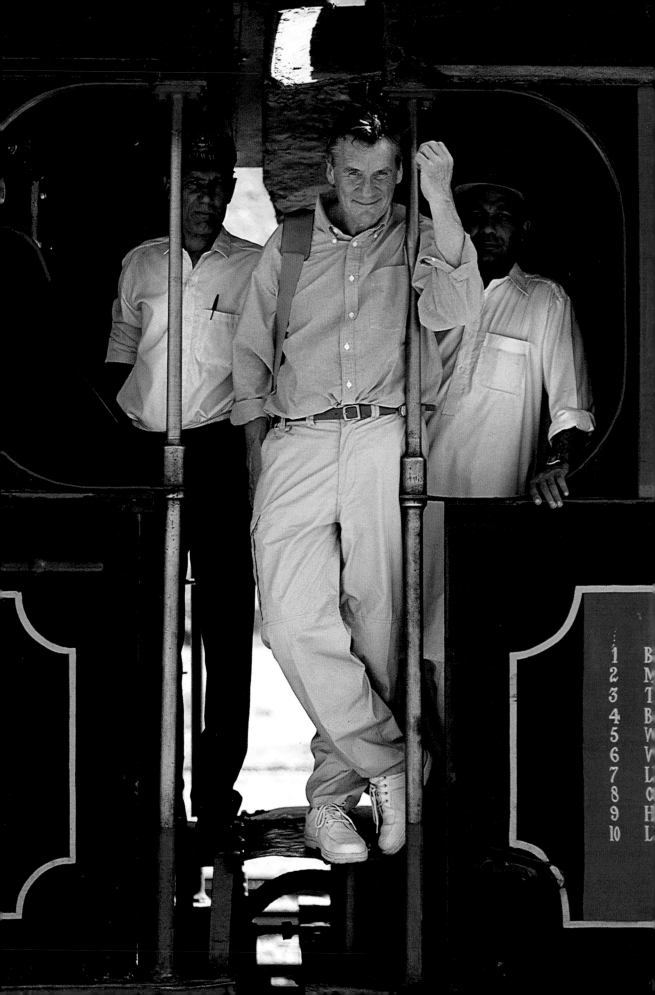

MICHAEL PALIN

HIMALAYA

PHOTOGRAPHS BY BASIL PAO

THOMAS DUNNE BOOKS
ST. MARTIN'S PRESS ♒ NEW YORK

Contents

Introduction

I'VE ALWAYS HAD a soft spot for my *Penguin Encyclopaedia of Places*. On a dull day when I should be talking to someone about tax returns I like to open it at random and set off a few quiet fantasies. Initial disappointment that you've opened it at Norwich and Nottingham can turn quickly to a frisson of excitement as, lower down the page, your eye alights on Noumea, Nova Lisboa and Novara, all places I'd leave for tomorrow if someone said I had to.

At the end of 2002, with *Sahara* still warm, as it were, Roger Mills came up with the idea of following it with a series on the Silk Route. When I looked at the map I saw an awful lot of desert along the way, and I was looking for something that would take me away from desert sands for a while. I was about to close the atlas regretfully when my eye drifted south and east to where the Silk Route becomes entangled with that long, white-tipped mass of mountains, hanging like a raised eyebrow above India, and connected by the single word: Himalaya.

Something began to tingle. I reached for the *Encyclopaedia of Places* and found the page I was looking for. '*Hillingdon*, Greater London Borough', '*Hinckley*, Urban District in Leicestershire' and there, snugly between the two, '*Himalaya*. In Sanskrit, "Abode Of Snow". Vast mountain system in central Asia lying along the S edge of the Plateau of Tibet, enclosed by the Indus and the Brahmaputra Rivers. It extends generally ESE in an immense curve about 1500 miles long.' There wasn't a word in that brief description that didn't thrill me, and by the time I shut the book I knew what the next two years were going to be about. (No, not Hillingdon in 12 one-hour episodes.)

What the Sahara is to desert, the Himalaya is to mountains. Both share the same contradictory attractions, appealing and appalling, tempting and terrifying in equal, and ultimately irresistible, measure.

By rights I should have followed up *Sahara* with something easier. Perhaps I should have taken more seriously our sound recordist John Pritchard's suggestion of a series called 'Death By Luxury'. But it's the mind as well as the body you have to look after, and that's where the Himalaya seemed to have the edge.

All the elements that appeal to me most about travel were on offer. The stimulus, mental and physical, of working at extremes, the breaking of new ground (I had never been to any of the places on our route), and the chance to go in by the back door, as it were, and see how lives are lived in a fascinatingly mixed bag of countries: superpowers of the future like India and China; countries like Pakistan, recently pushed to the centre of international politics; secretive, unconquered mountain kingdoms like Nepal and Bhutan; and remote lands on the margin of the world's consciousness like Nagaland and Ladakh.

The idea seemed to appeal to my team as instantly as it did to me, and setting aside advancing ages and hopes for quieter lives, we committed to a Himalayan journey at the beginning of 2003.

From the outset problems loomed as large as the mountains themselves. Pakistan was, though I'm glad to say no longer is, the subject of a Foreign Office advisory against all but essential travel. The whole Kashmir region was highly volatile, and the Maoists in Nepal were engaged in an increasingly threatening guerrilla war with the government. The Chinese were highly sensitive about allowing television crews into Tibet, and the Indian government was wary of our safety in Assam.

To their enormous credit, our production team soothed troubled brows successfully and we were able to leave for the Khyber Pass in May 2003.

There were crisis points, including a brush with the Maoists in Nepal, a nasty bout of illness halfway up Annapurna, and the loss, and subsequent recovery, of one of our crew to altitude sickness as we pushed up to Everest Base Camp. There were problems that could have been much worse, like the SARS epidemic in China, snowstorms in Bhutan and strikes in Bangladesh, but we were more or less intact by the time our tired little band emerged triumphant from a circuitous progress through six countries and 3000 miles of Himalaya at the beginning of April 2004.

The schedule was very tight, and I'm aware that these diaries are stronger on spontaneity than sober reflection.

What I feel we have achieved, none the less, is to put the Himalaya in a human perspective. We found people living at altitudes higher than the highest mountains in Europe; ancient civilizations surviving on arid, wind-scoured plateaux; gorges two and a half miles deep, through which traders have found their way for thousands of years and, everywhere, religion, vibrant and colourful, and thriving in adversity. In short, we found a Himalaya not reticent and forbidding, but permeated by every sort of human activity.

A battleground of immense geological forces that is a centre of human tectonics as well, with sacred and secular, tribal identity and national aspiration, tradition and technology, all pushing up against each other.

The scope of our journey means that this is not a mountaineer's account of the Himalaya, it's a traveller's account. This is Himalaya, not from top to bottom, but from one end to the other; from the Khyber Pass where in a tight knuckle of mountains the great ranges of the Hindu Kush, the Karakoram and the Himalaya are born, to Bangladesh, where the Himalaya, reduced to dust and sand, is swept out into the waters of the Bay of Bengal.

Great journeys tend to bring me out in a rash of over-used superlatives, so all I will say this time is that Himalaya was a wonderfully, magically, brilliant journey, with more gasps of astonishment per square mile than any other in my entire life. And for once, I think I might be right.

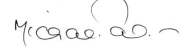

MICHAEL PALIN, LONDON, JUNE 2004.

A word about dates
We began our journey on 12 May 2003 and due to vagaries of the climate, timing of religious festivals and other key events like polo matches and Horse Fairs, returned to the region at various times before our final arrival home on 7 April 2004. We filmed for a total of six months. This account is based on notebooks and tape recordings kept at the time. Apart from missing out some rest days and days at airports, I've presented the journey as a continuous narrative, because that, in effect, is exactly what it was.

Postscript

SINCE I PUT these diaries together there have been significant changes in the region, mainly affecting India and Pakistan, and by and large hopeful. Even before the defeat of the BJP in the Indian elections in May 2004 cross-border relations with Pakistan had been improving, and both sides were pledged to a peaceful outcome in Kashmir, the most troubled area we went through. With the advent of India's first non-Hindu Prime Minister, Manmohan Singh, this process is expected to continue.

Indians are playing cricket in Pakistan again and the British Foreign Office has lifted its advice against non-essential travel to the country. On 22 May 2004 Pakistan was re-admitted to the Commonwealth after five years, a decision which India supported.

The day after that decision a bomb killed 33 people in Kashmir. Change clearly won't happen overnight, but there is cause for cautious optimism. Less so in Nepal where the Maoists and the government seem unable to sink their differences.

MP, JUNE 2004

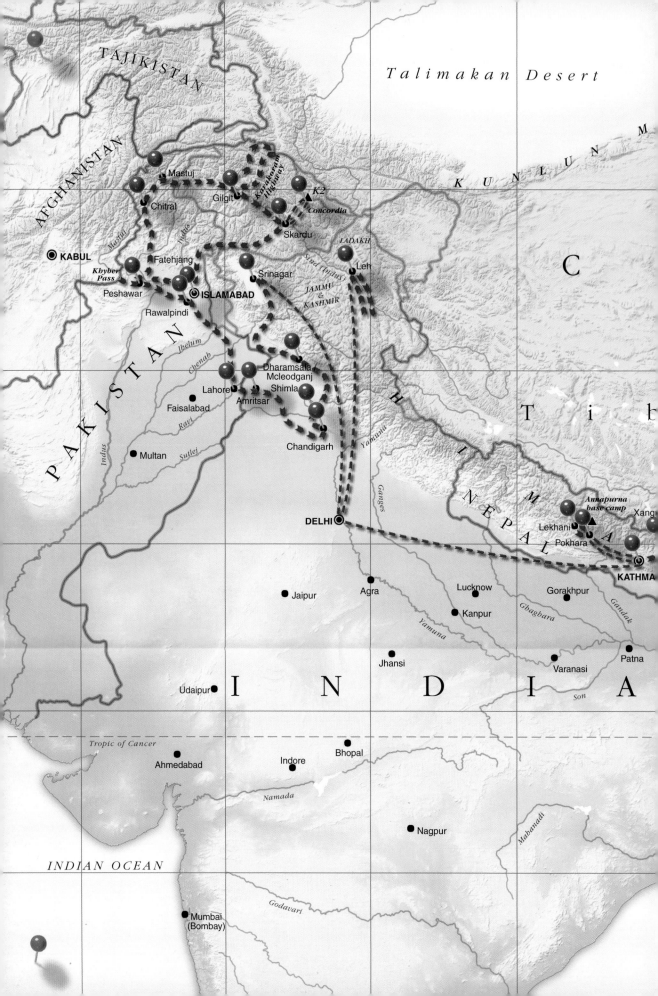

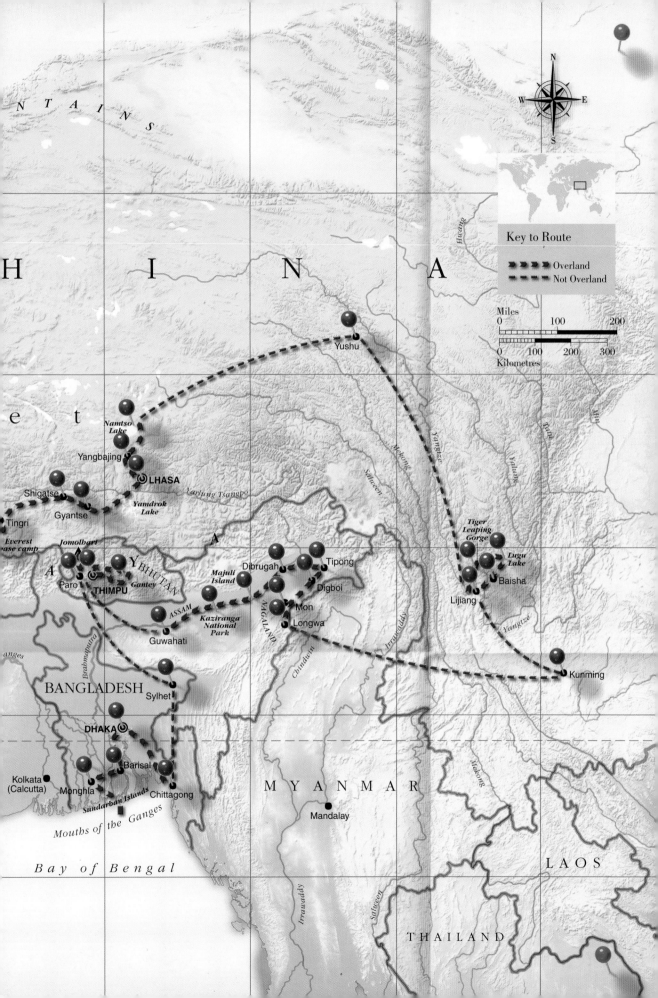

N T A I N S

H

I

N

A

Key to Route

Overland
Not Overland

Miles
0   100   200

0   100   200   300
Kilometres

Yushu

e   t

Namtso Lake

Yangbajing

◎LHASA

Yarlung Tsangpo

A

Shigatse

Gyantse

Yamdrok Lake

Tingri

Everest Base camp

Jomolhari

Y BHUTAN

Paro

THIMPU

Gantey

Majuli Island

Dibrugah

Tipong

Digboi

Kaziranga National Park

ASSAM

Mon

NAGALAND

Longwa

Tiger Leaping Gorge

Lugu Lake

Baisha

Lijiang

Guwahati

Chindwin

Irrawaddy

Yangtze

anges

Brahmaputra

BANGLADESH

Sylhet

Kunming

DHAKA◎

Barisal

Kolkata (Calcutta)

Monghla

Sundarban Islands

Chittagong

M Y A N M A R

Mekong

Mouths of the Ganges

Mandalay

Bay of Bengal

Irrawaddy

Salween

THAILAND

LAOS

Mekong

Huang

Yangtze

Yalung

Min

Yalong

Salween

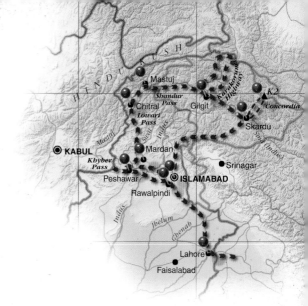

Pakistan

Day One : Up the Khyber

BELOW THE WALLS of the fort that guards the Khyber Pass there is a viewing platform on which rows of chairs are set out, facing Afghanistan, like circle seats at the theatre. They convey an air of expectation, of something about to happen, of a curtain about to rise on great events.

Casts of thousands have at one time or another filled the plains below, as greedy armies, seeking the great prize of India, gathered at this narrow western gateway. Darius I, King of Persia, led his soldiers through the Pass nearly 500 years before the birth of Christ. He was followed, nearly two centuries later, by Alexander the Great. Six hundred years ago I would have seen Tamburlaine's army, down from Samarkand, toiling up the hill towards me, and 400 years after that, the lone, exhausted figure of Army Surgeon Brydon bringing news of the annihilation of 17,000 of his colleagues who had set out to conquer Afghanistan for the British.

Despite the bloody nose of that terrible defeat in 1842, the British returned to Khyber almost 50 years later. Recognizing that the Afghans could not be subdued by war, they sought to keep them in their place by peaceful treaty. Having made a deal with Kabul, they instructed Algernon Durand to invent a border between Afghanistan and Queen Victoria's India.

To make things easier for everybody Durand marked the borderline with giant numerals engraved on the foothills, and they can still be seen on the Afghan side of the Pass. '1', '2', '3', '4'. The limits of the British Empire.

The Durand Line made no sense, then or now, to the Pathans who live on either side of it, nor does it appear to have made much sense to the generations of British squaddies sent to guard it, who accorded this bleak spot a memorable place in Cockney rhyming slang. Khyber Pass, Arse. (Khyber is locally pronounced with a soft 'K', so 'Carry On Up the Khyber' would, with Pashto inflection, become 'Harry On Up the Hyber'.)

But the Pakistan army of today takes the border very seriously, and they have provided an ambitious plaster model that mirrors the terrain ahead of me: the dark shadows of the mountains, the low brown hills, and the long and winding road that twists and turns between them.

'Such a river of life as nowhere else exists in the world', is how Kipling described the road that crosses the Khyber Pass. It was first laid nearly 500 years ago by the Mughal Emperor Sher Shah Suri to connect the extremes of his territory, Kabul in Afghanistan and Dacca in Bengal. In those

OPPOSITE

Sixty years on. Old vintage at the Murree Brewery, Rawalpindi.

RIGHT

*At the Khyber Pass.
The Grand Trunk
Road (to the right)
winds into
Afghanistan.*

days it was said that an unaccompanied woman could travel its 1500-mile (2400 km) length without fear or hindrance.

The British later paved it and christened it the Grand Trunk Road. Abbreviated to the colloquial 'GT Road', it remains to this day one of the most important transport arteries on the subcontinent.

Railways, rather than roads, were the status symbols of Britain's empire, and it was inevitable that there would eventually have to be a railway up to the Khyber. Construction began in the 1920s, amply fulfilling the criteria for a colonial railway, being both expensive and difficult to build.

At the cost of some £100,000 a mile, a line was squeezed for 27 miles through the rocky foothills between Peshawar and the Afghan border, an impressive burrowing job requiring 34 tunnels and 92 bridges and cuttings.

Though the last mile or two is now a spectacular no-man's land of abandoned viaducts and fallen arches, the line from Peshawar to Landi Khotal has been kept open for its tourist value.

Recent business has been badly hit by post 9/11 security scares and, for a while, the British Foreign Office was advising travellers not to come to Pakistan at all, so it's not surprising that Landi Khotal station is quiet as the breeze this morning as I wait for the train, which, I'm reliably informed, is the first to have left Peshawar for three months.

A group of teenage boys is fascinated by our presence. They form a circle around me, curious, unthreatening and very close.

'D'you live round here?' I ask their ringleader.

He replies in English with a toss of the head, confidently, if eccentrically.

'Why not?'

'D'you see many people from England here?'

'From England? Why not?'

I ask him if he's working.

'I have finished school. I have no job. There are no jobs here.'

'Have you brothers and sisters?'

'Why not?'

'How many?'

'We are 30 in our family.'

We're interrupted by a distant wheezing hiss and the whoop of a train whistle and as we turn, there, breasting the incline into the station, is a surreal snapshot of Empire.

Despite the silver-painted crescent moon and star of Islam on their noses, the breathless pair of geriatric locomotives that gasp to a halt beside me were built in Britain, in 1916. They draw two tankers of fuel and two coaches, from which descends a well-behaved group: workers from a bank in Islamabad, an imposing white-haired Welshman who is headmaster of an exclusive private school in Peshawar, prosperous-looking businessmen with cameras and binoculars and their unveiled wives. A band, immaculately turned out in plumed hats, tartan scarves and white gaiters, dismounts from the train. With a flourish of the bandmaster's silver-topped baton, the sound of drum and bagpipe mingles with the sighing of steam engines and the polite chatter of disembarked passengers. Only the presence of black-clad Pathan policemen with rifles spoils the powerful impression of having been transported back to an Edwardian house party.

A short, harassed man, carefully turned out in polo shirt and slacks, seeks me out and introduces himself as Zahoor Durrani, the man whose travel company keeps the Khyber Railway alive. He has organized today's outing. Included in the price of the ticket is a lunch and, there being no facilities of any kind at the station, Zahoor buses us to the Khyber Rifles Officers' Mess, where this normally arid landscape of rock and scree is cloaked with green lawns, rose-beds and ancient maple and walnut trees. A buffet lunch is served from a tent, after which we're entertained by military dancers in local costume. The dance seems a little camp at first, with much tossing of heads and raising of knees, when, quite suddenly, from among scarves and voluminous tunics the dancers produce rifles, which they loose off in time to the music. This, I'm assured, is how they celebrate in the Tribal Areas, and I'm just relieved that there are no US warplanes within range.

Back aboard the train, we pull out of Landi Khotal as the track cuts through successive outcrops of bare rock, amplifying the shriek of the bogies into ear-splitting howls. Then the walls of a longer gorge begin to close in, and the heat of the day and the stench of the furnace become almost unbearable.

We grind to a halt in one of the tunnels, trapped like bread in a toaster, and are only saved from suffocation at the very last minute, when the cow that was blocking the tunnel is persuaded to move.

The last miles of the journey are less fraught, a slow glide into the wide Vale of Peshawar, with time to indulge the voyeuristic pleasures of railway travel: surreptitious views over high walls into courtyards and back gardens, glimpses of life backstage, where mothers and wives prepare food and hang out the washing, and children carry bundles of wood and bring the cows and goats home. As the train passes it gives a look-at-me whistle. The animals run away from it, the children run towards it, and the women stare with a frank curiosity they'd never allow themselves if their men folk were about.

On the outskirts of Peshawar we pass one of the newest cities in Pakistan, the Kachi Gahi refugee camp, thought to be the largest in the world. It grew up in 1982 to deal with the displacement of Afghans after the Soviet invasion. Because the Afghans are great entrepreneurs, trade has thrived here and almost anything from guns to drugs to washing machines is available in Smuggler's Bazaar, the heart of this warren of sheds and shacks. Since the fall of the Taliban the trickle of overladen trucks returning to Afghanistan has become a flood, yet 1.5 million

refugees remain in this camp alone. And this is a fraction of the 18 million displaced people for whom Pakistan is their temporary home.

Zahoor Duranni tells me all this without any emotion, other than some quiet pride that his country has dealt with this enormous burden without complaint.

He gestures down towards the sprawling camp.

'We're all the same people.'

Day Two : Peshawar

It's 7.30 in the morning and the throng of humanity I saw at the refugee camps last night is reproduced on the streets of Peshawar. Beside the Grand Trunk Road is the Bala Hisar, a huge and sprawling pink brick fortress that seems to have squeezed civilian life into a crush of nearby side streets.

Zahoor tells me that most of the people here are small-farmers in town for the day to buy and sell. This is peasant capitalism, with no co-operatives or supermarket chains getting in the way as individuals set up stalls or simply open bundles of whatever they have, wherever they want.

There is a loose sort of organization. Chargan Mandi is the chicken market, Sabzi Mandi is the vegetable market and Chour Bazaar is basically Things Fallen Off The Back Of A Lorry market.

Zahoor advises us to remove all BBC stickers from our vehicles.

'Just to be safe,' he says, apologetically. There are plenty of Taliban sympathizers among these milling crowds, and with the highly unpopular Iraq war only recently over, our presence here in the conservative North-West Frontier Province makes us, though he never actually uses the word, targets. Hence our police escort and the armed guard deputed to stay by my side at all times.

I understand their concern, but emphasizing our separateness seems only to serve the purpose of those who want to keep people apart. It saddens me that extremists, on both sides, should have pre-empted the natural act of communication.

We drink some green tea at a smoky café with a dark and cheerful interior, and carry on regardless. There is so much to take in. The profusion of stuff. Mangoes from the Punjab piled up alongside bananas from Sind Province to the south, onions, squash, pears, peaches, a wheelbarrow of apricots being heaved through the crowd by a tiny old man, two young boys carrying nets to catch pigeons, which they will later sell. Beside a pick-up, a group of men are squatting down. One of them scoops up a half-dozen live chicks, stuffing them into a small cloth bag and pulling the drawstring tight. At a shop-front behind them a man sits cross-legged stirring rice and meat in a pan the size of a small pond.

There is a sudden flurry of movement. Traders pick up their wares and abandon their pitches, as, preceded by a lugubrious wail, a diesel locomotive looms up from nowhere, towering above the crowds and heading for the very heart of the market. At the very last minute, and with considerable reluctance, the throng parts to allow the nine o'clock to Karachi to continue its 1100-mile cross-country journey.

No sooner has the last coach rumbled through than the market reassembles, with little more than a vague irritation on the part of the traders that they should have to share *their* railway track with trains.

Peshawar, whose name means 'The Place at the Frontier', is the first big city on the Pakistan side of the Khyber Pass and was once encircled by a stout protective wall, with 16 gates to allow travellers and merchants through. One of the first places they gathered was Qissa Khwani Bazaar, which means Storyteller Street, for it was here that voyagers to and from the west would swap tales of the outside world.

Today, Storyteller Street has become Dental Alley. In between the photocopiers, money-changers and electric fan shops is a profusion of premises hung with painted signs depicting gleaming gnashers clamped tight between wholesomely pink gums.

I enter a tiny, hexagonal room at the base of one of the remaining stone towers of the Kabuli Gate. Most of the space is taken up by the impressive bulk of Abdul Wahid, proprietor of the Khyber Dentist Clinic.

Stone walls keep the clinic pleasantly cool, but it's impossible to keep out the roar of Peshawar's mighty traffic. An unbroken succession of private buses, turning out of the junction with Hospital Street, hoot furiously at each other while their conductors shout for business, yelling their destinations, selling tickets on the move and, when full, slapping the sides of their vehicles with cacophonous panache.

I've spent a lifetime in dental treatment of one kind or another, so I'm quite interested to see how Mr Wahid works. I squeeze into his chair, taking care not to dislodge the ominously placed green plastic bucket beside it. As I settle back I find myself staring at a wall decorated with a pair of dentures and a copy of the Koran.

The side walls are hung with various examples of gnasher-related art work: a collage of glamorous lady film stars with big toothy grins, a framed set of photos of drills at work in diseased mouths (fortunately in black and white) and a faded chart depicting 'The Four Steps Of Dental Decay'.

BELOW

Dental Alley, aka Qissa Khwani Bazaar, Peshawar. Abdul Wahid (far right) thinks the whole head might have to come off.

I avert my eyes, only to catch sight of an ancient rusty drill, standing to one side of the chair like a withered arm.

With fingers the size of small trees, Abdul Wahid stretches my mouth into a rictal grin and feels around inside, squeezing each tooth in a vice-like grip. He doesn't seem impressed by my Disneyland of caps and bridges, and suggests I give up using toothpaste and use powder and my finger instead.

His charges are reasonable: 100–300 rupees (£1–£3) for an extraction, fillings from as little as 50p and a full set of acrylic dentures from £15, though these look as though they may have been enjoyed by more than one previous owner.

If artistic self-expression has an outlet in Peshawar it seems to be in transport. Taxis, buses, auto-rickshaws and trucks are rampantly customized, bedecked with lurid colours, gleaming attachments, chrome strips, mirrors, glittering lights, prods, protuberances and general ornamentation that would have them instantly pulled over by the police in any Western city.

Zahoor takes me to a grimy yard on the outskirts of the city, where a half-dozen trucks are being beautified by teams of painters and mechanics, welders and artists, working side by side in Ruskinian harmony. They're assisted by a number of young boys, helping out fathers, uncles and cousins, and learning how to strip down gear-boxes long before their voices break.

Decoration is ubiquitous and uninhibited. No inch of the vehicle, apart from the windscreen and the tyres, remains unadorned. Everywhere else is covered in whatever the owner and artist agree on, from abstract shapes to animals, birds, flowers, vignettes of mountain scenery, roadside views, Koranic verses, names and Roman numerals.

A fringe of painted chains hangs down from the bumpers like beads on a flapper's dress. Multicoloured hubcaps protrude from the wheels, a combination of Damien Hirst and Boadicea.

We're offered tea in grubby enamel cups as one of the master painters begins work on the tailgate of a truck. A green base has already been applied (green being the colour of Islam) and he is now, with extraordinary speed and confidence, sketching the outline of a partridge, a bird held in high regard by the Pathans, who believe it has many powers including the exorcism of devils.

Less than an hour later the partridge is six feet high and standing proudly on top of a pile of stones in a romantic alpine landscape of lakes, snow-capped mountains, and houses set on tree-lined river banks, above which a name has been delicately picked out in Pashto. 'The Flower of Durband', a reference to the owner's home village.

The head and his team of seven take a week to decorate a truck from start to finish, for which they charge 15,000 rupees (£150).

By the time we get back to the hotel, exhausted but exhilarated by the intensity of life here, I'm ready for a beer at the Gulbar, about the only place in Peshawar where alcohol can legally be sold, to non-Muslims only of course. But the doors are firmly closed, bound together with adhesive tape. A sticker announces that the bar has been 'sealed off' until further notice, by order of the local authorities.

I learn later that this has nothing to do with hygiene or any trading malpractice. It's to do with moves by the MMA, the conservative Islamist majority in the local assembly, to introduce Sharia law on the North-West Frontier.

The Sharia law would not only ban alcohol for foreigners (hardly a nightmare) but close cinemas, ban non-religious music, forbid male doctors to examine women, forbid male tailors to make garments for women, and make failure to pray punishable by law.

Eat at the hotel's Chinese restaurant and, with only tea to linger over, am back in my room by nine. A small sticker is attached to the desktop in my bedroom. On it is an arrow indicating the direction of Mecca, and a card, which reads 'For Prayer Mat Dial 47'.

Day Three : South to Darra Adam Khel

Islam has been dominant in this part of the world since 711 AD, when Muhammad Bin Qasim of Damascus conquered the Indus valley, which had been Buddhist for hundreds of years. Islam was once at the forefront of cultural and political progress but now, it seems, up here on the North-West Frontier, it's being taken in the opposite direction.

Certainly the belligerence of the Iraq war and the incompetence of the peace has given the Islamists great new material as they pursue their goal of oppressive obedience.

The world is, fortunately, never clear and simple, and as we ride south to Darra Adam Khel, a town devoted almost entirely to the production of guns, I find myself confused by Zahoor's defence of such a place. Weapons, he says, have always been important to the proud, unconquered people who live on the North-West Frontier.

'For them,' he explains, 'a gun is a social necessity. Pathans carry guns the way Londoners carry umbrellas.'

What's more, he claims that the existence of and respect for the gun has reduced crime and kept order.

'Charlton Heston would be proud of them,' I suggest.

Zahoor nods seriously.

'He was in Peshawar.'

Why should I not be surprised that Charlton Heston was in Peshawar? The common ground is, of course, the West. The Wild West and the North-West Frontier have so much in common: proud, patriarchal societies with a marked dislike of outside interference, and strict moral codes of their own.

One of the twin pillars of Pathan tribal society is the concept of *melmastia* – hospitality.

Unfortunately, the other is *badal* – revenge – which can be swift and violent and provoked by as little as a glance at someone else's wife.

A few miles due south of Peshawar, we're halted at a barrier marking the transition between what are called the Settled Areas and the Tribal Areas. Beyond this our Peshawar police escort has no jurisdiction, so they are replaced by thinner, less well-equipped Tribal police who seem delighted to see us. We pull out behind them onto a busy road full of toiling over-loaded trucks heading south in the direction of Karachi.

In the fields veiled women bend in rows, cutting sheaves of corn, and beside the road schoolboys are playing cricket in their uniform blue *shalwar-kameez*, the combination of long shirt over loose baggy trousers that is Pakistan's national dress.

Darra High Street, described by Geoffrey Moorhouse as 'the noisiest street in the world', runs for almost a mile and is filled with the roar of horn-blaring, gear-changing trucks punctuated by the crackle of gun-fire.

You never quite know where the shots are coming from. As I cross the street a preoccupied figure in a white robe pops out of a shop behind me, raises an AK-47, blasts a few rounds into the air, shakes his head and disappears inside again to make adjustments.

Seeking relief from the din, I walk into a small arcade running at right angles off the main street. It is, to all intents and purposes, an arms mall, consisting of everything from workshops to carpeted rooms where you can select the weapon of your choice while taking tea with the management. In one establishment an earnest, bespectacled young man sits cross-legged, fashioning a trigger for a mini-Kalashnikov using pliers and a small hammer. Next door to him an older, bearded man scrutinizes a freshly made Mauser like a scholar bent over sacred texts.

The equipment may be low-tech but the standard of plagiarism is extremely high. Originally confined to making copies of the British Army's great standby, the Lee Enfield .303, Darra's retailers now offer brand-name pump-action rifles, revolvers, automatics and quite probably rocket-launchers. One man proudly shows me a James Bond pen that can fire real bullets (he proves this to me by stepping out into the street and loosing it off).

'Very popular with the tourists,' he assures me, adding regretfully, 'Until two years ago.'

Everything in Darra is faintly bizarre, so I'm not entirely surprised when, out of the corner of my eye, I spot an elderly man with a long white beard apparently climbing into a litter bin. Once inside he bobs down out of sight, and the crew think I've made the whole thing up until his face reappears over the top of the bin and, rearranging his robe, he steps out and proceeds on his way.

The grey, serrated steel tub that would in Britain be either a bin or a council flower bed turns out to be one of the smallest public lavatories I've ever seen. Barely three feet high, it sits astride a narrow concrete culvert along which water flows, though not, I notice, today.

A young man approaches and asks me where I'm from. Yesterday in Peshawar he would have been moved on pretty quickly, but today my police escort is nowhere to be seen. I later learn they're down the main street having their photo taken by Basil.

The young man speaks English well, but claims he's the exception. There is a lack of money for education and most men of his age have little option but to leave school early and go straight into the gun-making business. When he hears I'm from the BBC he is complimentary. Everyone listens to their Pashto service in the evenings. They are trusted, but less so after the Iraq war.

I bridle a little. Would he rather Saddam Hussein had remained in power?

He shakes his head vehemently. He hated Saddam Hussein. He hated him because he accepted American help to fight a fellow Islamic country, Iran.

I'm embarrassingly aware how much longer his memory is than mine.

Day Four : Fateh jang

We've already had to postpone our trip to see Prince Malik Ata. Mysterious objections from the government seem to centre around a security problem. Something vaguely to do with bombs and the military. As the Prince lives in the middle of agricultural countryside no-one can understand what all the fuss is about, least of all him.

After a volley of phone calls the objections have been withdrawn and he has promised to lay on a special welcome to make up for any inconvenience.

So we find ourselves heading east along the GT Road, crossing the great River Indus, which, along with the Tigris and Euphrates, nourished the first urban civilizations in the world. When Alexander the Great reached this point he ordered a half-mile bridge of boats to be built to carry his 50,000-strong army across. Today, much of the flow has been diverted for irrigation, but the sight of one of the world's great rivers rolling below the battlements of the old fort at Attock makes the heart beat a little faster.

Once off the Trunk Road we meander along country lanes. Brick kilns are the only signs of industry; otherwise it's quietly rural. At one point we pass a funeral. A small procession, led by a group of men dressed head to foot in white is carrying the body through the bush. They all appear to be hurrying.

The entrance to Prince Malik's country estate consists of modest cast-iron gates set between concrete posts. Once through them we follow a long, secretive track through acacia thickets, which, after almost half a mile, opens out onto a rather grand avenue of maples, beneath which a small crowd struggles to control a number of stocky, short-legged bulls wearing scarlet pom-pom hats and garlands round their necks. An open, four-wheeled carriage with a plumed and turbanned rider at the reins stands waiting behind two chestnut palominos. Fifteen elderly men in white *shalwars* and black-trimmed gold waistcoats are drawn to attention. One or two of them carry rifles. All are having orders barked at them by a figure in a brilliant white cotton *shalwar* and tight black sleeveless tunic sitting astride a black stallion. Beneath a bulbous turban, a

ABOVE

*Prince Malik and
friend prepare for a
traditional welcome.*

magnificently curled moustache dominates a fleshy face. A pair of watery, aristocratic eyes turns towards us.

'We must go soon, I cannot hold the bulls much longer.'

Roger steps down from the vehicle, exchanges greetings and begins to explain how he intends to shoot the sequence. But Malik Ata Muhammed Khan, Prince of the Awans, is not the slightest bit interested.

'You will put Michael in the coach over there!' he decides. 'Then I will tell them to begin the procession, and your camera will get a good shot from here.'

There is clearly no point in arguing, and I hurry back down the drive to the waiting carriage.

'Michael!' he bawls after me, 'Walk round the side! Those bulls are dangerous!'

As if to prove his point, one of them breaks free of its restraining rope, snorts, lowers its head and kicks out (maybe in protest at having to wear a scarlet pom-pom hat). Someone goes down.

'Right! Start now!'

It doesn't seem to matter that no-one really knows what they're doing. It all looks absurdly colourful and manically vibrant, like the opening scene of a musical. The bulls are led forward, the veteran guard of honour present whatever arms they can lay their hands on, and my two glorious palominos, who seem to be quietly giggling to each other throughout, set off at a canter that turns into an unstoppable gallop.

Cries of 'that's far enough!' fade into the distance as we hurtle through a set of grand gates, and up garden paths, eventually pulling to a halt at the front of a large white mansion with wide, presidential steps leading up to a towering columned portico.

I'm told it's modelled on the Royal Military College, Sandhurst, though it reminds me more of a plantation house in Louisiana.

Now that he's orchestrated the grand welcome the Prince is off his charger and visibly relaxed. He organizes drinks for us. Retainers (probably not the right word, but they behave exactly like retainers) carry trays of Pepsi Cola out into the garden. I suggest to him that a place of this size must be an awful burden to keep up.

'It is only one,' Prince Malik replies breezily, 'I have four others.'

I ask him about the episode with the bulls earlier.

'Was anyone hurt?'

'Yes,' he says, rather dismissively, as if it happened all the time. 'One old fellow had his arm broken. I've sent him to the hospital.'

The Prince calls forward one of the faithful fifteen who had mounted the guard of honour for my arrival.

'Here is a chap you must meet, Michael.'

A slightly stooped, handsome old man with lively eyes and a fine white beard steps out of the line.

'He fought in the First World War, you know. He's 104. He was a very big man.'

He turns a little towards me, lowering his voice.

'Much smaller now of course.'

The Prince seems to have a thing about height. He talks proudly of his great-grandfather, of whom he has a photograph taken at George V's coronation.

'He was a big man. Seven foot two.'

ABOVE

*Palatial hospitality at
Chateau Fatehjang.*

He has ordered lunch to be prepared for us. As we go inside he chides Vanessa about the problems we have had getting permission to come here.

'Always ask the army. It's the only discipline there is in this country. Did you not get my email?'

Vanessa shakes her head.

'Then your computer is wrong. Burn it.'

There seems to be almost too much space inside the house. Even without seeing any of the 28 bedrooms, I feel it in the dining room, with its high empty walls and giant table on which the eight places set out for us barely make an impression.

'D'you eat here even when you're on your own?' I ask the Prince.

'My father told me never to dine alone,' he replies briskly. 'If I have no-one to dine with, I go outside and find someone.'

At one end of the gloomy room, tall green electric fans are clustered together, heads bowed like dormant sunflowers. At the other, there is a marble mantelpiece on which is framed a front page of *The Times* with a photo of Prince Malik tent-pegging in Hyde Park.

'I was the champion tent-pegger in Pakistan. It is a very difficult thing to do you know.'

With some relish he describes the origins of the sport.

'When attacking a camp the first wave of horsemen would go in early in the morning and uproot the tent by its pegs, revealing the dazed occupants doing…' he pauses, 'whatever they might be doing. Then the next wave of slightly less skilful troops comes in and cuts off their heads.'

At this he rocks with laughter. A man in a turban, with all the aplomb of a *maître de vin*, tops

up my glass of Coca-Cola from a plastic bottle.

As the food is brought round Prince Malik enlarges on his life and reveals a keenly felt regret for the passing of the old ways. He is a countryman, not at all happy in the city. He loves country sports and rides at least twice a day for several hours.

'I am the last of the dinosaurs, who live like this. Who organize entertainments for the people. The new generation are only interested in becoming technocrats.'

More food issues forth from the Stygian gloom of the kitchen, ending up with a particularly delicious concoction of almond, egg and honey.

'The honey is off my land. It is very good. Have some more.' He pushes a bottle of Côtes du Rhône towards me. It's full of honey, not wine.

In the afternoon, despite the great heat, he insists that we visit the fort in Fatehjang. This is where the local *jerga*, or council of elders, meets. Recently they dealt with a vendetta that had gone on so long between two families that 13 had been killed on both sides. At the *jerga* they agreed that there would be no more killings, and, having forsworn further violence on the Holy Koran, the feud was declared to be at an end, with none of the murderers facing trial. Prince Malik shrugs.

'That is the way it works in the country.'

He insists that, if we are really interested in the rural life, we must come along as his guests to a bull-race in nearby Taxila tomorrow. Of course we can't say no. He wouldn't let us.

Day Five : Taxila

Taxila, at the axis of routes connecting Central Asia with Persia and the south, is one of the oldest continuously populated cities on earth. A university was thriving here 2500 years ago and remains of Buddhist temples, monasteries and stupas indicate its importance long before Islam or Christianity were born.

Following a narrow road through olive groves and fields of peanuts, we pull up a low hill until we reach an encampment where the animals are being unloaded from the back of trucks. Stalls selling food and soft drinks have been erected.

To get to the course means negotiating various ridges and ditches, behind, and sometimes alongside, swaying pairs of bulls, led out by owners and supporters to a relentless squealing of pipes and thumping of drums, each group trying to make more noise than their rivals.

There's such a squeeze that it's impossible to avoid bull contact. To my relief, they're smaller than the bulls I had a close encounter with in Pamplona. Of a breed called Dhanni, they have short legs, a distinctive fatty crest curling out from their shoulders and are mostly white with splodgy black markings that look as if someone has thrown a pot of paint at them. Today, each

one is turned out in their party best, their ferocity compromised by brightly coloured medallions and favours, ribbons and rosettes, gaudy horn-dressings and fluffy pom-poms. One wretched beast, with a tasselled, silver-trimmed, see-through muslin coat thrown over him, looks as if he's just stampeded through a lingerie department.

Ahead of the melee I can see the course, a wide stretch of open field, 600 yards long, marked by red flags on tall poles. Beside it and about halfway down the course a truck and trailer have been decked out with red chairs protected by a huge and ornate sun awning. Beneath it sits the unmistakable figure of the Prince.

He's in ebullient mood, which could be something to do with the presence of two tall, slim, European girls among his guests. He's already been out riding with them this morning.

With the racing about to begin, we ask if we can film up at the start, where a big crowd is milling around.

The Prince looks doubtful for a moment then barks an order and a man rushes over.

'He will go with you. He has a gun and speaks English.'

The bulls race in pairs, yoked together with heavy wooden frames called *joots*, from which the reins run back to a rider, who stands, as best he can, on a small board with a metal base, little more than a glorified tin-lid.

While dozens of people grapple to get the *joot* onto the two sets of shoulders, the bulls are kicking up the dust as they duck and weave and back up in a desperate attempt to avoid being involved in the racing in any way. Once harnessed, the animals are dragged unceremoniously to the starting line. Outriders heave them into position while the jockey, nervously clutching a flag on a stick, readies himself to spring onto the board the moment the bulls are released. This is where the race is won or lost. The bulls' desire to get away must be timed exactly with the attachment of the rider to his board. With luck the jockey retains his balance, and the bulls race off with the outriders running alongside to keep them in a straight line, before letting go, slapping the bulls' hides with a valedictory shout, and leaving the crouched figure to scud across the bumpy, uneven surface like a terrestrial water-skier, hanging on for dear life.

As if this isn't perilous enough, some enthusiastic teams throw firecrackers to 'panic' their bull into even greater speeds.

One team loses control at the start and the bulls make a 90-degree turn and plunge headfirst into the crowd. Two more hurtle off towards a flagpole that Basil has chosen as a photo-position, taking out the flag and almost Basil as well as they race off the course to the freedom of the fresh-cut wheat fields beyond.

Prince Malik says this only confirms that bulls aren't stupid. They know that their best interest lies in getting rid of their handlers as soon as possible, by any means possible. As he's explaining this a pair that seemed to be going well take an inexplicable left turn and head straight towards us. Nigel and Pete, filming with their backs to the course, are the last to notice. Grabbing

Bull-racing near Taxila. (from left) Going well; going badly; going the wrong way. At Prince Malik's travelling pavilion I meet an ex-jockey, on the left. The sport cost him an arm.

23

the camera and tripod they dive for cover as Prince Malik roars helpfully.

'Under the truck! Always under the truck!'

At the end of the day, as the racing is drawing to a close and the heat haze fades to reveal the low, reassuring contours of the Margalla Hills to the north, we're treated to a meal at a nearby village. It's laid out in suitably princely style, with dishes of tikkas and masalas in silver salvers on long tables and local specialities of partridge and quail.

'Now, quail racing,' the Prince enthuses, 'that is where the big money goes. You know, small fortunes are won or lost on quail races.'

As ever, I'm not entirely sure where fact and fiction merge in Prince Malik's stories, but before we can question him further, he shakes hands and apologizes that he must return to the course for the prize-giving.

'And those quails, Michael. They are not from a farm. They are shot in the forest.'

A countryman to the last.

Day Seven : Peshawar to the Kalash Valleys

It's a few minutes after five and just getting light as our convoy negotiates the suburbs of Peshawar. By the end of today, all being well, we should be off the plain and experiencing our first taste of big mountain scenery in the heart of the Hindu Kush range.

In the soft morning light pony and traps loaded with produce head for the city markets, boys cross a river on a gently undulating wooden bridge, a thin strip of black smoke drifts from a brick kiln, and in the fields figures are already at work bringing in the harvest.

We rumble across the wide and powerful waters of the River Kabul, swelled with snowmelt and curling back against the stanchions of a long steel bridge. It's joined in turn by the River Swat, creating a green and fertile plain, with fields of sugar cane and tobacco interspersed with orchards of plums, apricots and pears.

We pull off the road for something to eat at a hotel of very few stars but quite a lot of what the guides call charm. Beneath a wide verandah, tables with wonky legs are set out on a mud floor. Instead of chairs there are the ubiquitous charpoys, bedsteads with rope bases that are quite uncomfortable to sit on, but as soon as you pull your legs up and stretch out, make absolute sense.

Bleary staff appear from dark rooms and I realize that, although we've been on the road for more than two hours, it's still only half-past seven.

After a breakfast of bananas, hard-boiled eggs, green tea, fresh chapattis and malaria tablets I'm back in the jeep and climbing out of the plain and up to the Malakand Pass.

Here, on the endemically war-like North-West Frontier, almost any pass or prominence bears a fortification of some kind, ranging from fully-fledged fortresses to barricaded look-out points they call picquets or pickets. The best known of these is still called Churchill's Picket, where the great man, then a reporter for the *Daily Telegraph*, was holed up in 1897. A force of 1000 British and Sikh soldiers was defying an army of 10,000 Pathans, led by one Hajji Shaib Balee, whom the British press quickly, if predictably, christened the Mad Mullah. Young Winston sent back a blood-curdling account of the dangers they faced. 'Death by inches and hideous mutilation are the invariable measure of all who fall in battle into the hands of the Pathan tribesmen.'

I can hear him saying it.

The sun is well up now, but the roads badly kept and progress increasingly slow. My feeling of good fortune in being here at all is tempered by constant bumping and jarring and an enveloping cloud of dust and exhaust fumes from the vehicle in front.

Maqsood Ul-Mulk, who has organized our journey today, is a comfortably built man in his early forties with an amused air of quiet contentment, which may well come from being a member of the family who've ruled the Chitral Valley for several generations. He points across at the far bank of the River Panjkora, which runs beside us at a fast, muddy grey lick. The road is better over there, because it used to be a big poppy growing area. The central government, under a new policy headlined Poppy-Free Pakistan, offered new roads and houses if the locals agreed to change from opium to less controversial crops. They accepted the offer.

'What do they grow now?' I ask.

Maqsood gives the hint of a smile.

'Onions.'

A bad road becomes atrocious as we wind up to the 10,000-foot Lowari Pass. Closed by snow for six months of the year, this lifeline to the Chitral Valley has only just reopened and the soft-top track has wilted badly under the weight of over-loaded trucks struggling to restock the valley after the long winter.

The rapidly decomposing track climbs tortuously up above the snow line, slicing through sheer ice walls at the end of dirty brown glaciers, negotiating fast flowing streams of melt-water that tumble across the road before being flung into waterfalls below. The sun is blotted out by drifting grey clouds and hailstones scatter across the windscreen. With much blasting of horns and squeezing past trucks stalled on perilous precipices, we eventually obtain the top of the pass, marked by a small stone hut and a low wall of plastic-wrapped soft drinks.

Our drivers can't celebrate yet, for the road on the other side is even worse, a sheer plunge, which we ease down with the help of 47 sweaty-palmed hairpin bends. Tree trunks stripped bare by avalanche dot the route like tombstones.

Thirteen and a half hours after leaving Peshawar, we are down into the valley and gliding onto tarmacked road again.

By now it's dark and though it's frustratingly hard to see what's out there, I have a sense of being somewhere special. The stars are white as pearls and homes are lit by single lamps and the flicker of wood-fires.

A further three hours later one of the most spectacularly beautiful and consistently uncomfortable journeys I can remember draws to an end as we reach our home for the night, a plain and simple guesthouse above the tumbling waters of a young mountain river. And I was right. It is somewhere special. There are women without veils and wine to drink and villagers with clear blue eyes. This is a very unusual part of Pakistan.

Day Eight : The Kalash Valleys

All night long the river keeps up a light roar, which, in my semi-sleep, becomes transmogrified into the rumble of an ancient air-conditioner. Finally woken by sunlight as hard and bright as Excalibur, I take in the simple tongue and groove walls, flimsy curtains and bare floor of the cabin I'm sharing with Basil, and conclude that this is not air-con territory. Through the window I have my first glimpse of a narrow twisting valley and an extended village of stone-walled houses squeezed along it.

The village of Rumbur takes its name from the river that runs through it, one of a

number of steep and vigorous torrents cutting down through the mountains that separate the Chitral Valley from Afghanistan, chiselling out well-concealed canyons that have for centuries been the refuge of a tribe quite distinct from the rest of Pakistan. They have their own language, dress, customs and religion and because they are non-Muslim they have been historically known as Kafirs (Infidels), and this tight little land of theirs as Kafiristan.

Today they are better known as the Kalash ('black') after the colour of their clothes, despite the incidence of light skin, fair hair and blue eyes, which some say marks them out as descendants of Alexander the Great's soldiers.

Pale faces look curiously at us over the dry-stone wall that divides our compound from the lane outside. The fact that some of them are women is a great contrast with the rest of the North-West Frontier, where the rule of purdah is so strictly observed that no woman will look you in the face in public.

The Kalash ladies who peer so frankly at us, often dissolving into giggles at what they see, wear wide black dresses, tied with woollen scarves with multicoloured threads attached and strips of coloured ribbon on hems and cuffs. Their hair, which they never cut, is braided or plaited tight against the scalp and a long headdress, decorated with beads and cowrie shells, runs down from their crown to below their waist.

Saifullah Khan, a man of around 40 with grey threads in his thick dark hair and a face broad and olive-skinned as a Spanish farmer, is proprietor of the guesthouse and spokesman for the community. He's the only one of the Kalash to have received an education outside the village and after a breakfast of walnut bread he takes us on a walk around, pointing out this and that and constantly hitching up the pants of a grubby brown *shalwar-kameez* as he does so.

We're at 6500 feet (1980 m) and as the Kalash live in a largely pre-industrial state, with almost no modern gadgetry of any kind, the air is clear and fresh. Two small hydroelectric generators provide what electricity is needed; otherwise, life is entirely based around agriculture. The women till the fields in traditional costume while the men look after the

livestock. The houses, stout and stone-walled, are tiered up on top of each other to save space, with one person's roof another's front porch. They have neither gabled roofs nor chimneys and the smoke from the open fires has to find its way out of a hole in the ceiling.

It's picturesque and soothingly quiet, but as we walk through the village there are signs that all is not well. Children have runny noses and dirty faces, their clothes are grubby and their eyes often red and watery from the wood smoke that fills the houses. Faces show the effects of in-breeding and for each smile we get there will be another dull, dejected, vacant glance. Though Saifullah is proud and protective of his community, he can't disguise the problems. The Kalash, infidels, squeezed to the very edge of their country, are neither powerful nor numerous. Rumbur consists of 50 families, about 300 people, and the combined population of the Kalash villages is around 4000.

Their best hope of survival is tourism. Aware of the potential, the government has given them better roads and schools that teach Urdu and English, but of the money charged for permits to visit the Kalash valleys Saifullah reckons only five per cent finds its way through to the community.

In a stone hut with an irrigation channel running through it, an old man on his haunches watches barley being ground between two stones turned by the force of water. A few yards further on there is a handsome new suspension bridge that allows vehicles right up into the village. The road passes a long, low building with a high wall snaking around it. This is the menstruating hut. Kalash theology has very strong notions of purity and impurity. Menstruation is confirmation of women's impurity, and when their periods begin they must leave their homes and enter a communal house.

Mothers must give birth in the hut and remain there for 20 days afterwards. Only after undergoing a purification ceremony can they return home and rejoin village life.

We climb a hill above the village through glades of juniper and mulberry. Halfway up, I catch the sharp, sweet smell of something rotten. Ahead of me are small piles of wood and glass and I realize we're picking our way through a graveyard. Saifullah seems unconcerned as

OPPOSITE

Threading our way
through the Hindu
Kush. The rugged
route out of the Kalash
valleys.

he points out decomposing coffins on top of the ground. That's the Kalash way of death, he says. The bodies are never buried and the tops of the coffins are often left open to let the souls escape. I fear souls must have escaped quite recently.

At the top of the hill the modern world intrudes again in the shape of a long, open-sided building that looks like a bus shelter. This is another government perk, provided for the village as a permanent arena for the music and dancing for which the Kalash are renowned. Every year there is a music festival here that pulls in the tourists, many of whom come to see something unheard of in Pakistan: women dancing together in public. The emancipation of Kalash women has brought them the unwelcome attention of men from outside, seeking a sexual freedom denied to them in the rest of Pakistan.

Supper is very jolly. Saifullah's cooked some locally caught trout for us and produces a bottle of his home-brew, grape juice from last summer, which is still fermenting and tastes like fortified sherry.

Day Nine : To Chitral

Wake to the sound of water and the smell of wood-smoke. After a couple of nights here I no longer feel cut off from the world, but protected from it, and not particularly anxious to move away. I can understand why Saifullah values the isolation that has shaped and strengthened this tight-knit community, and why he loves visitors so long as they don't want to change anything.

As our jeep rolls over the bridge and down the hill, the Rumbur valley narrows behind us until the village and the thin strips of green fields that sustain it disappear altogether, and we find ourselves descending through a tight, treeless gorge onto whose steep sides the track hangs by its fingernails. Nadir Begh, my driver, anxious at the best of times, never unfurrows his brow. He's less concerned by the precipice below than the rock wall above. Recently descended loose grey shale lies scattered across the road and he peers up in the air, accelerating forward at the slightest trickle of dust.

We're all relieved as the valley widens and reveals a perspective of broad mountain slopes that lead the eye remorselessly upwards to the solitary bulk of Tirich Mir, 25,228 feet (7708 m), the highest mountain in the Hindu Kush and, I realize, the highest mountain I've ever seen.

As we near Chitral, orchards and tranquil stretches of woodland cluster beside the road. We pass groups of men shaking mulberries from the trees with long sticks, and a line of very small children coming out of school, all dressed in vivid green *shalwar-kameezes* and looking like a procession of parrots.

The Hindu Kush Heights Hotel is set on the side of a hill with a fine view the of the valley and Chitral town. Recently built, the emphasis is firmly on local design and craftsmanship at the expense of televisions and mini-bars. In the garden the heat smells of rosemary and jasmine.

The owners and creators of this remarkable hotel are both of that great Chitral dynasty, the Ul-Mulk family. Siraj, a man of my own age and a one-time Pakistan Airlines pilot, is one of several sons of the last ruler or Mehtar (Persian for prince) of Chitral. His father was married to Siraj's mother for 80 years.

'They were two and four when they got married.'

Clean-shaven and soft-spoken, and wearing a Western shirt and trousers, Siraj is pale

enough to pass for a suntanned Suffolk farmer, except for the flat, felt Pashtun cap, the *pakol*, which perches on top of the head in summer and rolls down for extra protection in the winter.

Though the Mehtar surrendered all his political powers to the Pakistani state in 1972, Siraj is still technically a prince and his wife Ghazala, with the piercing, dark eyes and intense good looks of the Pathan, a princess.

Three pet dogs help complete a sense of sharing a family house, rather than an impersonal hotel, and their guest book shows that they are by no means cut off up here in the valley. A framed photo shows the staff posing next to General Musharraf and on the wall by the door hangs a signed photo of thanks from Robert de Niro.

Ghazala is much amused that when De Niro came to stay, Siraj asked him what line of work he was in.

Despite their international clientele they observe the local custom. Ghazala, for instance, has elected to observe purdah and cannot walk into the town uncovered.

I join her and Siraj as they walk the dogs on the hillside behind the hotel. She enjoys this walk because she doesn't feel trapped by having to wear the veil. As we pick our way through artemisia scrub we talk about the two standards of behaviour. Though Pakistan's constitution makes no discrimination on grounds of gender, for traditional reasons most women choose to remain behind the veil. This cannot but result in some inequality, however self-inflicted, and it shows up in national literacy figures. For men literacy in Pakistan is around 60 per cent; for women, 35 per cent.

Chitral. With Siraj
Ul-Mulk at a madrassa
(a religious school) in
the mosque his
grandfather built.

Day Ten: Chitral

Chitral, a compact riverside town and centre of a close-knit valley community, has grown and prospered in recent years with the influx of Afghans, who came over the mountain passes during the Taliban years. Siraj reminds me that the border is less than 50 miles (80 km) to the west.

'You see, in winter we're cut off from the rest of Pakistan, but we're not cut off from Afghanistan.'

He's complimentary about the Afghan influence. They rejuvenated the sleepy town, bringing new cafés and restaurants, improving the choice of food in the shops, opening butchers, greengrocers, carpet-weaving and other businesses and generally demonstrating their talent as entrepreneurs. Now many of them are returning home and Chitral is once again reverting to its natural sleepiness.

There was a time, a hundred odd years ago, when it was the British who were the new arrivals in Chitral. Seeing Chitral's western passes as potentially vulnerable back doors through which the expansionist Russians might steal into their Indian empire, they installed a garrison at the fort. The Great Game, as the rivalry between the two 19th-century superpowers came to be known, saw one of its more dramatic moves played out in Chitral in 1895.

The Ul-Mulk family were at the centre of events. Siraj's great-grandfather Aman died in 1892 after a 35-year reign, instigating a vicious war of succession in which his various sons quarrelled with, plotted against and killed each other, until one decided his best hope of survival was to create a local alliance aimed at throwing the British out of their kingdom.

The siege of Chitral may not be as well known as those of Khartoum or Mafeking, but it was pretty heroic stuff, as the defenders, mainly Sikh troops under British officers, forced to eat their horses to survive, held out for 48 days before being relieved by a force of men, mules and cannons that had marched over the high passes of the Hindu Kush in the middle of winter.

The fort where the horse-eaters held out is still there, sitting low on a promontory round which the muddy grey river swirls. Its 25-foot-high, 240-foot-long walls still stand, but they look a little sad, with plaster cracked and fallen away, revealing the bare bones underneath. Groves of tall trees loom over the bedraggled ramparts and beneath them contented cows chomp their way through fields of wild cannabis.

Chitral's ageing fort is upstaged by its neighbour, an exuberantly decorated mosque in a central Asian style with onion domes and white stucco, paid for by Siraj's grandfather in the 1920s.

I ask him if it was common for ruling families to sponsor mosques.

He laughs.

'Well, I suppose, like in England, they wanted God on their side.'

The sound of chanting comes from a long, columned chamber off the courtyard. We step inside. Sixty young boys are learning the Koran by heart. They kneel before copies of the Book, rocking backwards and forwards on their haunches as they recite.

A mullah sits at a small table, peering myopically at a text as he listens to a boy sitting in front of him.

'These boys are being forced to learn the Koran in Arabic, a language quite foreign to them,' whispers Siraj, as we watch.

'It's like reading prayers in Latin.'

Many of the boys watch us back, clearly much more interested in what we're doing than what they're learning.

Repetition of the Koran, at the expense of other subjects like science and maths, has become the main discipline of these *madrassas*, religious schools, which have increased in number since the Taliban was thrown out of Afghanistan and fled across the border.

'It won't last,' says Siraj. 'They have nothing much to offer the people.'

Polo, on the other hand, seems to have a lot to offer. Chitral's polo ground is a long, green rectangle behind the Mountain Inn, sloping up quite markedly at both ends.

An early evening training game is in progress, and even this draws a crowd of several hundred. As Siraj explains:

'Over here you don't have to be a rich man to play polo. You could be the most important person in Chitral, but if you happen to be playing on the field here you could be written off by your barber or your shoemaker.'

Polo thrived here on the border country after being introduced from Persia, and was known to be played on occasions with enemies' heads and sheep carcasses.

Unlike the international game, invented by the British, which is broken into seven-minute segments, at the end of which horses can be substituted, they play what they call 'free-style' polo, with no referee and no rules. Each chukka lasts 25 minutes, with no change of horses, unless one is injured.

At half-time, Siraj introduces me to the captain of the Chitral team, his brother Sikander, ten years his junior. He's hot and sweating after a first half in which he's been evaluating his new horse, Bucephalus. (Another example of the resonance of Alexander the Great, Sikander being a derivation of Alexander, whose favourite horse was Bucephalus.)

This is one of the last trial games before selection of the team to take on arch-rivals Gilgit in the biggest free-style polo match in the world.

ABOVE

A boy recites the Koran, which he must learn by heart.

It's to be played on the top of the 12,000-foot (3660 m) Shandur Pass, the highest point of the mountain road that connects the two competing communities. At least 5000 Chitral fans will make the journey up to the pass to support their team.

Sikander grins broadly, and grips my hand in a firm Ul-Mulk handshake.

'See you there!'

Day Twelve : Chitral

Therapeutic recovery time at Hindu Kush Heights. The food is good and varied here, cooked with a light touch and the emphasis on home-grown vegetables and treats like mushrooms off the mountains, quite a relief from the heavy curries of Peshawar. The scenery is magnificent without being overpowering, mountains with a human face, and our last night in Chitral is to be marked by a visit to a *baipash*, an old Chitrali house where local music and dancing will be laid on. My heart sinks as the dreaded spectre of a 'folklorique' evening looms. Siraj is enthusiastic, though, and describes what we shall see and hear as the last of its kind, a style of music and poetry that is 'locked in the mountains'.

We drive out, crossing the river over a sturdy suspension bridge built by the British in the 1920s at the personal request of Siraj's grandfather. He'd been so excited by hearing of the invention of the car that he ordered a fleet of Baby Austins to be delivered to him in Chitral, without realizing that cars couldn't cross rivers. The bridge was obligingly completed by sappers from the garrison in two months.

His grandfather's ignorance of cars sounds pretty comprehensive. Apparently, when the tyres wore out, he just sold the cars. A lucky dealer from Karachi bought the whole lot, changed the tyres and sold the fleet in mint condition.

The *baipash* is a carefully preserved 300-year-old house, approached through a large garden with tall and immaculate dry-stone walls, reinforced with horizontal timbers to protect against earthquakes. The layout inside is the traditional single chamber with a central hearth and opening in the roof above for smoke to escape. Around the walls are darkened wooden stalls where cattle would once have been kept. The columns that support the roof are also wooden and carved with plant and flower motifs. It's dark, stuffy, cosy and presided over by a tall, gaunt man with white beard and thick, sprouting eyebrows. With a strong and piercing gaze, he reminds me of a manic Scots preacher.

He's 77 years old, with a wicked sense of humour. At some length, he expounds on the abundance of hallucinatory substances in the sylvan glades of Chitral.

'Did you ever try any of these drugs?' I ask him.

He shakes his head.

'Oh no. But I've been smoking hash for 40 years.'

Once the music begins I can't take my eyes off him. Like the venerable leader of a jazz band, he's at the very heart of the action, sometimes plucking skilfully at a sitar, sometimes singing, but always urging others on, holding out long thin arms and flicking his bony wrists in time to the beat of sitars, tambourines and a pink jerrycan that does for percussion.

The pattern is the same each time. The music starts slowly, then one of the audience gets up and begins to move with delicate shuffles of the feet and upraised arms, gradually becoming more animated. As the tempo of the music accelerates, so does the speed and intensity of the movement, until both merge into a stomping, exultant crescendo, which leaves everyone exhausted, ecstatic and applauding wildly.

There is a sense of real joy as the music and dancing goes on. The songs and the style of playing are improvisations on music that has been part of this isolated culture for centuries. Once small groups like these forget, it may disappear altogether.

Which explains the intensity of Siraj's pleasure as he listens, his description of the songs and the music as being 'locked in the mountains', and the infectious magical warmth that banishes my worst memories of things folklorique.

Day Thirteen: Chitral to Mastuj

On the road again. I have a different jeep, and a different driver. Raza Khan is younger and less earnest than Nadir Begh. Whereas Nadir used to comb his hair every time we did a shot, even if we were a tiny speck on a mountain panorama, Raza is a little more relaxed and wears a baseball cap, reversed. He's a Chitrali and everyone we meet on the road seems to be either an intimate friend of his or a member of his family.

Long before they were Chitralis, the inhabitants of these mountain areas were collectively known as the Kho, and I've acquired a modest, locally printed guide book that has a glossary of words in the language they still speak here, known as Khowar. It's pleasingly phonetic and in between gasping with awe at the scenery I try out a few words on Raza. Father is *tut*, mother is *nun*, grandfather is *bap*, grandmother is *wow* and foot is *pong*. This is the sort of language I like.

There is a page of Miscellaneous Phrases, which is short but has an interesting theme. 'Have you a wife?', 'Do you love your wife?' 'Is it late?', 'At what time shall we start?', 'Well done', 'Thank You', 'Don't go naked', 'There is a pain in my leg' and 'When will you come back?' It conjures up images of a lusty life in the mountains.

We climb slowly up the valley, the river rushing past us at great speed, huffing and puffing and occasionally leaping ostentatiously into the air as if trying to attract our attention.

As the road deteriorates the mountains grow more spectacular and quite suddenly we turn onto a flat saddle of land to be confronted by the dazzling white bulk of a massif called Buni Zum, 21,000 feet (6400 m) high, trailing glaciers and massive hanging slabs of snow. It provides a backdrop for a huge cricket match being played among the rocks, with dozens of boys fielding over a vast area.

We spend the night in the grounds of a crumbling, but still dignified fort, which commands the confluence of two rivers at the town of Mastuj. Another Ul-Mulk family house, given to them by the British in 1913 as thanks for their loyalty, it's currently run by Siraj's father Khushwaqt, a dapper, bright-eyed man who has just celebrated his 90th birthday, and who everyone knows as the Colonel. Hoping to attract tourists, they have built some handsome wood cabins around the perimeter of a luxurious greensward beside the fort, the sort of flat open ground where you can imagine tournaments taking place. Unfortunately, the builders have done a runner and all that's working are the bathroom fittings. So we sleep outside in tents and clamber into the empty buildings for a shower. Very odd.

I'm kept from deep sleep by an unlikely combination of cold wind and apricots. The window panel flaps of my tent don't zip up and the night breeze freshens to a chilly blow that provokes a gentle deluge of apricots dropping off the trees, bouncing onto the tin roofs of the unfinished chalets, rolling down the corrugated iron in interesting ways and plopping onto the roof of my tent.

FOLLOWING PAGES
On the way from Chitral to the Shandur Pass. Pakistan is cricket mad, even at 10,000 feet (3050 m). Buni Zum, 21,000 feet (6400 m) dominates the background.

RIGHT

Walking with the Colonel. Khushwaqt, grand old man of the Ul-Mulk dynasty, at Mastuj Fort.

Day Fifteen : From Mastuj Fort to the Shandur Pass

Three hours of dogged mountain driving out of Mastuj, our convoy is climbing out of the last cultivated valley, which now lies far below us, tucked into the massive rubble-strewn flanks of mountainside like a fig leaf on a grey marble statue. With a last heave of the gears we push through 12,000 feet (3650 m) and soon level out onto a grassy plateau with a blue lake spread along its length and saw-tooth mountains surrounding it. We've reached the Shandur Pass, the watershed between the valleys of Chitral in the Hindu Kush and Gilgit in the Karakoram.

Although the three-day festival doesn't begin till tomorrow, this normally desolate and lonely place is beginning to resemble a small town. Vehicles raise clouds of dust as they arrive on the plateau laden with people, food, bedding and tents. As many as 10,000 are expected for the big polo game and shops and businesses from the surrounding villages have moved up here to supply them.

Cafés are opening, offering the obligatory karaoke, stalls are selling rugs and blankets, generators are coughing into life, and special prayer areas are being marked out with stones.

A yak has just been slaughtered at an improvised butcher's shop, its throat cut with a foot-long curved knife. The severed head lies in a nearby stream, creamy-white innards spread out on a boulder. Customers are already queuing up to buy the cuts of meat, hanging from a horizontal wooden pole, a washing-line of flesh.

Our accommodation is in a small encampment conveniently close to the polo ground and next door to the Chitral team quarters, where I meet up again with Sikander Ul-Mulk.

The word is not good. One of the best horses they have has been hurt in training and another is lame after being hit by a ball in a practice game. News from the Gilgit team is of ominous confidence.

It might be something to do with altitude but by ten o'clock I'm blissfully tired and ready for bed. No sooner have I wriggled into the foetal warmth of my sleeping bag than the whole site explodes with noise. A thumping of drums, a squeaking of pipes, clapping, cheering and general encouragement fills the night air. When the party ends I'm aware of how bitterly cold it is. As the

LEFT

No lie-in when the band's around. Early morning music heralds the start of the Polo Festival at the Shandur Pass.

night goes on my tent seems to attract an icy chill and I have a short but powerful nightmare based on the scene in *The Long Good Friday* where recalcitrant gang members are strung from hooks in a cold store.

Day Sixteen : The Shandur Pass

A beautiful morning. The clear skies that made the night so cold are china blue and an unblinking sun shines down, mocking my night's misery.

There are three big polo games over the next three days. The two villages nearest the pass, Laspur on the Chitral side and Ghiza on the Gilgit side, play each other today. Tomorrow is the turn of the Chitral and Gilgit 'B' teams, and the final day is the big match between the 'A' sides.

The Laspur team is camped, modestly, a mile or so back towards the pass. With only an hour to go before the game, supporters are still arriving, many of them walking up the long steep road from the village. Before they leave for the ground each player seeks the blessing of the elders of the village. Meanwhile, their supporters sit around listening to music. Various men (there are no women to be seen) are moved to dance. One of them moves particularly gracefully. My guide whispers in my ear.

'He is Taliban.'

During a break in the dancing there is an address from a man in a dirty *shalwar-kameez*, with a stick, a pack and leathery, sun-scorched features. Whether he intends to look like the classic yokel or not I don't know, but it's clear from the way the audience listens that he is a star, and a comedy star at that. My guide tries to translate but the laughs come so thick and fast that he has trouble keeping up.

It's all good anti-government stuff. According to my guide, it's a popular grouse on both sides of the Pass that the government praises the spirit of the mountain communities but fails to put any money their way.

Like any good comedian his eyes flick round the audience, and pretty soon alight on me. To gales of laughter he tells me that his people pray constantly for the restoration of British rule and he asks me to tell the Queen that if she gives them each a thousand rupees she can have their village back.

Meanwhile, the players are emerging from a team talk and are getting ready to mount their horses. In their red jerseys, white *pakol* hats, red knee pads and black boots they stand out like mediaeval knights among the rough and ready dress of the villagers. The captain, a wiry middle-aged man wearing dark glasses, caresses his horse's head and talks soothingly into its ear.

A fiercely fought game sees Laspur coming in to win an 8-7 victory. The crowd pour onto the pitch and no-one tries to stop them. The quiet, rather studious figure I saw whispering soothing confidences to his horse two hours ago is the hero of the day, flung up onto the shoulders of rapturous supporters. First blood to the Chitral Valley. Hopefully, it will be a good omen.

Day Seventeen : The Shandur Pass

I've acquired a thick Chinese blanket from the temporary shopping mall up here on the Pass and though my tent remains an ice-box, I actually slept last night, after an unpromising start when I was kept awake, not by drums and pipes but by someone being very funny near my tent. I couldn't tell whether it was Urdu or Pashto they were speaking, but it didn't really matter. His total control of the audience was wonderfully infectious and I lay curled up in my many layers of thermals, shirts, sweaters and fleeces, giggling away, without understanding a word.

More people have arrived overnight and our encampment is now part of a growing community. Figures are scattered among the grassy boulders, cleaning teeth, scrubbing feet and washing faces in bowls of water heated on a brushwood fire, which Maboub, who is in charge of these matters, has to keep continually tended, as thinner air at this height make things harder to burn. In the kitchen tent, where a violent gas fire looks like an accident waiting to happen, Zahoor, the chef, produces scrambled eggs, fried potatoes and even porridge for our breakfast.

At the far end of the valley, away from the hustle and bustle of the ever-expanding encampment, the 'A' teams are out beside the lake practising shots, gallops, passes and tight-reined turns. Both sides exercise together in the cool of early morning, then return to their separate camps.

Gilgit's team is drawn entirely from the ranks of police and army. They're well-drilled, organized, efficient but institutional. Their captain, Bulbul Jan, is a tall middle-aged man with neat, short hair and the modest, kindly manner of an avuncular schoolmaster. Hard to believe as he talks softly to us that he is one half of the most successful combination in free-style polo. The other is his tall, black Punjabi stallion, Truc.

Bulbul is 55 and his horse is 21. Together they have played in 15 of these matches and have led Gilgit to victory for the last two years, proving that despite the Herculean efforts required of them up here on the plateau, guile and experience still count as much as youth and strength. Bulbul claims that Truc can tell him, within 24 hours of a game, just how things will work out.

'So what about your chances tomorrow?'

Truc bares his teeth and rears his head away, clearly impatient to end the interview.

'Truc is in a very good mood,' pronounces Bulbul Jan.

Chitral come across as the gentlemen amateurs, with an altogether more happy-go-lucky approach to their polo, but the mood at the camp today is subdued. Gilgit won the 'B' game this morning, though one of their horses collapsed and died of a heart attack at the end of the first chukka. Neither side wants this to happen, and Sikander admits that this is only one of several such deaths over the last few years, grim reminders of the demands of such a physical game at such a high altitude.

He concedes that Gilgit's 'A' team are the favourites. They are unchanged from last year, and unlike Chitral's series of misfortunes, have had no casualties among their horses. I ask about the rumours I've heard about black magic and spells being put on the teams.

He shrugs.

'I never used to believe it, but now since everyone does, I've also started believing it.'

'You think it's more than just coincidence?'

He nods.

'More, yes, more than coincidence.'

He thinks the only possible advantage for Chitral is that they have Afghan horses, tough and strong after apprenticeships carrying men and goods over the high border passes.

I ask what it will be like if they should lose tomorrow.

'Terrible. Terrible.'

He laughs, a little desperately.

'We try to go back in the dark. We pack up, get ready and leave at night.'

'Do they forgive quickly in Chitral?'

Sikander Ul-Mulk pauses, then shakes his head philosophically.

'It takes about a month or two.'

Day Eighteen: The Shandur Pass

The weather is perfect.

A crowd, estimated at around 15,000, has gathered at the ground well in advance of the game. Apart from a VIP area on top of the main stand, the accommodation is basic, ranging from purpose-built concrete terraces to standing room on the various low mounds of glacial debris that enclose the playing area. One of these, with perhaps the least good view, is reserved for women.

The six players of each side parade onto the pitch, Chitral in scarlet, Gilgit in blue and white. Protection is optional. None of the Gilgit side wears protective headgear, whereas three of the Chitralis have helmets and one wears a *pakul*.

I'm squeezed into one of the terraces. There are no seats and we just settle ourselves as best we can on mud and stones. My eyes meet those of a policeman with riot helmet, night stick and dark glasses, sitting at the end of our row. He pulls on a cigarette and turns away. Above us is a line of brightly coloured kites, strung together, stretching right across the ground. (I later learn that there are 105 of them, thus winning, for a Doctor Ejazul Haq of Islamabad, the world record for the number of kites 'aired on a single thread'.)

Silence falls as a prayer is read out from the Koran. The horses canter forwards to the centre-line to receive the ball. Bulbul Jan, bareheaded, looks every bit the midfield general, effortlessly in control at the centre of his team. Truc, less effortlessly in control, is the first to fertilize the pitch.

I don't blame him. If I was facing 50 minutes of constant running, sudden sprints, balls flying about and full-speed charges towards two-foot-high stone walls, I'd have probably done the same. In free-style polo the player is as much fair game as the ball and deliberate obstruction with either horse or mallet is a great skill. Nor are the horses and players the only ones taking risks. Mallets are dropped or broken with considerable frequency and stable boys take terrible risks rushing into the fray with replacements.

The game is non-stop, fast and even.

Predictably, Gilgit score first with Bulbul pushing in an easy goal after a furious build-up. He now gets to restart the game with a *tapokh*, which is very good to watch. The goal scorer races up the field at full gallop, holding both the ball and the mallet in the same hand, then, still with one hand only, releases the ball and strikes it ahead of him. It's often missed or half hit, but the apricot-wood hammer of Bulbul's stick meets the ball head on. It soars up the other end, bounces past the goal and is thrown back into play by a spectator, this keeping any interruption to the flow of play to a minimum. Maqbool pulls a goal back for Chitral and they go into the break unexpectedly level.

After a long interval display of ceremonial dancing, all hands and arms turning and twisting gracefully, the players are back on the pitch and a repeat of the first half is played out in the first few minutes. A Gilgit goal, then a Chitral equalizer. As a well-informed spectator next to me says it's now all about the stamina of the horses.

Gilgit's powerful ponies begin to outrun Chitral, racing after the long ball with breathtaking speed. Two more Gilgit goals, then Bulbul Jan and the ageing Truc first set up a superb through pass for the fifth goal before running in the next one themselves. 6-2.

The Chitral supporters simply disappear at this point, streaming off the mounds and emptying the stands. Their departing cars send up columns of dust that blow over the ground as if bringing down a final curtain over their team's efforts.

The departure of these fair-weather supporters seems, perversely, to spur on the Chitral team and they pull back two goals in an unexpectedly nail-biting finish.

Gilgit have made it a hat trick of wins and won best player award. For Chitral there is the consolation of Best Horse, won by a tireless grey called Computer, and not much else but a night-time skulk back down the mountain.

I'm sure someone somewhere will claim it's been a victory for black magic.

BELOW

The hills are alive. Pitch invasion after Gilgit's victory. The red roof of the permanent stand is in the far distance.

Day Nineteen : The Karakoram Highway

The view from my hotel window in Gilgit is an exercise in contrasts. Immediately outside is a carefully tended rose garden, of the sort you might see in a Best Kept Village in the Cotswolds. A half mile further away, this tidy view swells into a stupendous wall of mountain scenery, rising from the muddy cliffs carved out by the River Gilgit.

Soon we're running north, deeper into these mountains, along the road that bears their name – the Karakoram Highway, also known as the Eighth Wonder of the World.

A collaboration between the Chinese and the Pakistanis, the road winds 800 formidable and majestic miles, from Kashgar in western China almost to the Pakistan capital, Islamabad. It first took traffic in 1978 after 20 years of construction. Considering the obstacles in its course – some of the highest and least stable mountains in the world, fierce winds, temperature extremes ranging from icy cold to blazing summer heat – 20 years is pretty quick, but the human price paid was considerable. Between 500 and 800 Pakistanis and untold Chinese died in its construction, roughly one life for every kilometre.

Before there was the KKH there was the Silk Road, a network of trails and passes that led from Persia and Turkey through Afghanistan and into China, a commercial conduit following and enriching the precious routes through the mountains.

Apart from the increased prosperity brought by the road itself, many projects round here bear the name of the Aga Khan, spiritual head of the Ismaili Muslims, a Shiite sect who believe their leader to be a direct descendant of the Prophet's son-in-law. The Aga Khan Foundation provides money for education (especially girls' schools), healthcare and agricultural schemes. The results can be seen in the communities through which we pass. The settlements are tidy, with solid communal buildings and ingenious irrigation systems flowing between immaculately built dry-stone walls.

In the Hunza valley, believed to be the model for many Shangri-las and the inspiration for James Hilton's book *Lost Horizon*, the Karakoram Highway is quiet as a country lane, running beside neatly planted fields of spinach, potatoes and cabbage and sun-dappled orchards of apricot, apple, peach, pear and plum. Yet this is one of the geomorphic hot spots of the world. This tranquil countryside lies above the epicentre of a titanic geological upheaval. Around 50 million years ago India collided with the rest of Asia, or rather the great mass called the Indian plate drifted north and ran into the much larger mass of the Eurasian plate. The force of the impact pushed one over the other and thrust them both skywards, creating a momentum that is still at work, carrying India deeper into Asia at the rate of two inches a year. The Hindu Kush, the Karakoram, the Pamirs and the Himalaya are all, in a sense, wreckage from one of the great head-on collisions in the history of the planet.

A sign outside a modest little town reads simply, 'Chalt. Where Continents Collide'. Which certainly puts 'Artichoke Capital of the World' in its place.

There are few spots where the consequences of tectonic trauma are more dramatically visible than at the Rakaposhi View Restaurant in Ghulmet. Rakaposhi is one of the most imposing peaks of the Karakoram, rising to 25,500 feet (7772 m). As we sit at a table beneath a willow tree eating fresh-picked cherries we are looking at the highest unbroken mountainside on earth. From the River Hunza, just below us, to the summit of its western face far above us, a single slope rises 18,000 feet (5486 m). Three and a quarter miles of rock, glacier and gravity-defying terraces of snow and ice.

And the lavatory's spotless.

The KKH, like an earlier engineering marvel, the Forth Railway Bridge, needs constant attention as the road climbs higher and the ice cracks the rock and the snowmelt sends the rubble slithering down onto the highway. So it's no great surprise to hear that a landslide has blocked the road between here and the 16,000-foot (4877 m) Khunjerab Pass which leads into China. Even if we got there we couldn't go further, as the frontier has been closed due to the SARS epidemic. We detour up to the village of Altit.

The Altit road is not one for faint hearts; it's just an unfenced track of flattened debris dug across the middle of a 3000-foot spill of scree. Halfway along it someone tells me that the word Karakoram means 'crumbling rock' in Turkish.

I'm much relieved when we drop slowly down through the tree line, but just as I'm feeling secure we have to cross a slatted bridge of warped and bent timbers, between which I can see a lot more of the raging waters of the Hunza than I'd like to. Under the weight of each vehicle it bounces up and down as if it were made of elastic. Never have I been so happy to reach the other side of a bridge.

On the way back to Gilgit, the sun hits the eastern spires and ridges of the mountains and turns their tips the colour of molten metal. I only hope the Himalaya can live up to the magic of the Karakoram.

Day Twenty : Gilgit to Skardu

We have been given the go-ahead by the Pakistan military to join one of their helicopters on a service flight from Skardu in Baltistan, to Concordia, close to the Chinese border, where ten of the world's top 30 peaks are clustered, including K2 (Karakoram 2), the second highest mountain in the world.

It's mountaineering made easy but not to be sniffed at for all that. Last night I called my

OPPOSITE

The tenacity of life in the Karakoram mountains: a flat-topped spur is enough to create a village.

friend Hamish MacInnes in Scotland for the reactions of a world-class climber. He gave me various words of encouragement, among them the fact that the road to Skardu is known as 'the road that eats jeeps'.

Skardu is only 99 miles (160 km) from Gilgit, but we're told it will take most of the day. Progress is slowed down by rock falls and landslips at roughly one-mile intervals. Some bring us to a halt, some have to be negotiated with infinite care. Road gangs, muffled like mummies against the dust and heat, stop to watch us pass, then resume the Sisyphean task of fighting landslides with spades, shovels and wheelbarrows.

We turn off the KKH and stop for refreshment. Across the road a large man sprawls across the threshold of a very small shop. He's sunk deep in an armchair and has one leg up against the door-post. A sign above him announces 'Ahmad, Gems and Minerals. We Deals In Precious Stones'. Up here, mineral seams are routinely exposed by the massive geological upheavals. As they bring our tea they tell us we've had one big piece of luck. The road that eats jeeps reopened only two days earlier after unusually heavy spring rain closed it at 126 separate places.

As we set off along yet another gorge I'm aware that this is a significant moment for us. Dominating the mountains on the far side of the Indus is the westernmost bastion of the Himalaya. Nanga Parbat, an uncompromising, irregular giant of a mountain, rises to 26,650 feet (8125 m). It has wide flanks and a bad reputation. It's known as Killer Mountain, claiming 50 lives before it was first scaled by an Austrian, Hermann Buhl, in 1953. According to Hamish, Buhl was a very hard nut indeed. Those who came on his expeditions were issued with one-way tickets only.

Progress seems positively jaunty for a few miles. Then the walls of the gorge close in and the eating of the jeeps begins as we grind along, clinging to the roller-coaster track above the Indus, at one moment rising so high above the river that we can no longer hear its roar, at the next plunging to within range of its wind-tossed spray, and all the time bumping and juddering over half-cleared piles of rubble that fling me from side to side like someone in the terminal throes of fever.

The existence of a road at all in this desperately confined space is something of a miracle. It seems to be maintained by the army, and the different companies of engineers have their names engraved on a rock at the end of each section. A camouflaged vehicle comes at us round a tight bend and as we go through the elaborate ritual of manoeuvring past each other I notice the slogan on the side of its cab. 'Pakistan Army. Men At Their Best.'

At Skardu, the hyperactive River Indus, which has been leaping and writhing past us for most of the day, flattens out into a wide alluvial lagoon.

We find ourselves in a very singular hotel where the lights don't always work but the waiters wear white gloves to serve dinner.

It's called Shangri La.

Day Twenty One : Skardu to Concordia

There's a crashed DC-3 just outside my room. Apparently, it came down after take-off at Skardu 49 years ago and, spotting an opportunity, the owner of the Shangri La Resort bought it, rolled it into the gardens, took off the wings, fitted some tables and turned it into a café.

Contradictions are apparent again this morning. The gardens are tended with obsessive efficiency, each blade of grass individually manicured by a dedicated, well-equipped team, yet the breakfast is a very sad affair, with toast so pale and limp that we re-christen the wicker container it comes in the laundry basket.

Such trivial preoccupations are soon behind us as we assemble at the air base for a

BELOW
Not for the faint-hearted. A chair and pulley take a commuter across the Indus. The river is young and strong here, as it cleaves a way between the Himalaya and Karakoram ranges.

OPPOSITE

My first taste of the
high life. Dropping off
at Concordia, where
great glaciers meet K2
at three miles above
sea level.

briefing on today's flight up into the high mountains. The message here is macho, and our two pilots are from a team called 'The Fearless Five, M-17 pilots'.

I should imagine fearlessness is an asset if you have to fly M-17s. They're heavy-duty Russian supply helicopters, the very embodiment of brawn before beauty. We fan out along bench seats running around the side of the cabin. It's unpressurized and, as we're going up beyond 15,000 feet (4570 m), we've been warned that for the first time since we've been in Pakistan we may get really cold.

The helicopter roars into the air, and once in the air the roar is augmented by various rattles and groans. Communication is only possible by shouting into the ear from point blank range.

Below us, the green fields become sparse and scattered and eventually disappear altogether as we enter the valleys that lead to Concordia. What is for us a 90-minute flight would be an eight-day trek on the ground.

The mountains close in. Steep slopes and jagged summits rise above us, the clatter of the engines echoes back off the rocks and the M-17 that looked so bulky and secure on the ground seems suddenly small and vulnerable. At 11,000 feet (3350 m) the pen I'm making notes with explodes, spattering ink around like a nosebleed.

We're now over the imperceptibly moving tongue of the Baltoro glacier, not romantically blue and white but covered with a grey patina of dust and debris and dotted with lurid green pools where the snow and ice crust has collapsed.

Then all at once we're flying clear of the grey constraints of the canyons and out into crystal clear sunshine and over an ice plateau of staggering beauty, with razor-sharp peaks surrounding the confluence of the Baltoro and Godwin-Austen glaciers. A tricky landing. The crew are put off first, as they need to be on the ground to shoot me emerging. We pirouette up into the air and once again circle this astonishingly beautiful coming together of ice, snow and mighty mountain peaks. As they attempt the landing a second time no-one bothers to lower the steps, so I spill out of the plane with as much dignity as I can muster and run, fast and low, away from the rotors and towards the camera. My feet strike a soft patch and I plunge forward, headfirst into snow alarmingly deeper than anything I expected.

We know we have only a few minutes to shoot before the helicopter returns and yet the best full frontal view of K2 is almost half a mile away. Led by two army guides, who are actually stationed up here, we make our way through the snow. We try to hurry but it's hopeless, as the surface is melting in the sun. Every now and then people ahead of me drop down to their waist as if a trap door had opened beneath them.

I can't quite believe that all this is really happening. That I'm struggling in slapstick fashion through six feet of snow in a country where the average daytime temperatures have been around 40°C (104°F). That, only five hours after drinking a cup of coffee in a crashed DC-3, I should be a mere five miles from the second highest peak on earth, half a dozen miles from the Chinese border and 13 miles from where heavily armed Pakistani and Indian troops are eye-balling each other on the Line of Control.

The reward for all our efforts is an uninterrupted view of K2, standing with symmetrical grandeur to the northwest, straddling the Chinese border. Not a wisp of cloud obscures the summit, which I know has tempted many to risk, and in some cases give their lives on a mountain much harder and crueller than Everest.

I feel hugely lucky to be here at Concordia, even if we have done it the easy way. And the helicopter doesn't return for almost an hour, giving us time to take it all in, and, very slightly, to panic.

Day Twenty Three : Islamabad

The mountains where we've spent the last two weeks seem a distant memory. Everything is so different down here on the plain. And Islamabad is different again. Nothing stood here 45 years ago, when it was chosen to be Pakistan's new capital, replacing the original capital Karachi, which, 1550 miles (2480 km) away to the south, was considered to be too remote from the heart of the country. Now nearly a million people live here.

The crowds and turbulence we experienced in Peshawar's densely packed bazaars are absent. Islamabad is formal, with long wide avenues and comfortable residential houses laid out in numbered sectors. Instead of Storyteller Street, a typical address in Islamabad might be House 3, Street 18, H-8.

This experiment in New World orderliness has been remarkably successful. Its position certainly helps, on the border between the North-West Frontier and the Punjab, as does the presence of the ministries. Each with their competing landmark buildings, the grandiose Prime Minister's Secretariat in Neo-Mughal style, the Revenue Buildings in American Modern, and the Supreme Court in a mixture of both, they give Islamabad a sort of official liveliness.

It isn't a city to tempt you out for a stroll. That's not how it works. If you're staying in the Marriot the city comes to you, and our lobby is full of delegations, advisers, journalists, educationalists, air-con salesmen, arms dealers and anyone else wanting the ear of the government.

Islamabad is also home to one of Pakistan's national heroes, a cricketer who led his side to a never-to-be forgotten World Cup victory, founded a cancer hospital in memory of his mother, but failed to work his magic in the world of politics. His name is Imran Khan and his PTI, anti-corruption party has only one seat in the National Assembly, his own. It's said that the reasons why he picked up so few votes were that those he attracted were below the voting age of 21, and those he alienated, like the landowners, remain very powerful.

In today's morning paper, however, a disillusioned former colleague of Imran is more severe. He blames Imran's dictatorial tendencies. 'This is not cricket, this is politics. And Imran has never understood that fact.'

We turned up at an unostentatious detached house in a leafy street whose name I forget, but it might have been 14.

Imran is in a meeting but three amiable dogs rise to greet us, tails wagging vigorously, until that becomes too much of an effort and they collapse, bellies flat against warm stones or on their backs in the shade of the verandah, legs spread-eagled in abandon.

After a half-hour or so, Imran, unheralded by minders, secretaries or advisers, slips quietly onto the verandah, wearing a light blue *shalwar-kameez*. His complexion is clear and unlined and his long face has a few interesting angles, which makes him more than conventionally handsome. When we ask him if he minds us filming the house he waves his arm agreeably. He'll only be here another three months, and his wife Jemima is back in their house in London.

Tea and soft drinks are brought out. When I tell him of our visit to Skardu, his face lights up. 'The most beautiful country,' he says with feeling. 'The Baltis are friendly and decent folk.'

Imran scratches the luxuriating Labrador with his foot. He talks carefully, as economical with words as he was with runs, seldom raising his voice, but relying more on expressively graceful hands to emphasize or illustrate a point. His soft-voiced, unemotional delivery masks bracing views.

On matters of religion he feels the clergy, rather than the scholars, are the big problem. The Koran, he maintains, quoting from it with confidence, is an example for life, but the mullahs seek to reduce its message to fit their own interpretations.

'And some of them are decadent, you know,' he says with a real touch of anger.

He feels the Taliban began as a genuine people's movement, a reaction against the summary justice and tyranny of the warlords.

'But they were taken over by extremists.'

We talk about the British influence. He thinks it not only strong, but fundamental. India and Pakistan were created by the British, who saw the plethora of tribes, small rulers, languages and customs as unwieldy and difficult. By playing them off against each other they created a centralized administration that India had never known before. It was a classic case of divide and rule.

I ask him if many of the old institutions aren't still in place, or in the case of his alma mater, Aitcheson's College, the Eton of Pakistan, positively thriving.

'For the elite we had what's called the "English medium education" and for the masses the "Urdu medium education", so the elite became quite Westernized and the rest of society was not that much touched by Westernization, as you've seen as you travel around.'

'Are you tolerant of these schools still existing?'

'No, I think it's terrible this educational apartheid.'

I press him on whether a bright lad from the bazaars would ever make it to the top in Pakistan, and he shakes his head quite vigorously.

'Highly unlikely.'

He says he made the transition from cricket to politics because he felt that, with the way things were going, his country faced a bleak future. The population was the highest in the world, people weren't being educated and governments were corrupt and unconcerned with investment in human beings.

'It was pretty tough because I had to stand up to the status quo, which is very strong in this country.'

He doesn't mince words. 'Money in Pakistan is in the hands of crooks. The majority of people who go into politics make money through illegal means.'

Our government minder is listening in to all this and I fear the worst, but at the end of the interview all he asks of us is that we take a photograph of him with his hero.

ABOVE

Imran Khan. Sporting hero, political outsider.

Unlike the locked and barred Gulbar at the hotel in Peshawar, there is a place in the bowels of the Marriott where non-Muslims can enjoy an alcoholic beverage. It's called The Bassment, which may or may not be a spelling mistake, and we agree to meet down there after work. I'm the first to arrive. Disapproval, in the forbidding shape of an unsmiling hotel bouncer in a suit, begins at the top of the stairs. He stands, arms folded, legs apart, resolutely avoiding eye contact, guarding the heavy door that opens onto a dank stairwell whose walls give off a pervasive odour of tobacco smoke, long-since exhaled. At the bottom two swing doors open onto a long, apparently empty chamber sunk in Stygian gloom, pierced only by tiny disco lights sunk into the ceiling. Concrete walls increase the atmosphere of being in a bunker. At the bar is a Norwegian. We exchange a wary grunt of greeting, like two people who've come together to commit the same crime.

I order a beer. They have no international brands, only beer brewed in Pakistan.

Which is how I begin my acquaintance with the life-saving products of the Murree Brewery.

Day Twenty Four : Rawalpindi

Islamabad, its critics say, is 12 miles outside Pakistan, and this morning, as we drive out past the well-fenced government buildings and onto the wide, landscaped, highly under-used modern highway that surrounds the city I know what they mean. Everything is discreet, tidy, straight and planned, and it's not until we reach the outskirts of Islamabad's twin city, Rawalpindi, affectionately abbreviated to Pindi, that Pakistan comes back to life.

Not far from the airport, we're diverted off the main road by hundreds of police. After

*At Rawalpindi,
crossing the most
famous road in the
subcontinent. First laid
across north India
some 500 years ago.*

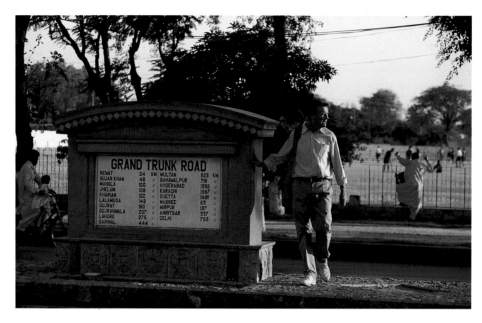

some time a convoy of outriders, some in open cars with gloriously conspicuous scarlet berets, races by on either side of three blacked-out Mercedes, any one of which, or possibly none, contains President Musharraf. Significantly, he doesn't live with the civil servants in Islamabad but in Rawalpindi, where the army is based, and this whole extravagant process, an entire six-lane highway closed for a half-hour, is a reminder of where the power lies in Pakistan.

At Independence in 1947, Mohammed Ali Jinnah, known to all as the Quaid-e-Azam, Father of the Nation, wanted Pakistan to remain a secular state but, divided as the country was into West Pakistan and East Pakistan (later to secede and become Bangladesh), the only real bond that held the disparate tribal groups together was religion. In 1956 the Constitution accepted this and declared Pakistan an Islamic Republic. The army, seeing power drifting away from them, staged their first coup two years after that and, despite various attempts to hand power to democratically elected leaders, Pakistan still is a military state, and one of the most hotly debated issues is whether or not Musharraf should give up his uniform and run for democratically elected office.

Turning off the Grand Trunk Road we pass the high, blotchy walls of the old barracks behind which one of Pakistan's experiments with democracy came to a grim end, when Zulfikhar Ali Bhutto, a populist, secular prime minister, was hanged on the orders of General Zia, leaving Zia free to accelerate the process of Islamization.

At the heart of this nerve centre of the Islamic Republic, sandwiched between the barracks and the military headquarters, is the Murree Brewery, Pakistan's largest purveyor of alcoholic beverages.

Originally established in 1861, up in the Murree Hills, north of Islamabad, by Henry Whymper, brother of the first man to climb the Matterhorn, it's a place steeped in irony. Ninety-five per cent of the brewery's 450-strong workforce is Muslim and officially not allowed to touch the product their lives depend on. The owner, Minoo Bhandara, is a scholarly Parsee who writes regular newspaper columns and his business card notes that he was 'adviser to the President 1982–1985' (that same President who hanged Bhutto). His office, dominated by a 150-year-old mahogany table, feels as if it would be more at home in an Oxbridge college than a brewery.

Minoo would make a good don. He is slightly stooped, and a large pair of glasses with thick lenses gives him an owlish air. He's soft-voiced, courteous, a touch pedantic and very much at home in a well-worn rattan chair.

His Muslim brew master, Muhammed Javed, has been here 17 years. More in the mould of the modern executive, he's a genial, youthful-looking man with degrees from universities in the Punjab and America.

His enthusiasm for the production of alcohol is abundant. He walks me past the beer production line, enthusing over the current output of 10,000 bottles an hour ranging from high strength Millennium at 7.5 per cent alcohol, through the popular and medal-winning Murree Classic at 5.5 to a Pils Light at 3.5.

This selfless Muslim workforce also produces 20 brands of spirit including gin and vodka.

Despite draconian laws on the possession of alcohol – a prison sentence of three to four years, un-bailable, and quite possibly a caning as well – it's pretty clear that the Murree Brewery wouldn't be in business if its customers were only non-Muslims.

Minoo argues that it's foolish to suppose there is no demand for alcohol in Pakistan and if he doesn't supply it then someone else will. Either the bootleggers smuggle foreign whisky in on dhows from places like Dubai, or for those who can't afford bootleg, there is moonshine liquor, often made from what he calls 'denatured alcohol'.

He looks over his glasses at me, rather severely.

'"Denature" is an old English word for poison.'

One of the outlets where non-Muslims can legally acquire Murree's output is at Flashman's Hotel in Rawalpindi. A run-down collection of white bungalows, looking a bit like a 1940s film studio, it stands just off the Grand Trunk Road and next to a handsome Victorian church with everything but the spire painted deep pink.

Round the back of Flashman's, if you know who to ask, you'll find two well-scuffed shutters, bordered with a patina of black grease from thousands of hands. A sign, in Urdu, announces that opening time is three o'clock. A line, looking suspiciously Muslim, has already formed. About 3.15 the shutters are opened and I soon find myself peering through a barred window into a gloomy little room full of storage boxes and men drinking tea.

Before I buy I have to fill in a permit, which requires me, among other things, to give my father's name and my religion.

'Agnostic?' I suggest, trying to be completely honest.

The man at the counter looks blankly back.

'Agnostic with doubts,' I write down, and hand back the form. This entitles me to six units of alcohol a month, a unit being one bottle of spirits or 20 bottles of beer. I buy a bottle of Vat No.1 Rawalpindi whisky at a cost of 350 rupees (about £3.50), which the attendant wraps in brown paper and hands through the bars to me.

BELOW

(left) Filling in the forms at Flashman's Hotel. (right) Cheer up! You're the proud owner of a bottle of Pakistan whisky.

'Drink only in room,' he cautions. 'Not in public.'

I nod, grateful for the advice. He must have got the measure of me, for as I turn away he shouts hopefully.

'I do gin!'

Day Twenty Five : Rawalpindi to Lahore

For a military state Pakistan has a remarkably free press. Or so it seems as I read an editorial this morning addressing what it calls the Military-Mullah alliance. The writer's argument is that since General Zia's time the military and the Islamists have sought each other's support against secular democracy.

The only difference between them, it argues, is that the clerics have beards and the army have moustaches.

A front page headline warns of the heatwave that waits for us tonight in Lahore. '50 Die As Punjab Boils.'

On our way to the station in Rawalpindi, there is reassuring evidence of the hopefully inextinguishable richness of Pakistani life. Run-down streets dotted with foreign language schools and computer shops, and looming above them hand-painted billboard ads for the latest movie adventures of Shaan Shahid, Pakistan's screen heart-throb, glowering menacingly, as blood courses from a head wound, or grinning, equally menacingly, as he brandishes a Kalashnikov. He seems to be the star of every film they make.

Stopping to buy provisions in the Rajah Bazaar, I'm approached by a heavily bearded man offering to sell me a CD of Mullah Omar and Osama Bin Laden praying together at a mosque in Idris. Never seen before, he says.

Another seems pleased that we represent the BBC. 'Everyone in Pakistan believe BBC, but not CNN,' he assures me, readjusting his New York Yankees baseball cap.

It's heating up as promised – 44°C (111°F) by the time we reach Rawalpindi Station, a huge conflation of Scottish baronial turrets and cupolas with a bland modern extension tacked on. Porters cluster around us and a thin-faced ascetic old man with a Gandalf-like white beard grabs one of my cases, hoists the other onto his head and, a little disappointed that I choose to carry my own shoulder bag, marches off through the crowds.

Our driver nods approvingly. This old man is a great character, he says. He was carrying bags for British officers before independence. That was 55 years ago.

There are three classes on the train, two with air-con and one without. We're in air-con, 2nd class and are made comfortable by an army of solicitous attendants marshalled by a man in a white suit, green peaked hat and a crimson arm band, grandly embroidered with the

words Conductor Guard. A rich cast of characters, all with titles clearly inscribed on jackets or lapels, come through offering refreshment of various kinds. My favourite is the Iceman, a stocky, embattled figure in a frayed white jacket, whose bulbous eyes and droopy moustache remind me of a small-time crook in a French gangster movie. He hauls a huge bucket in which is a block of ice with bottles squeezed around it. There is a tired, emaciated Sweet Seller and various perkier, smartly turned-out young men described on their lapel badges as either Buttlers (sic) or Waiters. Waiter No. 14 brings chai, sweet milky tea, and Buttler No. 7 collects the money.

The name Punjab is an elision of Paan, five, and Aab, waters, and refers to the five rivers on which the prosperity of the province depends. Connected up, under the British occupation, by a network of branch canals and distribution channels, the flows of the Indus, Chenab, Ravi, Sutlej and Jhelum support 70 million people, almost half the population of Pakistan. Seventy miles south of Pindi a mile-long railway bridge crosses the river into the town of Jhelum. Walking out on the station there I fall into conversation with a tall, irrepressibly cheery young man with wide, expressive eyes. His name is Asim and he's on his way to Lahore with his brother, Azam, an accountant who is having a weekend-long engagement party. They buy me pakoras, savoury fritters, from a stall on the platforms and we munch away in mutual enthusiasm. I will love Lahore, he promises.

'They are not fundamentalists there. Lahore is a city of very loving people, very wide-hearted, very loving.'

He puts away another pakora.

'Lahori people are very fond of eating,' confirms Asim.

'And is there a lot of night life?'

He nods animatedly.

'Oh yes, two, three, four o'clock in the morning, people are eating different dishes at different places.'

South of Jhelum the scenery changes from scrubby bush plateau to the freshly shorn fields of the Punjab plain.

Back on the train the Iceman is coming. I talk with a pale German girl who converted to Islam a year ago and two young, articulate computer programmers in shirts and trousers travelling with their father. He is shy, speaks no English, wears an embroidered skull cap and *shalwar-kameez* and looks steadily forward.

The light is softening and the day is cooling and people are out beside the railway; leading dusty-flanked water buffaloes to be fed, carrying goods home on the back of bicycles and playing cricket with breeze blocks for stumps.

It's dark when we reach Lahore. Outside the station, a colossal brick and stone fortified folly, I pick up an auto-rickshaw to the hotel. We grind off onto wide roads and through

ABOVE

Street cleaners take a photo break. In the background, Shaan Shahid, Lollywood heart-throb, dominates the billboards.

careless traffic, adding our own little cloud of pollution to a thick, hot, suffocating fug, tight as a strait-jacket.

Day Twenty Six : Lahore

Up at 5.45 to beat the heat. We make our way to the low hill that dominates the heart of this flat city and on which stand two of the most beautiful buildings in the subcontinent, Lahore Fort and the Badshahi Mosque. Both were built by the Mughal (the word derives from Mongol) emperors who came out of south central Asia and through Afghanistan around the time that Henry VIII was planning the Reformation. Using rifles, mortars and gunpowder, previously unheard of in India, they seized Lahore in 1524 and subdued Delhi two years later.

These two cities became the twin jewels of an empire that lasted almost 200 years and was characterized by blood, death, romantic tragedy and some of the most exquisite buildings, gardens, books and paintings in the world.

The Mughals were not the first to fortify Lahore. Some 13 or 14 strongholds have succeeded each other on this hill, but today's fort, completed by the Emperor Akbar, has stood solidly behind its mighty brick walls for 450 years.

It is a huge complex, but we find ourselves caught for some time in a small office, with a beamed roof and lots of tasteful antique furnishings, making the acquaintance of the curator, who has a bad cold.

I have the feeling the last thing he wants to do is to go outside. Two days ago Lahore had its highest temperature for 75 years, he tells us, reaching for a tissue. 'Forty-Nine Centigrade!'

Fortunately, it will be cooler today he prophesies. Perhaps 47 at most.

The appeal of the Lahore fort is a successful combination of intimacy and grandeur. Power with a human face. There is the massive Elephant Path, a wide flight of steps with long, shallow stairs designed to enable rich courtiers to bring their elephants into the heart of the fort without having to dismount. There are courtyards of immense size, criss-crossed with cooling water channels (sadly dry today), and audience chambers supported by forests of sandstone columns, and in among them, exquisite architectural miniatures.

The Shish Mahal, the Palace of Mirrors, is a series of cool, serene rooms open at one side and enclosed at the other by an exquisitely carved screen through which the breeze is drawn by a 17th-century carved marble air-con system. Narrow apertures on the outside widen out on the inside to draw the cool air in. And it does work. The walls are picked out with glass mosaics, paintings of gardens and countryside and complex mirrored panels.

It was in one of these, so the story goes, that Emperor Akbar noticed his son Jahangir exchange flirtatious glances with the Emperor's favourite courtesan, Anarkarli, aka Pomegranate Blossom. As a punishment Akbar ordered her to be walled-up, alive. When Jahangir became Emperor he built a grand tomb at the place where she died, on which were written the words:

'Ah, could I behold the face of my beloved once again, I would give thanks until the day of resurrection.'

The curator sniffs and sighs. Not because he's moved by the story, but because he says it never happened. True or false, Anarkali has become a folk hero for many Lahoreans and the main market of the city is named after her.

Another gem, the Naulaka Pavilion, has less gruesome romantic attachments. Its canopied roof, an exquisitely carved blanket of marble, said to be modelled on a Bengali hut, covers walls and pillars intricately decorated with tiny carved panels filled with stones of agate, lapis lazuli, gold, jade and cornelian. It was built by Emperor Shah Jahan for his wife Mumtaz, of whom he must have been pretty fond. When she died he built the Taj Mahal for her.

The view from this cool pavilion out towards the Badshahi Mosque is a reminder of what makes Mughal architecture so fine. It's all about balance and symmetry. Towers, domes, minarets, columns and cupolas, some in red stone, some in white marble, are all gracefully harmonized. The Mughal emperors set out to balance power and pleasure, and no-one ever

LEFT

Lahore Fort. Steps built wide and shallow enough for visitors arriving by elephant.

ABOVE

*Prayers at the 330-
year-old Badshahi
Mosque, Lahore.*

achieved this more successfully.

It's midday and in the mosque the sandstone slabs are so hot that a thin strip of carpet has been laid out, which is continually being hosed down. This requires a lot of water, as the 500 feet (160 m) square courtyard is one of the largest of any mosque in the world, and can hold upwards of 60,000 worshippers.

Today most of them are inside the shade of the tall Prayer Chamber, ten bays deep and topped by three white marble domes. The imam is giving his address but there seems to be little of the formality of worship in an English church. Some stand to listen, some kneel. People come and go, others talk to each other, some attend to their own devotions while young children run around at the back. Only when it comes to the holy prayer do they all come together to stand in line, barefoot, heads lowered. Then, moving as one, they bow to the waist, stand upright, kneel, press foreheads on the ground twice, then stand up and begin the process over again. There's something simple and powerful about such a communal act of humility in such splendid surroundings.

This evening we meet for a meal at the house of the well-connected Yusuf Salahuddin, who, hearing of our curiosity about Shaan Shahid, the actor on all the posters, is to take us to see him filming at the studios on the Multan Road, heart of Lahore's film industry, or Lollywood as it's known.

Yusuf's house is a warren of tastefully decorated rooms and courtyards in the Old Town. On antique tables stand photos of himself with Imran Khan, Jimmy Goldsmith and others. In the courtyard we eat the most delicious mangoes I've ever tasted and talk about what we've seen in Pakistan. His views on the trigger-happy North-West Frontier are far from reverential.

'They'll shoot you if they feel like it. Any excuse. If they don't like the food, or the way you smile, or farting. Farting, that's very bad. Farting is a crime on the North-West Frontier. And the older you are when you fart the worse it is.'

He insists we come back here for the Basant festival in April. Everyone in Lahore flies their kites for a day.

'It must be a beautiful sight.'

'Beautiful?' He shakes his head in mock horror. 'It's war!'

Apparently it gets seriously competitive, with rooftop rivals attaching knives and glass to their string to cut each other's kites adrift. (I've since heard that the mayor of Lahore has banned next year's kite festival because of risk of injury.)

It's late by the time we head down to the studios but Yusuf assures us that there is no point in getting there earlier. Because of the heat, all the shooting is done at night.

He explains that someone like Shaan will have several films on the go at once.

'What sort of films?'

'All the same,' he says. 'All Punjabi films have the same ingredients. One boy, two girls, one boy, one girl, two girls, one boy. We are a very emotional people, we like to cry our heart and soul out.'

Shaan arrives. A trim figure, early to mid-thirties, with black trousers and tunic and dyed blond hair. A good face, strong features, heavily muscled arms. Not unlike the young Brando.

A big wedding scene, in which Shahid plays an angry lover, is about to go before the cameras. There's the usual scrum of activity around the set. Turbanned figures on lighting gantries re-direct the lamps, extras wait nervously in a back room, a leading lady is applying the heavy and elaborate layers of make-up that seem to be obligatory for any heroine, while the director, Sangeeta, a big, fair-skinned, bespectacled woman, prowls around like the headmistress of a particularly troublesome comprehensive, cajoling, exhorting, upbraiding and generally trying to hurry the process along.

The set is all fairy lights and soft furnishings and fussy white balconies.

'This is what Punjabis want,' says Shaan, in quiet, fluent English. 'This is their fantasy of success.'

As he waits for his moment to be shot by the bride's father, he seems calm and quite happy to talk. He says he's been in the business 14 years and I ask him how many films he's made.

LEFT

My night with the stars. Shaan Shahid (left), and other top Pakistani thesps, on set at the Bari Studios, Lahore. This was one of nine films Shaan was making at the same time.

'223, I think, or is it 4?' He considers for a moment. 'And two of those years I spent in New York, so, yes, that's 224 in 12 years'.

His father was a director, producer and writer, his mother the leading actress in Pakistan, so Shaan has no illusions about the business, or his success. He's a family man. Loves to be woken by his daughter, he says.

'I wake up by 12.30, I go to my gym, I have breakfast, then I come to work. I do about nine projects a day.' He reckons he finishes a film every 28 days.

'Are you allowed to kiss on screen?'

'Not on the lips. On the hand or the forehead, or you know on the side cheek or something, but not on the lips. My wife's not going to agree to that, so forget it.'

'Does that seem unnatural to you?'

'No, that's very natural.'

I wonder if he fears any backlash from resurgent, conservative, Islamist elements in the country, who've made no secret of their dislike for the cinema.

'There's a bunch of people that need to be taught that this is something that has nothing to do with religion; it's a form of expression, it's a form of art and that's it.'

There are shouts from the set. The bride's father has been handed his gun and had his moustache reapplied, and pink spray is erupting from the fountain at the bottom of the stairs at the back. To my surprise Shaan calls me onto the set to have my photo taken with the actors.

'They are all big fans.'

I shake hands with the bridegroom, who beams with excitement.

'This is very exciting for us. We love British comedy.'

I shrug modestly.

'Oh yes. Mr Bean, Benny Hill. We love it!'

I think it's time for me to go to bed.

Day Twenty Seven : Lahore

A short night. Spend the morning at what has been described as the 'Versailles of the Punjab', the Shalimar Gardens, created 360 years ago by that prodigious creator of fine monuments Emperor Shah Jahan, the tasteful tyrant who gave the world, among other things, the Taj Mahal.

Long, metre-thick pink and cream sandstone walls protect the gardens from the commotion outside, and a great and soothing sense of space and tranquillity envelops you as you enter.

In a city bulging at the seams it is both gratifying and surprising that these 40 acres of royal pleasure gardens survive at all, even though it's clearly a struggle to maintain them to Shah Jahan's specifications.

The layout is formal, based on descriptions in the Koran, with three descending terraces and the ultimate in water features – streams, pools, cascades and waterfalls – all set in precise geometric harmony. In the days when the Emperor and Empress looked out at each other from their own personal pavilions, separated by shaded walkways and water channels, 400 fountains played in the gardens, kept at constant pressure by water from huge storage tanks continually topped up from a canal by a conveyor belt of wheels and buckets.

But that was the 17th century and modern technology just hasn't been able to keep up. The 20th century pumps are far less effective and water springs from the calcified fountains in dribbles rather than jets. An old man is wading around in the water tank unclogging non-performing fountains by hammering a wooden peg into their sclerotic spouts.

There is, sadly, no sign of the 128 gardeners recorded in an early description of the Shalimar Gardens. Instead there is a man cutting the grass with a small domestic lawnmower hauled by a water buffalo. Every now and then he brings the buffalo to a halt and empties the grass cuttings into the nearest ornamental lake, where they're devoured by large and slothful fish.

Eating being one of the preoccupations of Lahoris, I end the day in Food Street, on the recommendation of Asim and Azam, my friends from the train. I think they've slightly oversold the place. It's picturesque enough, with fresh-painted wooden verandahs and shiny, stuccoed

BELOW

Unblocking the fountains. Shalimar Gardens, Lahore.

balconies, but it's obviously designed for tourists and has that cheerful soulless glow of civic improvement. The food, especially the house speciality of Mutton Karahi, served in the wok it's cooked in, is good, strong and filling, but how I long for a beer to wash it down. The soda I'm allowed is just not the same.

The alcohol ban brings the conversation around to religion, and my assumption that because Asim and Azam are young 'modern' Pakistanis they would be less interested in matters of faith than their elders proves to be wrong.

Azam, the accountant, maintains that being a Muslim means that the Koran orders everything for him, offering guidance and instruction in every area of life.

He picks a glass up from the table.

'Even a simple thing like this glass. How I hold it. In my right hand, never my left. I should always drink sitting down, never standing up. I should look into the glass as I drink.'

He puts the glass down and looks across the table at me, almost defiantly.

'I do all these things not just because it says so in the Koran, but also because I know they are good for me.'

Tomorrow Azam will become engaged and they will have a big party. He doesn't know when they'll marry. It could be a year, two, or even three years.

'Will you live together until then?'

Both he and Asim shake their heads vehemently.

'Oh, no. No. Sex before marriage is out of the question.'

Day Twenty Eight : Lahore to Amritsar

On the front page of the newspaper there is a photograph of a man on a ladder painting black stripes over an advert that shows an unveiled woman holding an apple drink. He is described as a member of the Shabab-I-Milli Islamist Activist group. Lower down the page are pictures of two sisters, their faces disfigured by acid thrown by the husband of one of them. 'Acid attacks,' notes the report, 'are among the worst of the huge numbers of crimes against women committed in Pakistan.'

LEFT

Strangers from the train. With Azam the accountant, in foreground, and Asim the soldier, in Food Street, Lahore.

There could hardly be two more graphic reminders of the problems that loom ahead for the country as it tries to reconcile progress with deeply entrenched tradition.

As I pack for the last time before crossing the border to India, I have to say that Pakistan has been a revelation. Simplistic post 9/11 propaganda sought to equate it with terrorism, as if you could equate a population greater than that of France and Germany combined with any single thought or idea. I have found Pakistan to be infinitely more complex and diverse than I had been prepared for. Wilder and more beautiful too. Never once did I feel threatened. Give or take a few cold beers, I leave it with regret.

The Indian border is only 18 miles (30 km) from Lahore, an accident of politics that brought terrible suffering to the city when Pakistan was created in 1947. The exact details of where the frontier would run were not revealed by the British until a few hours before independence was declared. When it became clear that one of India's oldest and most prestigious cities was to become part of Pakistan an hysterical panic broke out. As half a million Hindus and Sikhs fled east and even more Muslims fled west, reprisals on both sides were swift and bloody.

Cross-border trains arrived at Lahore station full of massacred corpses. Men, women and children on both sides were attacked and killed. Law and order were paralysed as the communal violence took its course. The British refused to bring their army out onto the streets to help. Across the subcontinent as a whole it is estimated that partition resulted in over a million deaths.

The legacy of hatred still smoulders. The border post at Wagah is the only official land crossing between Pakistan and India, and even then Pakistanis and Indians are only allowed to cross in specially secure trains between Lahore and Amritsar. Foreigners, if they have the time and patience, can walk through from Pakistan to India, and this is what we intend to do.

The thermometer has fallen to a mere 41°C (106°F), but the humidity has risen. There was quite a storm across these plains last night and a combination of dust and moisture makes the air thick and sticky. It's what Roger calls a three-shirt day.

The canals that run along the side of the road to Wagah are thronged with people cooling off. Families picnicking on the banks watch children splashing in the mud, men wash rickshaws and bicycles in the water, women, veiled and sari-ed, take tentative dips. Hot-headed teenage boys fling their shirts off and leap from bridges. There seems to be a heightened devil-may-care mood

ABOVE

Wagah border
crossing. A red-letter
day for the local
porters as the BBC
leaves Pakistan.

along the roadside today. As the traffic grinds to a standstill boys who would not normally have dared approach us dance like scarecrows in front of our minibus and bang the sides as we move on. It's nice to have one last image of Pakistan with its hair down.

At the border the road peters out in an open assembly area, full of trucks. Beyond this rises a modern redbrick arch decorated with faux-Mughal columns and cupolas and flanked by terraced seating. Through the arch can be glimpsed two pairs of heavy metal gates, with a white line between them, which is the border itself. Beyond them rises another arched gateway inscribed with the single word 'India', the grandness of the gesture somewhat compromised by a row of threadbare potted plants arranged along the top of it.

This is the arena for a nightly display of nationalist feather ruffling, as both sides lower their flags in a ceremony deliberately designed to provoke unabashed jingoism in the assembled crowds.

Loudspeakers blare out. The terraces are filling up and a heavily perspiring man wearing a T-shirt in green and white national colours is warming up an already damp crowd.

'Pa-ki-stan!' he shouts.

'PA-KI-STAN!' they roar back.

Two very small children carrying flags are sent out by their mothers to join him. They're greeted with tumultuous applause.

We can hear the same sort of thing happening on the Indian side, the only noticeable difference being that they have music playing from their loudspeakers, while the Pakistanis have prayers and readings from the Koran.

At 6.05 precisely (this is, after all, a military ceremony) a bugle sounds, and, to resounding cheers, two of the tallest people I've seen in Pakistan march out towards the border gates. These are Punjabi Rangers and to say they march is an understatement. Every movement is executed with barely suppressed fury. Arms are snapped out like freshly drawn swords, legs fly into the air, high enough to brush the nose with the knee, before thudding into the ground with the force of a steam-hammer. This study in bellicosity is emphasized by uniforms as black as their smouldering eyes. Fan-shaped headdresses rise like hackles from their turbans.

They are followed by a squad of 12 more Rangers, who emerge with a splendid mixture of panache, aggression and bad acting that has the crowd roaring.

Speeding, slowing, high kicking, strutting, stamping, grimacing, leering and hissing with a finely honed ferocity, they create the impression of caged beasts ready at any moment to bite their opponents' heads off.

The Indian guard, in light khaki with red and gold turban plumes and white gaiters, march out to meet them. They try hard to be as theatrically aggressive as their Pakistani counterparts but somehow you don't feel their hearts are really in it.

Nevertheless, the show must go on and both sides, now eyeball to eyeball, contrive to present a quite surreal display of precision nastiness, raising their forearms like weapons, pawing the ground, baring their teeth and snarling at one another like turkey-cocks.

Even the lowering of the flag is conducted with a tight-lipped, carefully choreographed, competitive swagger, the final flourish of which is the controlled slamming of the gates between the two countries.

Applause and cheers follow the two flag parties as they march rabidly back towards their respective arches.

After this the whole thing degenerates into a PR exercise as the men who have terrified us for the last 30 minutes reappear to mingle with the crowd and have their photograph taken with kiddies and members of Parliament.

This pantomime at the border sends out confusing signals. Beyond the arches and the terraces where this carefully calculated piece of theatre has taken place is the reality of the Indo-Pakistan border: a mile-wide strip of no-man's land, guarded and patrolled as far as the eye can see by troops armed with more than high kicks and grimaces. Follow this line north into Kashmir and you will find several hundred thousand heavily armed men facing each other, not for entertainment, but because 56 years after independence, the line of partition remains a deep, unhealed wound.

BELOW

Pakistan's Punjabi Rangers strut their stuff at the border. (right) With their Indian counterparts, they prepare for competitive flag-lowering.

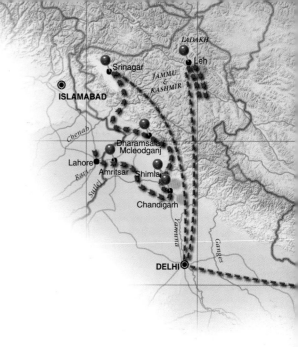

India

Day Thirty : Amritsar

A SIGN GREETS the traveller who makes the long walk across no-man's land and through the easternmost archway. 'India, the Largest Democracy in the World, Welcomes You'. As if to emphasize what a difference a half-mile makes, cold beer salesmen assail you and you are liable to be overtaken on the road by women on motorbikes. But the difference between the severity and discipline of Islamic Pakistan and the liberalism of secular India seems nowhere better demonstrated than in the border city of Amritsar.

Muslim and Hindu live reasonably happily together here (indeed, it's a fact that, despite Partition, there are more Muslims in India than in Pakistan), but the predominant religion in the first big city on the Indian side of the border is neither Muslim nor Hindu. Amritsar is a Sikh town.

Sikhism, professed by 65 per cent of the population here, is one of the world's newer faiths. It was founded by one Guru Nanak, in the early years of the 16th century. After a lifetime of travel, he concluded from what he saw that 'God is to be found neither in the Koran or the Puranas' (the sacred Hindu texts). Unable to accept the Hindu caste system, or what he saw as the intolerance of Islam, Guru Nanak came up with an admirably pragmatic solution. One God for all, rich or poor, with no human hierarchies or priesthoods, idols or icons coming in between.

In a nod towards another religion, the Sikh gurus chose a pool visited by Lord Buddha around which to build their first temple. It was called Amrit Sovar (The Nectar Pool) and though the name was elided to Amritsar, the pool, much extended, still exists and the temple built around it is now one of the most famous shrines in the world.

To get to the Golden Temple I take a motorcycle rickshaw into the centre of the city. The bracing, or exhausting, anarchy of Indian streets begins as soon as we leave the hotel. Cars veer out of side roads without stopping, lame dogs hop gamely across your bows, bicycles and buses appear from nowhere and blasts of the horn mingle with blasts from exhausts. At a roundabout we are forced into the middle of the road to avoid not just a cow, but a cow feeding its calf. As we pull out, a scooter with three small children concertinaed in between their mother and father hoots indignantly at us before disappearing in a cloud of fumes from the back of a passing truck.

OPPOSITE

More Tibet than India. The gompa *(monastery) at Chemrey, Ladakh.*

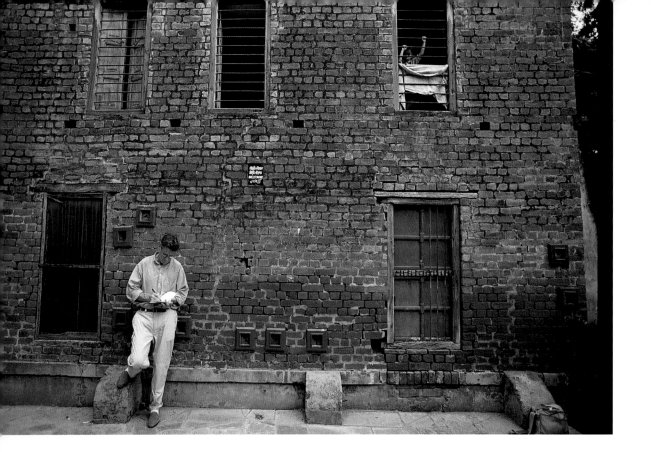

ABOVE

In the Jallianwala
Bagh. Thirteen framed
bullet holes on the
walls are said to date
back to the Amritsar
Massacre of 1919.

Road safety signs with slogans like 'Hell or Helmet!' and 'Stay Married! Divorce Speed!' are partially obscured and universally ignored.

An additional discomfort for an Englishman driving into Amritsar is a series of very public reminders of how much we were once disliked.

On one roundabout is a statue of a dashing figure in a theatrical moustache, a *puja* garland around his neck, running forward pointing a gun. This celebrates the assassin Udham Singh, who shot and killed Sir Michael O'Dwyer, a hated governor of the Punjab, in London in 1940.

Around the next corner is a statue to S. C. Bose, who felt so strongly about getting the British out of India that he tried to ally his Indian National Army with the Germans and Japanese in the Second World War. A half-mile further on is the alleyway leading to the Jallianwala Bagh, where 400 peacefully but illegally protesting Indians were massacred on the orders of Brigadier-General Reginald Dyer in April 1919, an outrage considered by many to mark the beginning of the end of British rule. Today the site is a park where a sacred flame burns, sponsored by Indian Oil.

The complex of buildings that contains the Golden Temple is called a Gurudwara (Gateway to the Gurus), the name given to all places of worship of the 20 million or so Sikhs in India. This, the holiest and grandest of them all, dominates the centre of Amritsar, its balconied, white stucco facade and flamboyantly domed roof rising exotically above a clutter of stalls, billboards, shops and crowded pavements where groups of Dalits ('the oppressed') squat inches from the traffic.

There is a strict dress code for the Golden Temple. First of all the head must be covered at all times. Scarves of various colours are readily available for non-Sikhs, either from any one of the 17 young lads who converge on you as soon as you pull up outside, or more cheaply from one of the stalls inside the forecourt. Shoes and socks must be removed. By the time we have deposited them at special lockers (a lady takes mine, something that would never have

happened in Pakistan), we look like a line of pantomime pirates. Hands must then be washed at marble-lined public basins and bare feet passed through a trough of water at the bottom of the steps.

ABOVE

Ablutions in the Amrit Sarover, the 'pool of nectar', at the Golden Temple, Amritsar.

The combination of the heat of the day, the constant crowd moving in and out and the carrying of film gear makes all these preliminaries rather a trial, but the sight that greets us when we finally reach the gateway arch banishes thoughts of discomfort, at least for a minute or two.

The Golden Temple itself, called by Sikhs the Hari Mandir (God's Temple) sits, like a great glittering barge, in the centre of a huge tank of water, with one narrow causeway (jammed with people throughout the day) connecting it with the promenade and the dazzling white temple buildings that enclose it on all four sides.

Four gates, one on each side, symbolize the inclusivity of Sikhism, the temple's openness to all, irrespective of religion, caste, creed or sex. The four equal entrances are not all that distinguish it from other religious buildings. Instead of climbing to an altar, the stairs to the Golden Temple lead downwards to the holy place, an encouragement to approach with humility.

Once down the steps to the waterside, there isn't much encouragement to sit around. Most of the pilgrims are moving, in a remorseless clockwise flow, around the marble-flagged promenade, some strolling, some bustling purposefully, some dodging the mops and buckets of the cleaners, most squeezed onto coconut matting to avoid burning their feet, while hymns from the Holy Book are sung over booming loudspeakers. Some men are stripped down, bathing in the holy water, which seems to be largely full of fat carp with gulping, Jagger-like mouths. Very few visitors, apart from a one-legged man lying asleep, head resting on his crutches, are doing nothing.

I notice how much more openly curious people are here than in Pakistan.

'What is the country in which you are residing?' they ask. 'For what purpose have you come?'

Occasionally, a passing family group will quite unapologetically insert themselves alongside

ABOVE

With two guardians of the temple. Their robes and spears symbolize the dual nature of the Sikhs: service and defence. In the background the Hari Mandir (Hari is God, Mandir is temple) has 1100 lb (500 kg) of gold on its walls.

us and get a friend to take a photo, as if we too are part of the tourist attractions. Helpful explanations of what's going on are given, whether solicited or not.

An elderly gentleman with a long beard points in the direction of the Hari Mandir.

'Whatever you require from God he is giving you. That is what they are singing about.'

There is a brisk, businesslike pragmatism about the Sikhs. They don't seem over-concerned with the mysteries of belief.

Philanthropy, along with business enterprise and physical bravery, is a vital part of Sikhism and all their temples have a *langar*, a kitchen preparing free meals around the clock, financed through the one-tenth of their income that all Sikhs are expected to give to good works. It's a huge operation, with an estimated 50,000 meals prepared each weekday and twice that at weekends. The work is all done by volunteers, and any Sikh, whether surgeon or street cleaner, is expected to come and help chop onions or wash dishes. In the words of one of the ten holy Gurus on whose teachings Sikhism is based: 'If you want to understand me, come into my kitchen.' This we do.

The kitchen is spread through several buildings. One is entirely devoted to a chapatti production line. A rat skips nimbly out of the way as fresh sacks of flour are cut open and fed into the bowels of a slowly turning machine, which regurgitates the flour as dough. One group of helpers rolls the dough into balls, another flattens each ball out into a pancake, and another lays them out on hotplates the size of double beds, made from cast-iron sheets laid on bricks with gas fires underneath, and capable of taking a couple of hundred chapattis at a time. When one side is done the chapattis are flipped over in quick, dexterous movements of a long thin implement with a half-moon end. When the flipper is satisfied both sides are right he gives an extra strong flick, which sends the chapatti flying off the hotplate to land neatly on a pile on the floor. The piles are then removed and carried out to the refectory.

The chapatti production line shares a tall barn-like space with dal cauldrons, the largest cooking vessels I've ever seen. Vats like giant tympana are set above gas jets and stirred with mighty ladles.

I pick my way through the kitchens, across a terrace where 30 or 40 people sit slicing onions and garlic, green peppers and ginger, and up the stairs to take a meal in one of the spartan communal dining rooms. Each floor is the size of a warehouse and can accommodate 3000 covers at any one time. I join a line of people who file in and sit cross-legged at a long coir mat, soggy from periodic washing. Volunteers pass through, giving out segmented stainless steel trays, which others then fill up with chapatti, dollops of pickle and dal ladled out of steel buckets. Water is poured into our mugs from another bucket.

As a helpful man next to me says, this whole process embodies the Sikh teaching that we are all equal and we must learn to serve each other.

This high-volume soup kitchen is not the only service; there are also free dormitories here providing accommodation for 25,000 people a night.

It looks and sounds like a fine and good thing but there have been abuses of the system. I notice a sign advising 'Pilgrims must not accept eatables from strangers', which refers to a recent spate of cases of people being drugged and their belongings stolen.

Twenty years ago this altruistic environment saw dreadful violence when a group of Sikhs demanding their own state barricaded themselves in the Akhal Takht, the second most sacred building on the site.

The siege was lifted in the infamous Operation Bluestar, when the Indian army brought tanks into the temple and pulverized the building. It's estimated that several thousand died in the fighting. Such was the strength of feeling that a few months later Prime Minister Indira Ghandi, who authorized the attack, was assassinated by Sikh members of her own bodyguards.

Such trauma seems almost inconceivable tonight as a setting sun burnishes the 500 kilograms of gold that sheath the marble walls of the Hari Mandir, hymns echo around the arcades and turbanned and bearded Sikh men and their families move slowly in through its doors to pay homage to the Holy Book, the most precious object in a religion that rejects idolatry.

Day Thirty One : Amritsar to Chandigarh

India is much concerned these days with behavioural improvement. Yesterday I noticed the road safety campaign (though I seemed to be the only one who did) and this morning I see that the government is tackling the vexed subject of 'night soil', or open-air defecation, which is such a feature of life here. A series of adverts in the morning papers appeals to people to stop 'easing themselves' in public places. 'Easing oneself' is a new euphemism to me, but I rather like it and will use it whenever possible.

Heading south from Amritsar on the main road to Chandigarh we pass an horrific accident. Two trucks have collided head-on with such force that one of them has burst, oozing a load of gravel from its ruptured sides. My driver says that truck-drivers not only don't have to take a test, they don't even have to be able to read.

The road we're on is a four-lane intercity highway, yet it's also a country road with farm vehicles, and indeed farm animals, crossing it whenever they feel like it.

Waiting for the Grand Prix? Pit stop on the road to Chandigarh.

At any given time we're sharing the NH-1 with cars, trucks, battered Tata buses (driven like the wind), auto-rickshaws, pedal rickshaws, scooters, horse-drawn carts, buffalo-drawn carts, tractors, dogs, bicycles, motorbikes, pedestrians and unattended cows, sheep and goats.

A roadside billboard cheers me up. 'Youghal and Sons. Where Fashion Ends.'

We take a short cut off the main road along an avenue of eucalyptus trees, which leads promisingly quietly through a green and pleasant countryside of rice and barley fields dotted with elegant white cattle egrets. Quite out of the blue we're brought to a halt by a traffic jam ahead of us. I ask my driver what's going on and he shakes his head in exasperation. It's a police check.

When we finally pull up alongside the policeman he swaggers slowly over to our driver. He looks like the corrupt cop out of central casting. Overweight, ponderous and self-important. He sniffs loudly as he examines our driver's papers, but when he sees us in the back he becomes a little more animated. After a couple more questions he hands the papers back and waves us quickly on.

My driver chuckles.

'He's fleecing people. Taking their money to drive along his road. I told him we were making a film for BBC Television. That's why we got through so fast!'

Arrive on the leafy ring roads of Chandigarh about six. And, miraculously, in one piece.

Day Thirty Two : Chandigarh to Shimla

Chandigarh seems to consist entirely of roundabouts. Beautiful, well-kept, florally abundant roundabouts, sending the traffic spinning from one to another like some endless Scottish reel.

Verdant avenues of peepul, ashoka and mango trees connect this gently swirling system, leading, presumably, to a city of some substance, for Chandigarh is the capital of two states, Punjab and Haryana. I say presumably, because in our short stay here it is difficult to see much beyond the roundabouts and dead-straight, repetitive avenues.

LEFT

Kalka, Himachal Pradesh (Himalaya Province). The public pump still has a vital role in Indian life. And the railways are the single biggest employer in the world.

What I do see reminds me of Islamabad. Both are post-Independence cities, built in a self-consciously modern style to replace the architecture of the Raj with something new and fresh, and more in keeping with what Nehru called 'the nation's faith in the future'. Both are discreet, tidy and a little cheerless.

At least Chandigarh secured the services of the top man. Swiss architect Le Corbusier designed the grid-plan layout and the boxy, modular buildings in concrete and red brick that can be glimpsed every now and then between the trees.

When I enquire what sort of person lives in this mecca of modernism I'm told that it's mostly wealthy Punjabi farmers approaching retirement.

My local informant summed up Chandigarh as 'a town of white beards and green hedges'. And sadly I'm not here long enough to disprove it.

It's time to return to the mountains, and we begin the journey dramatically, aboard the Himalayan Queen railway service to Shimla, a town high in the Shiwalik foothills, from where the British Empire in India was run during the hot summer months and which is now the capital of Himachal Pradesh (Himalaya Province).

The 2'6" narrow-gauge railway to Shimla climbs 7000 feet (2130 m) in 57 miles (92 km) and there is barely a level stretch of track on the entire route.

Midday at Kalka station. Ten minutes before the Queen leaves, the express from Delhi arrives, disgorging yet more passengers for the Shimla train. Half-term holidays have just begun and sturdy schoolgirls with backpacks and walking sticks are fighting with harassed family groups for a place in one of the seven small coaches.

The stationmaster, a stout man with a shiny bald head ignores the helpless cries of his staff as he rolls out a liturgy of statistics.

'Indian Railways is the biggest employer in the world, you know. We move ten million people a day, over 6000 kilometres of track.' He dabs a handkerchief at his forehead, then tucks it in his pocket and produces a small scrapbook.

'You want to film the viaduct?' he asks. 'You can do that.'

He opens the book to reveal a grainy photograph of the railway line running over a multi-

71

storey stone bridge, and holds it up to the camera.

'There,' he smoothes down the page, 'you film that.'

'We'd rather film the real thing,' says Nigel with a trace of irritation. The stationmaster, undeterred, riffles through the pages.

'Look at that!' he holds the book up again. A wintry scene of the same viaduct. 'That is *snow*!'

Somehow, everyone squeezes aboard and, on time at 12.10, the Himalayan Queen pulls out past Kalka signal box, rounds a curve and heads for the hills, passing by a mix of factories and rust-stained housing blocks surrounded by lush sub-tropical vegetation. A lineside tree sways beneath the weight of a family of monkeys the size of small Labradors.

'Langurs,' says the woman opposite me. 'They're the biggest monkeys of all.'

I offer some sweets to her and her family and we start talking. She's a large very jolly lady and her name is Deepti. She works for the ministry of defence in Delhi and is on a week's holiday with her husband and two boys. I ask her if the Britishness of Shimla is still an attraction for Indian tourists.

She frowns and shakes her head.

'They're not so interested in all that, no.'

She reminds me that vital conferences between Ghandi, Nehru and Jinnah aimed at getting the British out of India also took place in Shimla.

We rattle into a tunnel. One of 103 on the line, their entrances all numbered and marked with the exact length.

Deepti opens plastic containers and gets out lunch for the family. She was up at four this morning, she says, preparing *pooris* and *aloo* for the journey, and she insists on sharing them with me.

The deep-fried fluffy *pooris* mix deliciously with the curried potato. There are four more hours of the journey to go and I feel in no hurry at all, which is just as well, for the progress of the Himalayan Queen is dogged rather than dashing. We rarely make much more than 20 miles an

ABOVE

*First glimpse of the
scale of Shimla, 7260
feet (2213 m) above
sea level. Provincial
capital of Himachal
Pradesh.*

hour, which is all you want with good food, good company and a good view.

I stand at the open door and let the gradually cooling air blow over me as we snake round corners and in and out of trim stone tunnels dug into the hillside like rabbit holes. As we climb, the date palms, rubber trees and bougainvillea give way to grassy meadows, oak scrub and then spindly deciduous woodland.

I have a knowledgeable companion in Raaja Bhasin, a neat, theatrical, young man who has written books on Shimla. The British, he tells me, had discovered the spot in the 1820s, and it was so much to their liking that in 1864 it was declared their summer capital.

'At that time one-fifth of the human race was administered from Shimla.'

As the railway was not opened for another 39 years, the entire apparatus of government had to be moved up from Calcutta on bullock carts.

When it was eventually decided to go ahead with a railway they moved fast. The line was built in little more than two years, and the basic structures remain in good order a hundred years later. The high standards expected took their toll. Raaja tells the story of a Colonel Barog who supervised the construction of one of the tunnels working from each end simultaneously. Unfortunately, they failed to meet in the middle and Barog, distraught at the miscalculation, shot himself.

Half an hour out of Shimla we're into alpine forest and there is a cool, refreshing scent of pine in the air. The railway runs between tall rhododendron trees and the big cedars they call deodars, until all at once we're among the half-timbered villas and cottages with verandahs and cast-iron canopies that comfortably conform to my image of Shimla. But as we pull away clear of the trees and get our first glimpse of the town itself I realize I've got it very wrong.

Modern Shimla is no cosy retreat in the mountains but a city of considerable scale, home to 150,000, spread out over five hills and liberally sprinkled with concrete apartment blocks.

On the steep street outside the station there is a chaos of drivers, passengers and vehicles manoeuvring in an impossibly small space. Once away from this bottleneck our taxi crawls slowly round the side of the hill and along the Mall until we reach the Cecil Hotel.

This famous Shimla landmark has been extensively and, I should imagine, expensively, restored.

The room is lovely and, as darkness falls, I just want to throw open the balcony doors and taste the freshest air since we left the mountain valleys of the Karakoram.

As soon as I do so my telephone rings and I'm politely but firmly requested not to, as monkeys will get into my room. Monkeys are a big problem, they assure me. Big enough to install sensors in my tall, tempting balcony doors to sound an alarm whenever I open them.

Day Thirty Four : Shimla

Wake to grey skies and rain. Filming delayed till the weather clears. Retire to the best bed on the journey so far and read the Dalai Lama's book *The Art of Happiness*. We have been granted an audience with him in a few days time and I began the book a little out of duty. Now I find I'm getting a lot out of it. There is something infectious about his optimism, an optimism which comes from confronting rather than avoiding the unacceptable and acknowledging, understanding and demystifying it.

An hour later the clouds have passed over and I can see a crystal clear sky beyond my monkey-besieged windows.

I can see the enemy clearly. They move in family groups along the wall opposite, scratching themselves and ambling rather cockily along, until some commotion breaks out and they race in all directions, shrieking and snarling.

I gaze out in frustration, feeling an unlikely empathy with those mega popstars, besieged in hotel rooms by their fans.

From being just a summer hideaway, Shimla grew to become the nerve centre of Britain's

ABOVE

Keeping out of the sun or keeping out of the book? Shy ladies on the Ridge at Shimla.

Indian empire for eight months of the year and in 1888 a building considered appropriate for this role was completed. The Vice-Regal Lodge is an extraordinary edifice. Built at the top of a hill and the peak of Victorian self-confidence, it is authority made manifest, superiority set in stone. The British relationship with India changed in the 1860s, after the bloodshed of the Indian Mutiny, or the first War of Independence, as most Indians call it. What had been a loosely commercial enterprise, a sort of mercantile laissez-faire, began to be seen as a moral obligation. Previously relaxed relations between British and Indians were discouraged. Better communications meant that wives and families could come out to India, ending inter-marriage with locals. The army was strengthened and concentrated in well-armed cantonments.

'Keeping India at bay', is how my friend Raaja sums up this new imperial vision, as we walk in the gardens of the Lodge this morning. In his view, the sombre grey walls that rise above us represented a deliberate attempt by the British to recreate the island mentality in India. The Vice-Regal Lodge stood not just for power, but for permanence.

Permanence lasted less than 60 years and to add insult to injury many of the most important talks that led to the departure of the British took place behind these grandiose faux-baronial walls. All the founders and future leaders of India and Pakistan at one time trooped in below the lions rampant that stand guard above the carved stone portals.

'Ghandi disliked it,' says Raaja. 'While everybody else came in rickshaws, two men pushing and two men pulling, Ghandi walked.'

Mountbatten, the man charged with giving India its independence, met the leaders of the Princely States here, reminding himself of who the most important ones were by using the mnemonic 'Hot kippers make good breakfast'. Hyderabad, Kashmir, Mysore, Gwalior and Baroda.

The fact that the monumental Vice-Regal Lodge still stands is hardly surprising. It would probably need some controlled nuclear device to take down these massive walls, but the fact that it is so well maintained, with gardeners sweeping immaculate lawns and carefully raking the gravel on the forecourt, says a lot about the attitude of the Indians after independence.

'There was no wholesale desecration of imperial buildings in Shimla,' says Raaja. 'Everything was left pretty much as it was.'

The Vice-Regal Lodge has been reborn as an Institute for South-East Asian Affairs. The Ballroom is now a library. Functional shelf stacks fill a floor that in its heyday had hundreds of dancers swirling across it, themed perhaps in Chinese or Regency fancy dress. Though chandeliers still hang from its ceiling, the spot where the orchestra played is now marked by a large sign that reads 'Silence'.

An index board showing where books can be located still uses vice-regal descriptions like State Lounge and Fan Room. Social Sciences can be found in the Ballroom, the Tibetan Collection in the Pantry, and copies of *The Muslim World* and *American Scientist* sit side by side in the Dining Hall.

Modesty and earnestness has replaced display and grandeur. Entertainment has given way to enlightenment. This bastion of British certainty has become a place of enquiry, curiosity and debate. Three very Indian preoccupations.

The imposing site on which Shimla is built can best be seen from the Ridge, a long, thin, open area that stands at the narrowest point of the bluff. It's a watershed, with rivers on one side running east to the Bay of Bengal, and on the other, west into the Arabian Sea.

This afternoon it's thronged with holiday strollers eating pizza and ice cream. Though the milling tourists are almost entirely Indian, the centre of the town still lives up to its description as 'a little bit of Cheltenham in India'. Statues of Mahatma and Indira Ghandi are overshadowed by the tall Gothic Revival tower of Christ Church dominating one end of the Ridge, looking yellow, blotchy and feverish with plants pushing up out of holes in its red, corrugated-iron roof. A little way down the hill is the Arts and Crafts Style Town Hall, about the only building in town with a slate roof (Raaja tells me that corrugated iron is preferred because monkeys pull the tiles out).

A flight of steps leads down from the Ridge to another Cheltenham-ish landmark, the Gaiety Theatre. It was built about the same time as the Vice-Regal Lodge, as a home for a thriving amateur dramatic club in Shimla, which gave its first performance in 1838. With few women around at that time, the female roles had to be taken by army officers, one of whom refused to shave his moustache off for a love scene.

A heavy stone exterior gives little indication of the little gem of an auditorium inside. Horseshoe shaped and decorated with carved wood and plaster of Paris stucco, it has a dress circle supported by slender columns with gold-leaf capitals. The stage, spacious for a theatre that only seats 200, has been graced by Kipling, Baden-Powell, who later founded the Boy Scouts, and more recently Felicity Kendall and legendary Indian stars like the singer K. L. Saighal and the Bollywood actor Anupam Kher.

Our visit has coincided with a performance of an early play by Michael Frayn, called *Chinamen*. With huge successes running currently on Broadway and in the West End, I imagine this is quite a coup for them, and have taken the trouble to ring Michael and solicit a message of support for the cast.

The director, Mrs Neelam Dewan, thanks me profusely for this, as she had been given a copy of the play without a front page and didn't know who the author was.

She seems a little harassed. Last night's performance had been spoiled by mass amnesia on the part of the actors.

Had they not had time to learn their lines, I asked her.

Oh yes, they had time, but they are all in the army and very busy.

ABOVE

On the same stage as Kipling and Baden-Powell. Another Englishman hams it up at the lovely Gaiety Theatre.

So I stumbled on the truth. This pretty little theatre survives as a sort of social club for the military. The activities of the Green Room bar and lounge upstairs subsidize the thespian activities below, the quid pro quo being that the army are offered the best parts, and the best seats.

As curtain up approaches, men trained to lead hundreds into battle are pacing about backstage, like schoolboys about to go before the headmaster, repeating the same lines over and over again. It's a full house tonight with the local commander in chief attending. This only seems to ratchet up the tension.

I have been asked to give a short address before the play begins.

'What is your name again, please?' asks the young captain who's been asked to introduce me. 'Palin…Palin.' He tries it out a few times before giving me an apologetic smile.

'I'm the entertainments officer. I do bingo, mainly.'

At 7.30 precisely he pushes aside the decaying velvet curtain, tells a few nervous jokes and then I hear my moment of glory approach.

'Ladies and Gentlemen, may I ask you to give a very warm welcome for our special celebrity guest, Mr Michael Plain!'

This sort of sets the tone for the evening. Despite the best efforts of Mrs Neelam Dewan, both as director and leading actress, some of the colonels and majors in the cast do have recollection problems, and I understand now why the two prompters are given such prominent mention in the programme and why, when they come on stage at the end, Mrs Punam Gupta and Mrs Vijaylaksmi Sood receive thunderous applause and garlands of flowers.

Afterwards we all repair to the Green Room and tell each other how wonderful we were and the Commanding Officer, Lt-General Singh, a Sikh in a handsome rose-pink turban insists that we return to his house for a drink. It's a short walk from the hotel and Roger is much impressed that the guards on the gate snap to attention and present arms as we enter. It's after midnight when we leave, and they totally ignore us.

ABOVE

On the road to Dharamsala. Our well-hennaed driver, 'Red', and a lunch bristling with green chillies.

Day Thirty Five : Shimla to Dharamsala

Pack up. Take a last look out of the French windows I'm not supposed to open. Expect the monkeys to at least look up, but they're all gathered around a rubbish skip, picking around in the contents as if it were the first day of Harrods' sale.

Or perhaps they've heard what's happening to their brothers and sisters in Delhi. *The Times of India* reports that the authorities there have decided to start rounding up some of the monkeys that roam the city and deport them. More controversially, they're to take 2000 cows out of circulation as well. Not, I notice, to improve road safety, but, so they say, to curb the illegal milk trade.

We leave the bow windows, pebble-dash walls and wrought-iron balconies behind and continue north by car to another hill station, Dharamsala, best known for being the headquarters of the Dalai Lama and the Tibetan government in exile.

Our driver, like many middle-aged men in India and Pakistan, has coloured his greying hair with henna, in his case so generously that it's almost bright scarlet and a tell-tale contrast with his grey moustache. Basil has christened him 'Red'.

Outside the village of Ghumarwin Red gives an agonized cry and swings the wheel frantically.

'That is very bad,' he says, in genuine distress. 'That was a snake on the road.'

Basil is unsympathetic.

'You swerved to avoid a snake?'

'It is Monday. Shiva's day. It is very bad luck.'

'No, it's not, it's Tuesday.'

A great weight seems to fall from Red's shoulder.

'Ah, yes, that's good. That is Hanuman's day. He is the monkey god.'

'So you've got to watch out for monkeys.'

'Oh yes.'

Basil, proud owner of a lovely wheaten terrier called Ed, asks which day he should avoid dogs.

'Dogs?' Red laughs dismissively. 'No. Always killing dogs.'

The country road is undulating and undramatic, rising and falling as we cross the valleys of modest rivers running down from the mountains into the Punjab. Reminders of worship are never far away, from brightly painted roadside shrines daubed in mauve, bright pink or orange, to busloads of pilgrims in yellow robes with red and gold sashes. They're causing traffic jams as they converge on the temple at a place called Jawalamukhi. The attraction here is that natural gas issues from the cliff in the form of an 'eternal' blue flame and feeds a constantly boiling pool of water. This is considered magical proof of the power of the local gods.

By evening we've reached our hotel, once a tea-planter's bungalow, with fine views over the green Kangra valley below and the Dhauladar mountains above, on whose wooded slopes Dharamsala and its sister McLeodganj are set like Tuscan hill villages.

No monkeys to besiege us down here but caged dogs bark all night long.

Read *The Art of Happiness* and try to avoid feeling murderous.

Day Thirty Six : Dharamsala and McLeodganj

It's six o'clock in the morning and the first streaks of light are in the sky as we drive along the narrow streets of Dharamsala and continue up the road that climbs through pine, oak and rhododendron woods to the less mellifluous sounding village of McLeodganj. ('Ganj' means market and McLeod, presumably, was a Scotsman.) To complicate matters, this place with a Hindu-Scots name is filled with Tibetans.

The reason they're here is that the Chinese, having invaded Tibet in 1949, began to consolidate their political power by eliminating any opposition. In 1959 this resulted in an uprising in Lhasa, which was put down with such force that, fearing for his life, the Dalai Lama, leader of Tibetan Buddhism and Head of State, decided to flee his country.

He crossed the Himalaya into India and in a brave gesture of generosity, Prime Minister Nehru gave him sanctuary and later a more permanent home in Dharamsala. (Many other countries would have had misgivings about what this would do to their relations with China.) Chinese oppression of Buddhists is less virulent now than it was at the height of the Cultural Revolution, but they have tightened their economic and political hold on Tibet and 44 years after his flight, the Dalai Lama, and the Tibetan government, remain in exile.

We're up this early to catch a dawn ceremony at the Lhagyal Ri Temple, just a short walk down the hill from the monastery where the Dalai Lama now lives.

On a terrace of land with tall pines falling away to one side are a series of stupas, the dome-shaped shrines in which are kept scriptures or remains or clay likenesses of the gods. A great wall of prayer flags forms a backdrop behind them. There's a residual night-time chill in the air but

LEFT

Country life in Himachal Pradesh. Rich land, poor farmers.

already a line of devotees are quietly moving along a line of brightly painted prayer wheels, which culminates in one huge wheel about eight feet high. They spin them and murmur prayers as they go. They then feed sprigs of juniper branch into small open ovens and leave gifts by the fire, a flask of tea or a bottle of barley wine. The aromatic, spicy smell of the wood smoke mingles with the pines to give a strong heady flavour to the dawn.

As the sun rises its rays hit the columns of smoke and turn them into long diagonal shafts of light. At that moment four monks, cross-legged on the floor before a microphone, begin to recite prayers.

Dogs sniff around. A herd of cows plods slowly across the front of the temple past the prayer wheels and on into the woods. No-one seems to bat an eyelid. It's part of life and all life is sacred to the Buddhist.

The only organized part of what seems to me a delightfully laid-back, unstructured ceremony is a ritual throwing of *tsampa*, barley flour. I'm encouraged to join in and, picking up a handful of the flour, I take my place in line facing the stupas. Prayers are recited, hands are raised three times and then, altogether, we toss the flour forwards, an offering to the gods, and a wake-up call to their protectors.

On the way back up the hill a driveway turns sharply right, up to the Namgyal monastery, or Little Lhasa, as it's known, where the Dalai Lama is currently in residence. An inveterate traveller, he's just returned from a five-city tour of the US. Our appointment to see him is in two days' time, but there is a flurry of activity around the buildings and word comes through that he is leading prayers in the temple and if we're lucky we might be able to get in and film the ceremony. From then on everything happens very quickly. We're introduced to one of the Dalai Lama's private secretaries, a tall young man in immaculate grey suit, with a Tibetan waistcoat to match, who ushers us through a side entrance, up a flight of steps and through a metal detector. We're then body-searched quite thoroughly and led up into a light, airy courtyard, half covered with a

ABOVE

*Tibet in India.
Hanging prayer flags
out near the Lhagyal
Ri temple at
McLeodganj. Flags
should be hung in
exposed places so the
wind can blow the
prayers up to the gods.*

corrugated plastic sun-roof. The floor is packed with people, many of them robed and beaded Westerners, but we are led on past them to the edge of an inner area, where, surrounded by a sea of shaven-headed, saffron-robed monks, the familiar bespectacled figure of the best known Buddhist in the world, the incarnation of Avalokiteshvara, the Bodhisattva of Love and Great Compassion, sits on a cushioned platform leading the prayers. Every eye and ear is concentrated on him and yet he seems a modest figure, swaying slowly as he speaks and sounding profoundly weary. Occasionally he leans forward to shake a small bell.

We watch all this from a side door, not 20 feet away from him, which gives onto a stage, dominated by a statue of the Buddha and stacked with piles of sweets, biscuits and fruit such as you might find in a church at Harvest Festival. When we have finished filming we're moved smartly away, as the prayers come to an end and the assembled throng rises to its feet and begins to move forward for a glimpse of the great man as he leaves, preceded, I notice, by a guard with a sub-machine gun.

In the crush, I lose sight of the crew and find myself at the bottom of a wide flight of stairs, with everything apparently going on above me. Then, out of the melee, the Dalai Lama appears, descending the stairs on the arms of two assistants. I step back out of the way but my retreat is blocked by a crash barrier, so I just bow my head and try to look invisible.

As he comes down off the steps I notice that the set gaze with which he intoned the prayers earlier has gone and he's looking around him with an animated smile, seemingly delighted to make eye contact. A few feet away from me he stops, looks over in my direction and waves. I cast a quick look behind me, but there's no-one there. I look back and he's waving again, almost as if he'd seen an old friend. I take one last quick look round then walk forward and shake his hand. I seem to have done the right thing, as he beams at me and, behind heavy dark spectacle frames, his eyes sparkle.

I mutter something about looking forward to talking to him later in the week. He nods, squeezes my hand and looks at me again in that pleased-to-see-you sort of way before moving on. The crowd, temporarily halted, passes by after him and I reassume my role as man at the crash barrier.

'He probably did recognize you,' says someone as we eat breakfast on the terrace of a pretty guesthouse overlooking the monastery. 'He loves showbiz folk.'

This barbed compliment comes with little evidence other than his wearily over-quoted association with Richard Gere, who has stayed at this guesthouse and whose name appears, interestingly, among a list of sponsors of the Sulabh Public Toilets, Baths and Sanitary Complex by the temple car park. Among the other dozen or so donors listed I couldn't help noticing the name of Mae Loo.

Public relations are important to the Tibetans, for McLeodganj is more than just temples and the Dalai Lama's residence. It is home to a flourishing number of enterprises, political, religious and commercial, all of which are designed to demonstrate the seriousness and competence of the government in exile. Everywhere we go we are handed well-produced information sheets by well-dressed, knowledgeable and patient young men, who do a thoroughly professional job of marketing the mysteries of Tibet. I discover a perfect example of old traditions and modern delivery when I visit the Tibetan Medical and Astrology Centre. Though there are beggars at the door, inside all is clean, whitewashed and businesslike. The ground floor is more like a warehouse, with sacks of herbs coming in and boxes of medicine going out. Upstairs the astrologers work away on quietly humming computers surrounded by the intricate Buddhist paintings on cloth that they call *thangkas* (pronounced 'tankers').

Outside the window prayer flags are tied to nests of satellite dishes. One sending out messages, the other receiving them.

Knowing I was coming here, I sent details of my place and time of birth to the Astrology Centre so that they could prepare a chart for me. The service costs around £50 a time and is available to anyone, as are the protective amulets that I notice they sell here (with instructions to wrap in yellow cloth and wear around the neck).

A young man, with curly dark hair, introduces himself as Phurbu Tsering, the astrologer in charge of my case. He is, like most of the young men here, neatly turned out in western style, with sports jacket, jeans and Gap shirt.

He it is who has calculated my incarnation prospects. As reincarnation is one of the basic beliefs of Buddhism (the Dalai Lama is a reincarnation of the last Dalai Lama, who was a reincarnation of the Dalai Lama before that, and so on), it helps to know what your chances are. There are six realms in which you can end up. God, Demi-God and Human Being are all good and Animal, Hell and Bad Spirits all less good.

With a certain amount of apprehension I open my chart, which is headed with my Tibetan birthdate, the 1st day of the 3rd month of Water-Sheep year. With mixed feelings (mainly of relief) I read on. 'You were likely to be an elephant in your previous life, but you are going to be born as a daughter of a rich family in the West.'

Basil finds this particularly funny and is convinced that I'll be reincarnated as one of John Cleese's grandchildren.

The rest of the chart has mixed news. I'm told I 'believe in honesty and logic feeling, not emotion' and 'never indulge in meaningless gossips and talks'. That doesn't sound right.

Blue, red and white are my lucky colours (which presumably means I can support Sheffield Wednesday and Sheffield United at the same time). Thursday is my worst day, Fridays and Mondays my best and my marriage has been 'disheartening'. How can I tell Helen this after 38 years?

Phurbu Tsering is sincere, friendly and speaks excellent English, and clearly believes in the truth of what he's found in my chart. He takes me to one side as we leave and urges me to be particularly careful this year. He sees change and a crisis ahead. As I'm about to spend the next two months crossing the highest mountain range on earth, this is not exactly what I need to hear.

I ask Phurbu if he has had his own astrological chart made. He shakes his head. There is no record of his date or time of birth. All this information, and everything else his family owned, was left behind when his parents fled Tibet.

He smiles gravely.

'I was born on the roadside.'

Perhaps the crown jewel of the exiles' achievement is the Norbulingka Institute, named after the Dalai Lama's summer palace in Lhasa, and dedicated to the preservation of Tibetan craft and culture. Once through the gates we're in lush, beautifully ordered gardens rising gently in a series of terraces to the gold-tipped temple at the top of the hill. The paths are paved with slate slabs, and soft, gently swaying stands of bamboo are both protective and mysterious. Flowers trail round columns and arches and water flows artfully down, bubbling from gargoyle mouths into a series of fishponds. The air is charged with the constant high-pitched trill of insects.

It's described to me as 'a campus' but with cell-phone beeps and a constant quiet coming and going between departments, another description comes to mind.

This is a highly motivated Garden of Eden.

It nevertheless retains a typically Buddhist character. There is an amiable sense of tranquillity, people don't shout and everyone works with seraphic concentration, whether in the *thangka* workshop, painting fine detail on a banner of beasts, angry gods and flying horses, or in the metal shop, hammering out the base of a sitting Buddha from a sheet of copper, or in an inscription room, sitting beneath a framed picture of the Dalai Lama and copying onto long, thin, rectangular plates the text of Buddhist scriptures picked out in gold, coral and silver.

Everywhere we go we are received with quiet cordiality and politely but persistently followed by a video camera recording our every move.

It's impressive, if a little tiring, all this courtesy and hospitality, and I'm not quite sure where it will all lead. The Tibetans in exile are skilful operators and I admire the tenacity and persistence with which they court world opinion, but as time goes by the Chinese are strengthening their hold on Tibet, while adopting more liberal policies towards the Buddhists and better relations with the rest of the world. It's hard to see where the leverage might be applied to get them to change their policy and allow a meaningful Tibetan government to work from Lhasa rather than McLeodganj.

Another problem is that over the last 44 years increasing numbers of the people who are running the government in exile have been born and bred in India and have never seen the country they represent.

As we saw at Norbulingka this afternoon, life is comfortable for the cultural executives and it would surely not be easy to uproot themselves from this congenial corner and relocate to a cold plateau on the far side of the Himalayan wall.

Day Thirty Eight : Dharansala and McLeodganj

Our audience with the Dalai Lama is at 2.15 this afternoon. We arrive early and film in the streets of McLeodganj. It's Ghandi's birthday and a public holiday, but no day off for the desperate figures in vests and cotton trousers trying to mend roads as cars continue to drive along them, or for the limbless beggars squatting beneath a Western Union sign, or the bundles of rags with hands protruding outside the cyber café. I've never seen so many mutilated and deformed people in one place, and there's not much you can do but walk on and try to avoid eye contact. Their own people, I notice, ignore them completely.

I stop to make some notes leaning up against a metal post crowned with a thick mesh of unprotected electric cabling. A boy, not more than five or six, holds out his hand.

'Hello,' he repeats softly, 'Hello.'

An older man with a stick simply stands there with a small pail, whimpering soundlessly. Passing these wraith-like figures are the substantial, muscular, Western backpackers who home in on these places, looking for cheap accommodation while sporting designer shades that would cost a street mender six months' wages.

Poverty is corrosive, but it's always worse when it is found side by side with wealth. Occupants of shanty towns in the Philippines or South America are as poor as this but they have their own, fierce, communal pride, and (apart from BBC film crews) they don't have rich foreigners walking their streets every day.

We're at the Tsechokling temple in good time. The Dalai Lama is giving a public audience before he speaks to us and security is tight. A beagle sniffer-dog is led along the line by a Sikh policeman. In the outer office leading to the Dalai Lama's private quarters we're politely asked to sit and wait while our papers are checked. A poster on the opposite wall makes depressing reading. 'China's Record in Tibet' is blazoned across the top. 'More than a Million Killed, More than 6000 Monasteries Destroyed, Thousands in Prison, Hundreds Still Missing', and in big red letters at the bottom, 'China Get Out of Tibet'.

The Dalai Lama's bungalow is spacious but not ostentatious. A room full of the various medals, awards and citations he's been given from all over the world gives onto a long, cool, marble-tiled verandah, from which a few steps lead down to a driveway that snakes around an oval garden bed full of conventional roses and marigolds. A desk has been set up at the bottom of these steps, beneath the protective shade of bushy bougainvillea. A long line of visitors is being led in, at its head an Indian Catholic priest in white robe with a prominent crucifix around his neck.

Monks line the drive, a most benevolent form of crowd control.

At 12.40, dead on time, the man they've been waiting for appears and without fuss or bother he begins to greet them, going through all 700, showing interest in every individual, catching the eye, trying to avoid identical responses. Whereas a lot of the Westerners pass by quite briskly, like students collecting passing-out degrees, the Tibetan monks approach slowly, utterly awed, some bent double in their supplication. Though I have the impression that the Dalai Lama is not comfortable with too much respect, he listens earnestly and at length to their requests and has a nice way of rubbing his hand across their shaven heads and, occasionally, bending forward to brush his lips against their foreheads.

By two o'clock the last of the line has gone through, and he is escorted away by his efficient, ever so slightly severe minders, only to reappear on the verandah minutes later to address a group of 60 new arrivals from Tibet, refugees who, have just made the difficult and dangerous crossing through the mountains as he did 45 years ago. One of his private secretaries translates his remarks for me. Very interesting they are too. He begins in a folksy way, sitting, hands on hips, trying to draw these cowed and respectful new arrivals out. He starts by asking if any of them had been caught by the border police, or lost money and valuables on the way. He asks about the current state of the hospitals and schools. Do they teach Tibetan? How many lumberjacks are there in Tibet these days (a reference to the massive deforestation since the Chinese arrived)? Then he talks to them quietly but with authority. He tells them that since September last year the government in exile has renewed official contact with the Chinese. Though he hears that the Chinese occupation is even more repressive than the year before, he notes that more Chinese are visiting Tibet, both as tourists and pilgrims, and that there is a growing interest in things Tibetan around the world, which is putting pressure on the Chinese.

It is important that they retain their Tibetan culture and language but Buddhism is far from being an irrelevant, unchanging religion. Buddhists and scientists have much in common, while in the field of psychology the Buddhists are well ahead. He grins. By 2000 years.

We will win, he assures them, because we have truth and truth will ultimately prevail. Don't worry. Educate yourselves. Learn Chinese. Learn about the world outside Tibet, because if he ever returns to Lhasa he will not go back to a feudal society. Go back, he says to the ones who plan to return home, and tell them that.

It's a sober, realistic, pragmatic message, implying, quite clearly, that the past is past. He has accepted the fact, if not all the practices, of the Chinese occupation. It echoes the mix of Buddhist spirituality and 21st-century savvy that characterizes the operation here in McLeodganj.

Meanwhile we have set up our cameras and lights in the audience room, hung with *thangkas* with a finely modelled shrine to the Buddha at one end, but as our time comes round, the secretary appears, eyebrows raised apologetically, to tell us that a group of local worthies have to be accommodated, but his Holiness hopes to get them through in five minutes. It sounds as if he'll be exhausted.

At 2.25 we are advised that he will be coming. I arm myself with a *katag*, a thin white scarf, which is a mark of greeting and respect among Tibetans. Try not to dwell on the fact that I am about to embark on a 40-minute talk with the spiritual leader of one of the great religions and can't remember a single one of the questions I rehearsed in my room last night. The only warning I am given is to avoid asking specific questions about his current relations with the Chinese. Two of his closest advisers will sit in on the interview, to help translate, they say, but I know they're there to keep an eye on us.

The 14th Dalai Lama, born Llamo Thondup, the son of peasant farmers, confirmed as the incarnation of the 13th Dalai Lama when only two years old, arrives without fuss or fanfare, entering the room unescorted and looking pretty good for a 68-year-old who must have shaken a thousand hands already today. His presence is powerful, but in no way intimidating.

He pauses in the doorway, bringing his hands together and bowing his head towards me in traditional Buddhist greeting. His skin is clear and healthy, his complexion barely lined. He holds his head slightly forward, giving the impression of someone who likes to listen as much as command. Pushing his maroon and yellow robes back up onto his left shoulder, he comes towards me. His arms, like those of any Buddhist monk, are bare, save for a chunky watch on his right wrist, and noticeably hairless. Almost brushing aside my offer of the *katag*, he gives me a firm Western handshake. His grip is strong and his palms noticeably cool. He sets me at ease straightaway, grinning broadly.

'Your face very familiar because of TV.'

Well, what can I say to the man who has stared at me from his book cover this past week.

'You watch the BBC then?'

'Practically every day'.

I'm genuinely surprised. This is a monk I'm talking to.

'Because I have more trust.'

'Yes?'

'And…some beautiful documentaries on film, including your own sort of film.'

My head is swimming. This is turning into some fantasy commercial, and there seems to be no stopping him.

'And sometimes…I wish to journey with you,' says the Dalai Lama. 'I could see many places, and meet different people.'

I can't remember the exact details of the fact sheet I was given earlier, but I think that, since he first travelled outside India in 1973, the Dalai Lama has been to 50 countries or more.

'From my childhood I always have curiosity…to know more about different people, different culture, and as a Buddhist monk I also, you see, have an interest to learn more about different religious traditions.'

I tell him we're going to Tibet next.

'But I don't think you'd want to come with us.'

He laughs very hard at this, then says quietly and seriously, 'Although I'm here outside Tibet, not inside Tibet, as a Tibetan I want to extend my welcome to you to visit my old country.'

There's pathos in this remark. A reminder that he speaks for 120,000 Tibetans living in exile.

I ask what we will find there, what may have changed most.

He cites Chinese immigration. Tibetans are a minority in Lhasa now.

'These people find it very, very difficult to preserve their own cultural heritage. So that's on the negative side.'

Unexpectedly, he picks out the modern buildings in Lhasa as a positive, but is worried that the big new blocks are being filled up by Chinese, not Tibetan workers. The unskilled Chinese make money more easily.

Another positive is, he says, the growing interest in spirituality in China. There is great interest in Buddhism in 'China proper', as he calls it. Especially, he notes, among the richer Chinese.

He's engagingly happy to talk about everyday life.

'One week ago I return from United States. Sleep not much problem, but my stomach still on American time.'

He pats his midriff.

'Toilet usually morning, but nowadays it's evening.'

He beams mischievously.

'That can't change through prayer.'

I learn that he gets up at 3.30 every morning, but goes to bed around 8.30, and that he recently lost his temper, in a dream.

I ask him if he ever loses his temper in real life.

'Sometimes yes, but not remain long.'

For his relatively robust health he thanks his parents for giving him a good body and his general peace of mind.

'Sleep without sleeping pill, happy without tranquilizer.'

For a world leader he seems extraordinarily well-balanced, natural and unaffected. His emotions are spontaneous, his judgements carefully pragmatic. He would justify the violence of a World War II or a Korean War on the grounds of just causes, but not Vietnam, nor I sense Iraq.

He feels that not enough was done to negotiate a peaceful solution with Iraq. He suggests that some council of wise men should perhaps have gone to Saddam Hussein. Those he admires and would have included, along with Muslim leaders, are Vaclav Havel, Bishop Tutu, Nelson Mandela and Jimmy Carter.

He believes it is very important to enlist with everyone, high or low, on a personal level. To communicate the positive.

Does he worry about his own safety when he travels?

'Generally no. Friendly atmosphere should immediately happen. When I'm passing through a street I always smile, when I look at another…nice smile. But then sometimes you see the other side, no smile.'

It all begins to sound a bit Mary Poppins when I write this down, but there is nothing remotely weak or woolly about the man himself. He just doesn't do cynicism.

We talk on well over our allotted 40 minutes, and even when an hour's up he is happy to pose for a photograph. (I have it on the wall beside me as I write up these notes. The Dalai Lama is in

ABOVE

Surely the most approachable of all world leaders, the Dalai Lama is a powerful man, totally lacking the trappings, or the presumptions, of the powerful.

the middle, clasping Nigel's hand on one side and mine on the other. The crew are spread out on either side and I don't think I've ever seen this hard-worked unit looking so happy.)

The only sign of any tension is after he's gone, when both the Dalai Lama's private secretaries lay aside their two-way radios and pitch in to help us de-rig our lamps, wires and cables. The next interview (with an Israeli crew) is already 20 minutes late.

Day Forty : Srinagar, Kashmir

An hour and a half after the azan (the Muslim call to prayer) has woken me, replacing the barking of dog packs as the sound of the night, I'm reclining like a maharajah's mistress on the soft cushions of a long flat-bottomed boat with a canopy above my head. Behind me a small, tightly built figure is propelling me slowly forward with a single paddle.

A heron perches elegantly on a thin pole, ignoring us as we slip slowly through lotus beds towards a robust stone bridge beyond which I can dimly see and hear a clutter of canoes and the distant sound of voices.

My hooded skiff, known as a *shikara*, has an English name board fitted above the bows. 'Stranger In Paradise', it reads, and it's very suitable.

Stranger I certainly am and Dal Lake in Srinagar, long, wide and lazy, with high mountains protecting its northeasterly shore, would give many paradises a run for their money. Except that this one is in Kashmir, where, nowadays, heaven and hell come pretty close.

To get to this idyllic place we have had to undergo tighter security checks than anywhere else on the journey. Police and army posts, baggage and permit checks dot the road to Srinagar with increasing frequency.

It's not cosmetic, either. Within a couple of miles of this aqueous paradise 16 people have been killed by bomb and bullet in this last month alone, and to that figure can be added another 60,000 who have died in Kashmir since the conflict began.

Why?

In 1947, when India and Pakistan became independent, Kashmir was a Princely State of

RIGHT

The early morning vegetable market on Dal Lake. Business is all done from boats.

India, ruled by Maharajah Hari Singh. All 565 Princely States, comprising 100 million people, were required to sign instruments of accession to the newly formed country. What made Kashmir different was that 80 per cent of its population was Muslim.

Hari Singh hummed and hawed and eventually decided, two months after independence, (and not without some heavy pressure from Nehru) that his state would stay a part of India.

The outrage of the new Pakistan government was predictable. After all, their country was set up as a homeland for Muslims and indeed the letter 'K' in its name stands for Kashmir. (The 'P' is for Punjab, the 'A' for Afghania (a romantic synonym for the North-West Frontier), the 'S' for Sind and the 'Stan' is an abbreviation of Baluchistan.)

Some Pathans took the law into their own hands and moved into Kashmir, taking over an area which has since become known as Azad (Free) Kashmir. Indian troops moved in to counter them and the long cycle of violence began.

In 1949 a ceasefire came into force, one of whose conditions was that a plebiscite should be held for the inhabitants of all Kashmir to decide on their future. It's never happened. Instead, this spectacularly lovely land has become the arena in which all the fear and loathing between Pakistan and India has come to a head. Thousands of soldiers face one another across a Line of Control. By the late 1990s the potential of the Kashmir dispute escalated from destructive to catastrophic as the Pakistanis confirmed that, like India, they now had the power to wage a nuclear conflict.

The houseboats that can still be found clinging to the shores of the lake are symbols of the days when Kashmir was not the problem, but a hideaway from all the problems elsewhere. If you can forget the roadblocks and the army patrols, the magic spell remains.

Among reasons to be thankful for being on Dal Lake this morning is the ban on outboard motors, which keeps the mood of the place as reflective as its still waters. There's time to take in the passing scene, admire majestic chinnar trees on the shoreline, the white walls and domes of an impressive waterside mosque and, alongside it, a run of multi-windowed three- or four-storey wood and brick houses that would not be out of place in a Baltic seaport.

For hundreds of years the lake has been farmed by the Mihrbari people, market gardeners living on islands only accessible by boat. Thirty-five thousand of them still live on the water,

LEFT

*Flower sellers give me
the once-over on
Dal Lake.*

89

farming lotus beds for food, cattle feed and the famed Kashmiri honey that comes from their pink flowers. Willow and poplar trees on the islands are cut for thatching and building materials, vegetables are cultivated in hydroponic gardens set among compressed bulrushes and all commerce is conducted from boat to boat in a floating market that starts at daybreak every morning. Suppliers from the city bring their barges down and bargain for turnips, potatoes, spinach, pumpkins, shallots, big fat radishes, aubergines, mint and okra.

We're here within an hour of dawn and the market is in full swing. Several boatloads of flower sellers, pushing through the jam make a beeline for us (we are, apart from an Israeli couple, the only people resembling tourists here today). It doesn't stop at buying flowers. This merely spurs them on to sell you seeds as well. The more you resist the more they like it.

'I have blue sunflower seeds.'

'No, thank you.'

'I have lotus seeds.'

'I've bought some already.'

'What lotus seeds you have bought?'

'Blue.'

'I have six-colour lotus seeds. And wild orchid and wild tulip.'

'I have no money.'

'You buy and send me the money.'

At this point one would normally wind up the window and roar off as fast as possible, but as we're both in paddle boats there is no prospect of a quick getaway and either you drift along together for several miles or, as I did, you buy six-colour lotus seeds for all your friends. These disappeared mysteriously into a hotel wastepaper basket about a week later.

It's still only breakfast time as I get back to the houseboat moored on the western shore of the lake, which will be our home for the next couple of days. Mr Butt, the owner of Butt's Clermont

BELOW

Stars of Srinagar. The dashingly decorative Clermont Houseboats, originally built by the British because they weren't allowed to buy land here.

LEFT

*Mr Gulam Butt,
proprietor of Clermont
Houseboats through
thick and thin times,
runs through a list of
previous guests,
including Nelson
Rockefeller and George
Harrison.*

Houseboats is worrying away at a table laid out in what was an old Mughal garden, believed to have been built by the Emperor Akbar and called the Garden of the Morning Breeze. Soon we're chomping on eggs, pancakes, thick toasted bread, honey and Kashmiri tea, a fragrant alternative to the straight cuppa, made with saffron and almonds.

Mr Butt circles nervously. He is a man of immense enthusiasm, very responsive to compliments and given to hugging the bearer of them with delight. On the other hand, the slightest thing that goes wrong produces intense anguish and much shouting at the staff. There seems to be no middle ground between euphoric happiness and utter despair.

This makes him an anxious but attentive host and even before I'd checked in he was proudly showing off the signed photographs of previous guests that adorn the walls of his office. They range from Lord Louis Mountbatten, the man who partitioned India and Pakistan, to George Harrison, who stayed here in 1966 to learn the sitar from his friend and guru Ravi Shankar. I ask which boat George had stayed in and a small cloud passes over Mr Butt's beaming features.

Later I could see why. It lies in a side channel, half submerged with water. Mr Butt couldn't afford to keep it afloat.

Newspaper cuttings are displayed alongside the photos: recommendations from the *Washington Post* and the *New York Times* and a flattering inclusion, together with such high-tone places as the Regent in Hong Kong and the Lowell, New York, in Charles Michener's 'Hotels You Won't Want to Leave'. These clippings are now yellowing and curled at the edges and there is none much later than the early 90s. When the troubles in Kashmir escalated, the press reviews turned to scare stories and the only foreign visitors were journalists covering the conflict.

Mr Butt admits there were times when he was near to tears. Staff he'd known all his working life had to be laid off, and at the nadir of his fortunes the army commandeered his property and set up camp in the Garden of the Morning Breeze. Things improved briefly from 1995 to 1999 but any hope of a steady recovery is stymied by every fresh atrocity, every fresh confrontation.

I can only feel grateful to this cheerful, distracted man for keeping going, for his boats are neither functional nor cheap to run. Mine is very splendid, with elaborately carved woodwork inside and out, a carpeted sitting room with very fine crewel-work embroidery and a grand dining room with cedar panelling, chandeliers, cut glass and an oval rosewood dining table.

This evening the skies darken, the lake empties of boats and after a brief and eerie period of silence and total calm the heavens open and there's nothing to do but sit tight and watch the rain splashing in great glassy drops on the water lily beds that surround the boats.

If anything, Dal Lake is even more beautiful in the rain.

Day Forty One : Srinagar

The storm rumbles on through the night and as the growls of retreating thunder merge with the cries of the muezzin I reach for my torch (there has been no mains power since the rain began). It's five o'clock, but I feel wide awake. I dreamt very vividly last night. Super-charged dreams, as if the electricity in the air had given them an extra intensity. I saw my father very clearly and I rushed up and hugged him, something I never did when he was alive, and heard myself say 'Hello Dad!' except it wasn't my voice at all but the voice of my son.

An hour later dawn is breaking and we're driving out onto the wet and windswept streets of Srinagar. The night-time curfew has only just ended and the streets are empty save for foot patrols and packs of stray dogs. Srinagar must have been a handsome city once. There are still many tall, steeply gabled, half-timber, half-brick buildings, a few onion domes and a magnificent mosque with roofs, turrets and spires with echoes of Russia and lands to the north.

The Indian government has 600,000 army and security forces in Kashmir and their ubiquitous presence has coarsened the city and compromised whatever beauty it might have had. Apart from bunkers and armoured patrol cars, there are barbwired and sandbagged surveillance posts, sports pitches that have been turned into army camps, and I'm told there's not a single cinema operating in Kashmir's capital now. All have been requisitioned for military accommodation.

On the corner of the busy main street, Lal Chowk, and opposite the heavily fortified Telegraph Office stands the Greenway Hotel. Two weeks ago two suspected Islamic militants holed up here and withstood a siege for 20 hours before police blew the building apart with mortar fire. Ten people were killed and 40 wounded and the Greenway now consists of little more than half a roof, scorched black walls and a crumpled framework of charred and blistered timbers. Around the time this happened six more people were killed when a car blew up in the vegetable market.

On the edge of the old town is a patch of green grass and a stagnant rubbish-filled pond. Horses graze and dogs chase, snarl, fight and mate amongst the filth. Next door to this soiled little field is a small cemetery, neatly walled and fenced. Inside, gravestones fringed in green and topped with sturdy metal pennants mark the resting place of those who have died in the struggle. An arch over the entrance announces it as the Kashmir Martyrs' Graveyard. Most of the graves

ABOVE

*The remains of the
Greenway Hotel,
Srinagar, destroyed by
the Indian army after
Islamic militants holed
up there.*

are inscribed in Urdu, but beneath a cypress a neglected metal sign in English reads:

'Master Shaheed Yawar Says
Do Not Shun The Gun
My Dear Younger Ones
The War For Freedom
Is Yet To Be Won.'

It's rusty and fading and must have been there for some time, unlike two freshly dug mounds, crudely decorated with a border of pebbles, containing a mother and a three-month-old baby killed in crossfire outside the Greenway Hotel. There are some 400 graves here and many more lie in similar plots throughout Kashmir. Flowers have been planted around the place, perhaps to represent on earth the gardens the martyrs are promised in heaven. Though governments may see the Kashmir struggle as the troubles, most of those who lie here saw it as a war.

This is brought forcibly and uncomfortably home to me by the bizarre conflation of our own patriotic rhetoric that is inscribed above the arched gateway of the Kashmir Martyrs' Graveyard: 'Lest You Forget We Have Given Our Today for Tomorrow of Yours'.

The only place where the violence seems not to have made a mark is on the water, and along one arm of the lake 60 or 70 houseboats, with jolly names like 'King of Kashmir', 'Himalayan Fantasies' and 'Buckingham Palace', still court the tourists. They're moored up cheek by jowl, end on to the bank, cabins tweely curtained, fenced sundecks ringed with pot plants, waiting for the next boom. Their design is cosy and old-fashioned and can't have changed much since the houseboat era began in the 1880s, when the British got around laws preventing outsiders from buying lakeside property by building their mansions on the water instead.

A white-crested kingfisher studies the limpid surface of the lake. Our presence on the bank has already attracted a flotilla of water taxis and eager salesmen flaunting jewellery, papier-mâché and various ethnic trinkets.

OPPOSITE

A selection of the famous and much sought-after houseboats of Srinagar. The names suggest happier times before conflict traumatized Kashmir.

'Where are you from?' shouts one man.

When we tell him he shouts manically back.

'England! Fish and Chips! Bangers and Mash! Marmite Sandwiches! Good Heavens!'

August, they say, had been a good month for Indian tourists. Then came the September violence and 30 per cent of the bookings were cancelled immediately.

I go out again on the lake at dusk. The rain has cleared the air and the water is a mirror, reflecting a huge golden sunset. It's ironic that of all the places I've been on my journey so far, this should be the closest I've come to perfect peace.

Day Forty Two : Ladakh

The looming presence of the mountains around two sides of Dal Lake reminded me that, after almost two weeks, we were once again getting close to the high Himalaya. This morning, as we land at Leh after a complicated flight from Srinagar via Delhi, the change from foothills to mountains is complete. Nature is not generous up here. The air is powder dry and the rocky slopes all round us are bare and deeply gullied. For the first time in a long while I feel my lungs working, pumping a little harder to pull in the oxygen, for we are at 11,650 feet (3550 m), nearly two and a quarter miles above sea level.

Sonia Ghandi, daughter-in-law of one premier and wife of another, is visiting this remote province and her convoy of chunky white Ambassador cars, honest but unglamorous, winds its way through the security chicane and out of the airport, while we are still waiting for our bags.

Nothing is quite as I expected. The porters and baggage handlers are stocky thick-set women wrapped in red cardigans, headscarves and baggy blue pantaloons and they jostle with each other for the heaviest bags. Their features are more Mongolian than Indo-Aryan, with darker, berry-brown complexions and broad cheeks.

The only similarity with where we've come from is the heavy military presence: jet fighters in revetments at the airport, a sprawling barracks on the way into Leh. Once again there is a sensitive border nearby, only this time it's not Pakistan they're worried about, but China.

Ladakh, meaning 'many passes', is a part of Jammu and Kashmir but has little in common with the rest of India, nor indeed with the rest of the state. Over half the population is Buddhist and its strategic position on the old Silk Road means it shares more with Tibet and Central Asia.

The architecture, too, is different from anything I've seen so far: stone walls and rugged houses with flat roofs that seem to have bushy undergrowth piled on top of them. (I never worked out if these rooftop toupees were fuel stores or a form of insulation.) The run-down palace that dominates the centre of Leh is on a grand scale and has the same upwardly tapering walls that I've seen in pictures of the Potala Palace in Lhasa.

The streets of Leh are busy, in a low-tech way. A row of men, some holding prayer wheels, sit cross-legged on the pavements behind sacks rolled back to show off various nuts and spices and fruits. I buy rather a lot of apricot kernels, because someone said they make you live longer, and am tempted by the piles of shawls, scarves and rugs made from *pashm*, the fine underfleece of goat's wool that is the speciality of this part of India. The pashmina salesmen look particularly doleful, as their trade, like everyone else's in Kashmir, is heavily affected by the troubles. They seem to face the situation with remarkable stoicism. I'm back among mountain people – patient, taciturn and politely wary of outsiders. Masters of survival.

There is evidence that their independence is being compromised by various life-improvement campaigns, from tidiness to road safety. At a busy road junction a prominent and

*Road safety campaigns
have yet to bear fruit
in Ladakh.*

colourful display board advises the locals to 'Learn and Repeat, Signs and Traffic Signals'.

As I'm reading it a black cow, followed by her calf, emerges from behind the board and, without signals of any kind, saunters off into the rush-hour traffic.

I think we should use cows for traffic calming at home. They're much more effective than sleeping policemen. And they give milk.

The road safety campaign extends beyond Leh. As we drive across the desert, following the slim green band of cultivation along the River Indus, we're treated to an assortment of useful warnings: 'Peep Peep, Don't Sleep', 'Drive Like Hell – You'll Be There' and 'Be Mr Late Rather Than the Late Mr', which is marginally our favourite. The road surface is good, better than you'd expect in such a remote place. The reason, of course, is that the highway is built and maintained by the army, or 'The Mountain Tamers', as they like to call themselves.

It's not road safety they're worried about up here, it's invasion.

The scenery has a spare and minimal beauty and the buildings along the way, though few and far between, are very dramatic. Some ten miles along the highway to Manali, the walls of the old palace of the kings of Leh rear up along a prominent ridge to the north of the road. A king hasn't lived there for 400 years, but the evidence of power and wealth still clings to the place, both in the scale of the ruins and, on a nearby hillside, row upon row of crumbling white monuments. From a distance they resemble lines of half-melted snowmen, with the outlines of once square bases, conical middles and pointed tops now soft and imprecise. These stupas, or *chortens*, as they're called in Tibetan, contain the remains of lamas and monks from the monastery attached to the palace as well as members of the royal family and their possessions.

They vary in size, the highest being almost 20 feet tall. Usually situated in favourable geomantic locations, their design represents steps to enlightenment. They are constructed on five levels, with the square base symbolizing the earth and the tapering tops the sky and stars. As I wander among them I can see that few are intact. Most are leaning or cracked down the sides and all look as if they may have been opened up at some time. Intriguingly, many seem to have been freshly whitewashed, suggesting someone is still looking after them.

I have the feeling, as I stand in the middle of this field of whited sepulchres with little more than a stand of poplars growing in the valley below, that there was a time when these bare hills on the banks of the Indus must have supported a small empire. What was so different then? More water perhaps, a wider flood plain or perhaps just the power and influence that came from living on the Silk Route.

As we head east more stunning monasteries and temples appear out of nowhere. Thikse straddles an outcrop of rock with the smaller outbuildings that are the monks' quarters wrapped around the steep sides below it. This has been a working monastery (or *gompa*, in Tibetan) for nearly 1000 years and 60 lamas still live here.

The richest and most striking of the great Indus valley *gompas* is Hemis, another half-hour's drive along the main road and then by a side track up into a narrow gorge squeezed between walls of striped granite, folded and thrust upwards at 45 degrees to the plain below.

The last part of the climb to the monastery is up a long stone staircase. By the time I reach the top my breathing is shallow and my legs feel like lead, but the dramatic entrance makes me glad I persevered.

Despite the narrow site, the courtyard that opens out beyond the main gateway gives a heady sense of space. High stone walls rise on three sides while the fourth is open to the bare rock slopes beyond. The walls are covered in paintings and a line of prayer wheels runs along one side. Another mighty flight of steps leads to the prayer hall, whose entrance is flanked by wooden pillars with carved figure-heads and richly coloured paintings of dragons and gods. A wooden gallery runs around the walls and an arcade below has what look like very ancient wall paintings of the Buddha. Among the treasures of Hemis is a *thangka* so precious and huge that it is only displayed in public every 12 years. 2004 is the next time it will be exhibited. We've missed it by a matter of months.

We drive on as far as Chemrey Gompa, another monastery topping a carefully selected crag. Can't help but marvel at the careful painting of these monastery walls and the way the white, brown and maroon, and the timber and stone construction, harmonize so elegantly with the dry and tawny landscape around.

By now, all of us are feeling the press of altitude and by the time we've returned to Leh and eaten *momos* (Tibetan stuffed dumplings) and noodles, none of us has much energy left. There only remains one thing to do before bed and that's to raise a glass of beer to Roger and Nigel, who were both with me exactly 15 years ago today, filming my departure from the Reform Club and the start of *Around the World in Eighty Days*.

BELOW

(left) At Shey, once the home of the Kings of Leh, ruins of the fort and palace ride the crest of a hill, and, in foreground, a field of chortens *(burial monuments) stand out from the arid slopes like half-melted snowmen. (right) Murals of Buddha's life at Hemis* gompa *(monastery).*

Nepal

Day Forty Four : Kathmandu

WE ARRIVED HERE last night from Delhi on the penultimate night of Dasain, a big Nepali festival, and though badly in need of some rest and recuperation after our Indian adventure, the final day's celebrations cannot be missed.

To start the day we've been asked by Pratima Pande, a formidable, energetic, Gordonstoun-educated Nepali, to watch a *puja*, a ritual act of worship, at the home of one of her in-laws. This being the first time I've ever been to Nepal, I'm craning my head out of the car window as we drive there. I have a sense of streets that are less hectic and a city much easier on the eye than those we've seen these past few weeks. Buildings look like buildings rather than structures for supporting billboards.

The house is comfortable but not opulent. As we arrive a group of musicians are parading around the garden before taking up a position on the far side of a small swimming pool. It's a bit of a squeeze, as two of them are wielding large, curved horns.

I'm told that this is Bijaya Dasami, the 'victorious tenth day' of the Dasain festival and Pratima and her husband, mother-in-law, brothers-in-law, nephews, nieces and cousins are here to celebrate King Rama's victory over the demon Ravana, helped by Shiva's consort, Durga.

I'm desperately trying to get all this down in my notebook when the music starts and the family priest, an unassuming, modestly dressed figure, who looks as if he might have come to fix the plumbing, steps forward. The exact timing of the *puja* is very auspicious and it cannot be delayed for foreign film crews. He sets the ball rolling by applying a dab of yellow to the forehead of the oldest member of the family, Pratima's 82-year-old mother-in-law. Today, Pratima tells me, everyone in Nepal, from the King downwards, will wear this mark, the *tika*.

After some light family argument over the exact order of things, the ceremony continues, in strictly hierarchical fashion, with the five brothers, and then the children, kissing the feet of their elders and giving each other the male *tika*, made from a preparation of curd, rice and vermillion powder. *Jamara*, shoots of barley, are placed on the head or in a garland around the neck as a symbol of fertility and longevity.

As an outsider I'm struck by how seriously all this is taken. Pratima's brothers-in-law are hard-nosed, professional people, one a doctor, one a banker, two others in the army. They're

OPPOSITE

Hindu Nepal. In Patan's Durbar Square stone elephants, carved 380 years ago, guard the entrance to Shiva's temple.

dressed in the *labada salwar*, a knee-length tunic, with tight leggings and black leather shoes, but over it they wear a Western-style sports jacket.

Many of them have been educated in Britain or America, their children speak fluent English and go to private schools. Yet here they are taking part in an ancient and rural ritual with a thoroughness that one can't imagine among their counterparts in the West.

The first thing to remember, says Pratima, is that not only is Hinduism the religion of 90 per cent of Nepal, the Nepalis take pride in being more scrupulous in their observance of festivals. The Indians, she says, have shortened their ceremonies.

'We take three days to get married. They do it in a day!'

She herself is off to a private audience at which she will be given *tika* and blessed by the King, who is some sort of relative (they're both from the Rana family). This afternoon, he will be doing the same for the public in the grounds of the palace. Would I like to come along?

The prospect of meeting the king of a country I've only been in for 12 hours appeals in a surreal sort of way, and I scurry back to the Yak and Yeti Hotel to find a tie and get my only jacket pressed.

There is a certain amount of morbid curiosity here, for the Nepali monarchy was very nearly wiped out in June 2001, when the King and Queen and seven other members of the family were murdered by the Crown Prince, who then turned a gun on himself. Rumours abound as to what really happened but it seems he was a heavy drinker, loved guns and flew into an hysterical rage when his father refused him permission to marry the girl he wanted.

At three o'clock I'm with Pratima in the grounds of the Royal Palace, blinking a little wearily in the bright sunshine as King Gyanendra Bir Bikram Shah Dev, the late Crown Prince's uncle and incarnation of Vishnu the preserver, descends his front steps between statues of guardian animals – dragons, horses, peacocks, dolphins and elephants – to the strains, and in this case strains is the right word, of a Scottish-sounding dirge weirdly played by a pipe band in red and white plaid scarves and white gaiters.

The palace, with its Potala-like central tower, Hindu temple shapes, Tibetan loggias, red brick skin and clusters of concrete columns that hang down without touching the ground, seems to have been built in a style that might best be described as Himalayan Fantasy. Which might also apply to the rest of the day.

The King takes his place behind a red, padded leather desk, which makes him look a bit like a hotel receptionist. At a given signal his subjects begin to move forward and he sets to work applying *tika* to the nation's foreheads. Having so recently seen the Dalai Lama work a line, I know that it's possible to combine gravitas and jollity, but King Gyanendra maintains one expression throughout, and that is a sort of jowly glumness, as if being ruler of Nepal is absolutely the worst job in the world.

The line is slowed down ahead of me by a succession of middle-brass army officers whose huge, peaked caps have

to be pushed back before the *tika* can be applied, then repositioned to enable them to salute. It all takes time and the King looks even more bored by the time my turn comes. Pratima moves forward to introduce me. I don't know what's said, but a flicker of animation crosses the royal features and after applying the royal *tika* to my deeply incised brow, the King extends a hand (his own) for me to shake and, leaning forward, wishes me a happy stay in Nepal.

'It could be the highlight of his afternoon,' says a Brit, working in the country. 'He needs all the friends he can get.'

Whatever his personal popularity, the institution of monarchy seems strong enough to attract a queue of people that extends all the way back to the heavy iron gates and for a few hundred yards out along the road, and those at the end of the line must be among the poorest in the kingdom.

No sooner are we back in the Yak and Yeti looking at laundry lists for the first time in a week than word comes through that a special ceremony, happening only once every 12 years, will be taking place in the heart of the old city later tonight. It's being kept very secret because it involves the King, who, because of the fear of attacks from the Maoist guerillas, rarely goes out in public within the city.

It sounds a long-shot but we follow it up and make our way to Hanuman Dhoka, the Old Royal Palace. Although it is dimly lit and hard to distinguish individual buildings, the complex of streets and squares has an extraordinary atmosphere. I'm reminded of walking at night in St Petersburg or Rome. There is a theatrical unreality to the place. Astonishing buildings, unlike anything I've seen before, are silhouetted against the night sky. Towering pagodas with long wide-eaved roofs, stacked one above the other, are topped with Hapsburg-like spires. Deep balconies cantilever out on long poles, the lintels and sills of the windows are thick timber beams. A fairytale kind of architecture, the more magical for being first encountered at night.

The general public seems conspicuously absent. We walk through empty squares until we come upon a small crowd that seems to consist mainly of flak-jacketed military, armed police and press photographers in dark suits.

The authorities look nervous, their eyes constantly scanning us and each other. Nigel grabs a camera position a few feet off the ground beneath a lamppost, and defends it against all comers as we wait for the production to begin.

After some time a procession can be heard approaching. Led by women with lamps and incense sticks and musicians playing cymbals and drums, a group of masked figures enters the square. The masks are big, elaborate and brightly coloured and their arrival provokes a mad rush as the press photographers, closely ringed by police, scoot across towards them like a squad of black beetles, thrusting people aside with their cameras as they try to get close. The masked dancers, some of them with towering headdresses and wearing animal skins like African witch doctors, seem to have been at it some time, and they twist and turn to the music as if in a trance.

There is still no sign of the King. The photographers have taken their pictures, the dancers have made their spectacular entrance and by the time the royal motorcade looms out of the darkness, the energy and spontaneity has all but evaporated. Army, police and plain-clothes security men with fingers at their ears move in around the King and escort him forwards. The most impressive of the masked figures, a representation of the goddess Bhadrakali, with a blue face, staring eyes, and scarlet lips, moves up close to the King. She blesses him with divine powers, hands over a sword, flashbulbs erupt and moments later it's all over.

The press pack close in; the King, tiny and insignificant beside the great blue head of the goddess, gives a brief and nervous smile, before being rushed back to his Mercedes and away.

This combined display of paranoia and celebration puzzles me greatly. Why was it so important to take such a risk with the King's safety? If it was so important why weren't the public invited? What is it that frightens King Gyanendra so much?

Perhaps I shall learn more as we go along. If this is the overture, my stay in Nepal promises to be a very rich piece indeed.

Day Forty Six : Kathmandu to Lekhani

Kathmandu airport is busy. Next door to the long, modern, red-brick sweep of the international terminal, domestic flights are checking in at a functional, concrete building with yellow-stained walls. The slip-slap of sandals mingles with the ring of discordant announcements as tiny Nepali porters carry in the bags of strapping Western hikers bound for the mountains. We're travelling to nearby Pokhara on Buddha Air, one of a string of local carriers with vaguely unconvincing names, like Cosmic Air, Shangri-La Air and Yeti Airlines. The crowds here this morning, indeed the existence of the airport itself, are still a relatively new thing for Nepal, which was only opened to foreigners in the 1950s.

A twin-prop Beech 1900 carries us out over the Kathmandu Valley, the widest valley in the Himalaya. Over a third of Nepal's urban population lives here and more are moving all the time; from the air the buildings expand along the main roads like concrete tentacles squeezing the green out of the rice paddies.

On our starboard side the peaks of the high Himalaya drift tantalizingly in and out of cloud cover, and by the time we begin our descent the cover is burnt off and the long, irregular, snow-capped ramparts of the Annapurna Ridge define the northern horizon.

In the days to come we shall be walking up there but today, as we skim down over the glittering lake, which, combined with the mountains, lures the tourists to Pokhara, we have only time to transfer our bags to vehicles and move on.

We are heading away from the tourist trails into the mountains west of Pokhara to the rural heartlands, where of one of Nepal's most famous exports comes from. Described variously as 'tough', 'hardy' and 'indomitable', the Gurkhas have long punched above their weight in the British Army. Since the first battalions were formed in 1815, these Nepali mercenaries have been fierce and faithful servants of the Crown, with a reputation for unwavering loyalty and unquestioning ruthlessness.

There are 3500 Gurkhas in the British Army at the moment (and 50,000 in the Indian army) and they have served all over the world, including recently in the Falklands and Iraq. The Nepali government allows a certain number to be recruited each year and Lt-Colonel Adrian Griffith, the Gurkha Chief of Staff in Nepal, has suggested we accompany him to the village of Lekhani to see how the recruiting process works. Adrian, slim, straight-backed and a couple of decades older than he looks, is the epitome of the decent Englishman abroad. At the age of eight, he first read the Johnny Gurkha stories in *Victor* magazine and the fascination that developed led him to join the regiment 15 years later.

Until recently there were no roads west of Pokhara and among the predominantly poor farmers in this inaccessible network of valleys and foothills one of the world's few surviving Communist parties is alive and well.

Succoured by poverty and feeble administration, the Communist Party of Nepal (Maoist) demands the removal of the monarchy, the setting up of a constituent assembly and the re-writing of the constitution. Since 1996 they have chosen to pursue the class struggle through guerrilla warfare. Over 7000 people have been killed, 10,000 injured and many more forced out of their homes as they took on the police and the army. No-one seems quite sure what their leadership is up to at the moment. Prachandra, leader of the insurgents, has sounded more conciliatory recently and they have observed a ceasefire for the Dasain festival. But that, as I know, ended the day before yesterday.

It's a soft, warmish morning. We stop at a police checkpoint. Beside the road a group of women in saris are breaking rocks. (Female road gangs were quite common in north India, but this is the first I've seen here.) At Baglung the good road runs out, and we have to pull over for a moment while our Gurkha escort checks out reports that a bomb has been found on the track ahead. We order a cup of chai from a roadside shack. A woman with a jewel in her nose sloshes milk from a kettle into a saucepan thick with ancient deposits, adding spoonfuls of sugar from what looks like an old tin of black paint. This is all boiled up with a touch of cardamom and, I presume, some tea inserted at some stage. It tastes rather good.

West of Baglung the road becomes a slow, muddy, rutted track. In the absence of drains or culverts, water runs off the paddy fields and onto the road. At one stage my driver refuses point

LEFT

Into the Nepali outback. Looking for Lekhani with Adrian Griffith, Gurkha comrades and 45 porters.

blank to take his nice, clean four-wheel drive through a lake of unspecified depth.

One of the Gurkha officers has a quiet word with him, then a slightly louder word, after which he drops all his objections and drives through the lake.

After two hours of painfully slow progress the track runs out. Everything is unloaded and re-packed in cone-shaped wicker baskets, *dokos*, which are then loaded onto the backs of porters and, looking like something out of the archives of the Royal Geographical Society, our 44-man, and one woman, procession, complete with everything, including the kitchen sink, sets off across the hills to find Lekhani. Worryingly, its name doesn't appear on any of the maps I have and the Sherpas who are organizing our transport are from a completely different part of Nepal. Local enquiries have to be made, which usually means chatting up someone half-buried in a paddy field.

Eventually, winding down across slippery, vertiginous rocks, between terraced fields of sorghum and millet, we come to our village, with attractive stone houses, some thatched, some tiled, spread along the hill, between spurs of rock running down to a valley far below. On the northern horizon a spectacular panorama of Annapurna, Machhapuchhre with its distinctive twin summits and the 26,750-foot (8150 m) Dhaulagiri massif looks sublime in the late afternoon sunlight.

The only disadvantage of this precipitous location is that there are only two unoccupied flat places in Lekhani. One is a sports ground, where the recruiting will take place tomorrow, and the other is an old cow patch, corrugated with dried mud. This is where we pitch our tents.

Day Forty Seven: Lekhani

It's not just dried mud I was sleeping on last night. As I made my way to the makeshift toilet, my torch picked out evidence that a menagerie of beasts had been easing themselves on our campsite for quite some time. When it also picked out a trail of bones and an abandoned flip-

flop I decided to switch it off.

Up at six. Nawang Dorjee, who I think may be the nicest person in the world, brings me tea and a little while later a small bowl of hot water for washing. Check the view. Yes, everything's still there. The Himalayas, the rocky slopes, the wooded spurs, the village without roads or streets. Poinsettia, oleander, frangipani and dry-stone walls. Farmhouses, simple and solid, as beautiful as any Italian hill village. When you look more closely, though, you can see that none of them has glass in the windows, only wooden shutters to keep out the winter cold, and the living space, though picturesque, is squeezed on one level, with space below reserved for stores of grain, firewood, animal feed and the animals themselves. A number of the houses have water buffaloes in the basement, big and black, like old vintage cars.

As I clean my teeth I look up the hill. A buffalo, being milked by an old woman, her head resting against its wide grey flanks, gazes impassively back. Prayer flags move lazily on their poles (there must be a Tibetan influence here), smoke drifts from the rooftops below and a pair of young women, with long dark hair, coming slowly up the hill, stop for a moment to adjust the headbands that carry the full weight of their baskets and to give us a good looking over.

At breakfast Adrian tells me about Long Noses and Flat Noses, something I've heard our Sherpas talking about. Nepal, he says, has a fundamental ethnic division between the Indo-Aryan with origins in the south and the Mongolian who originates from the north. Sherpas think of themselves as Flat Noses and superior to the Long Noses, who in turn think of themselves as more urban and intellectual than the Flat Noses.

'Traditionally, but not exclusively, it's been the Mongolian hill men who we've recruited,' Adrian explains.

'The hill farmer lives a very hard existence, and he comes from a hierarchical society and if you superimpose military discipline and military training you've got the makings of a very good soldier.'

He reckons there will be 100, maybe 150 potential recruits today, many of whom will have

ABOVE

*Some of the 251
would-be Gurkhas
start stretching the
sinews. Only 44 will
get to the next stage
of testing.*

walked as much as eight or ten hours to get here. There seem to be many more than that already, clustered in groups lower down the hillside, around the old volleyball pitch, which has been adapted for the recruiting, with gallows-like structures put up for the exercises and schoolroom desks brought out for the officials.

The whole event is organized by the local recruiting officer, the *galla-wallah*. He is a local man who will have been given instructions as to how many recruits are needed and scoured the villages to find likely candidates. The most that can be selected today will be 44. The *galla* is paid a small basic salary and a bounty for every successful recruit.

The Gurkha regiment has to walk a delicate tightrope between offending the Nepali army and provoking the Maoists, so the *galla* deliberately keeps the procedure informal and unmilitary. There are no weapons or uniforms in evidence. Sporting a baseball cap and a blue and red striped rugby shirt he gives an introductory talk, which, despite general squeaks, laughs and shouts from the local children, meanders on for some 25 minutes. He's followed by the village headman and then Adrian.

Adrian's much shorter speech, in fluent Nepali, is greeted with loud applause. He's garlanded by the local women and then cuts a red ribbon to mark the start of proceedings.

After the young men are registered and their height measured, they have to perform a series of physical tests. The first are heaves up onto a bar (the British Army requirement is six, the Gurkhas demand 12), after which they have to show that they can expand their chests by two inches. According to Adrian, this is a rule of thumb way of anticipating possible tuberculosis problems later on. The disease is prevalent here.

The boys puff their chests out to bursting point, and those who fail the first time are allowed to take strenuous exercise and try again. One of them completes a frenetic routine of 40 or 50 push-ups before leaping up, panting like a racehorse, and rejoining the queue.

He scrapes through the two-inch test next time, but his chances of being among the final 44 are still slim and, even if he gets through, this is only the first phase of the process. Successful applicants here go for a gruelling Hill Selection later in the year and only the best of those will go through to Central Selection in Pokhara after that. Some five months from now, the 24,000 original applicants will be reduced to a lucky 230, who will then leave Nepal for induction training in Singapore or at Catterick in North Yorkshire.

'It's a big culture shock,' Adrian admits, before adding, a trifle ruefully, 'But the army's a culture shock anyway.'

The rewards are substantial. As a serving soldier, the Gurkha gets the same pay as a British soldier, around £1000 a month. By comparison, a captain in the Royal Nepal Army is paid around £100 a month. On retirement many Gurkhas come back to Nepal and make a good living in the tourist business, buying hotels and guesthouses.

Adrian brushes off any suggestion that there might be local resentment at having these elite fighters poached by a foreign power. Adding up pensions, welfare schemes, direct expenditure, as well as the return of money earned abroad, he reckons the Gurkhas are worth £68 million a year to the Nepali economy.

Because the turnout out has been much higher than expected, with 251 applicants registered, they are only halfway through the programme by the end of the day. The *galla* seems pleased as he brings the results up to date. Twenty-three failed in the heaves, 40 in the sit-ups (in which one boy managed 98 in less than 2 minutes), 13 failed the eye-test and 7 were deemed too short. This leaves 168 still in the running for 44 places.

It's been a long hot day for everyone, so we discreetly open a bottle of whisky to celebrate

with Adrian and the organizers up in our dining tent.

After a while the *galla* comes in to join us. He looks decidedly uncomfortable and mopping his brow with a handkerchief, he talks rapidly to the others in Nepali. I can see expressions change.

Adrian translates for us. Some 'visitors from the forest' have approached the *galla*. They now want to talk to the rest of us. He nods, anticipating my question. They're Maoists.

A delegation, including our director J-P, follows two young men who look like students, one with a colourful embroidered shoulder bag, the other carrying documents of some sort in plastic folders. They look quite harmless, as if they might be on their way to a tutorial, but the submissiveness of everyone concerned suggests they have something more than moral authority.

They lead our people out of earshot, off behind a small temple, beside which a gnarled old bo tree grows. After half an hour they're back. J-P reports they met with four of them, all young, the same sort of age as the recruits, two of whom were polite and reasonable and two 'a bit nasty'.

They have asked the *galla*, Adrian and two other Gurkha officers, to go with them to meet what they call their high command, two hours' walk away into the forest. While we are taking all this in, three of the Maoists appear at the door of our tent. One, in a white shirt, is short and chunky and wears glasses reminiscent of Piggy in *Lord of the Flies*. He has a row of pens clipped in his top pocket. Another holds a radio. We mask the whisky bottle as they peer round the tent. Once they've gone another boy appears. He wears a baseball cap and speaks to the Sherpa Nawang, expecting him to translate. Nawang's eyes simply grow wide and he seems transfixed, speechless with anxiety. The boy's tone seems apologetic. Cradling a silver torch, he puts his hands together in the traditional greeting.

'Namaste.'

At that moment the stocky accomplice appears once again. He is less charming and, having scrutinized us all one last time, he makes a remark and goes.

Nawang eventually recovers enough to translate.

'He said he has the tape measure.'

The *galla*, together with all his records and the tape he used to measure the chests has gone, along with Adrian and his two fellow-officers. Though there appeared to be no physical threat, there seemed no question of their not going, nor of who they were going with. I walk outside. The sun has set and the distant peaks of the Himalaya, a moment ago blood-red and magnificent, are now cold, grey and remote. I find myself scanning the faces of the villagers. Everything seems very different from this morning. Perhaps they all hate us, stirred to anger by the Maoists, who've portrayed us as friends of a corrupt and oppressive government?

I realize, rather pathetically, how easily I project my own feelings onto others. If I'm happy, they must be happy. Now I'm suspicious, they must be too. Their expressions give nothing back. They get on with their work and I get on with my insecurities.

To complete a rotten end to the day, our cooks serve us goat in batter with tuna sauce.

Day Forty Eight : Lekhani to Pokhara

ABOVE

Crossing the cable bridge at Dopali, having been forced to abandon Gurkha recruiting after Maoist guerrillas abducted Adrian and other senior officers.

Adrian and his companions have not returned. Wongchu, our experienced Sherpa leader, doesn't want to stay here a moment longer than we have to, and in truth, there's nothing much we can do.

We wait until nine, then strike camp and head off down to the valley. As we leave the village we pass groups of young men standing around. Faces that were so eager yesterday, are either blank or confused as they wait to be told what they probably know already, that all their efforts were wasted.

I feel we've let them down and try to avoid catching their eye.

Soon Lekhani passes out of sight, and we pick our way down steep and precarious clay tracks through tiny settlements where we are the objects of considerable curiosity. The sticky heat of the valley replaces the cool of Lekhani, and I'm pouring sweat by the time we step carefully along the knife-edge rim of a rice paddy and out onto a level but half-finished highway, which in happier circumstances might have prompted mass whistling of the River Kwai march.

The road-head, over two hours' walk from Lekhani, is at a pretty village called Dopali, surrounded by silent, wooded slopes and a clean, fast-rushing stream. Life seems utterly restful here. An old lady cradles a cat, a family sit on the steps of a beautifully carved timber-frame house whose long doors are folded open to reveal slanting rays of sun spilling onto a cool, clay floor. Dopali is like something in a dream, a vision of delicious drowsiness and lethargy sent to subvert the purposeful and debilitate the dedicated.

We pick up vehicles here and, once away from the villages, J-P calls Adrian's superiors in Kathmandu to tell them the bad news. Absurdly, whoever he gets through to is not helpful. It's a Sunday, the commanding officer is having lunch and can't be disturbed. As J-P won't disclose details of what's happened, they seem to presume he hasn't any, and the harder he tries to convince them, the harder they stonewall.

It is a credit to J-P's persistence that eventually the word gets through.

By the time we're back in Pokhara all hell is let loose. At least three separate calls from the British Embassy ask us not to breathe a word of what has happened at Lekhani to anyone. This is the first time the Maoists have abducted a serving British officer, and may mark a significant change in policy. We eat, but, for once, no-one's terribly hungry.

By evening there is still no word of Adrian and the others.

Day Forty Nine : Pokhara to Chomrung

Early morning microlite flight over the lake and up towards the mountains. Myself in one tiny craft, Nigel filming me from another. Feel terrifyingly unsafe. Tucked in behind a Russian pilot with a big Seventies moustache who speaks only in thumbs-up signs, with thin air on either side. Cavorting at 10,000 feet above the ground, secured only by a car seat-belt across my lap, I experience pure terror for the first half-hour, and for the next, as we come down low over the shining lake and wooded hills, pure joy.

When I get back to breakfast, someone shows me the front page of the *Kathmandu Times*. So much for secrecy. 'Maoists abduct British Army Officers', reads the headline. Below is a jumbled report, which not only includes our director among the abducted, but has promoted him as well. He appears in the story as 'Brigadier General John Paul', which I hope won't go to his head.

And still no word on their whereabouts.

While we're in Pokhara a good opportunity arises to try and glean a little more insight into just what's going on in the country. John Cross, born in London and at various times in his life a soldier, diplomat and author of eleven books, including *Whatabouts and Wherabouts in Asia*, is an ex-Gurkha and expert in jungle warfare. He lives in a comfortable house in the quieter part of Pokhara with his adopted Nepali family.

We talk beside a small Hindu temple in his garden. It's an esoteric affair, containing a Buddha, a picture of the Blarney Stone, and a figure of St Jerome, the patron saint of languages.

'Cover all our options,' he grins.

John is a wiry, sharp-eyed 78-year-old. He still looks and sounds military, with a clipped delivery, straight back, green shorts and socks pulled up to the knee, but his replies are never predictable. He speaks ten Asian languages.

'I learnt one in seven days. Mind you, I wasn't eating.'

He sees an historical pattern in what's happening here.

'This is my third revolution,' he tells me. 'The first one was in Malaya, the second was in Laos. The first one the government won, one-zero, the second the communists won, one-all, and this is my third. Third time lucky for who?'

He sees it as something that's been bubbling for a long time.

'The poor have been marginalized.'

Law and order and a strong political base are prerequisites for defeating the rebels, but understanding the poor, as he has tried to do by travelling up and down the country, is also vital.

Wearing thick, dark glasses for his fading eyesight, John brushes off my query as to whether he's been tempted to try and help the Nepali government sort this one out.

'I've got to keep a low profile here.' He smiles. 'The doctor said get hit on the head, you're blind for life.'

We leave Pokhara this morning for our first serious assault on the mountains. Brigadier General John Paul, mindful of the fact that we will soon be crossing into Tibet and operating for several days above 16,400 feet (5000 m), has scheduled a five-day, altitude-training trek to Annapurna Base Camp.

The one sop is that, because of time constraints, we shall be taken by helicopter to our start point at Chomrung. A 20-minute flight instead of what would be a two-day walk.

Once the helicopter has delivered us we're left in deep and almost sensuous silence, hemmed in by the steep and thickly wooded walls of a valley, one side in brilliant sunshine, the other in deep, impenetrable shade.

At this height – we're at just over 7000 feet (2130 m) – even the most precipitous slopes are cultivated. Across the valley, I can see a farmhouse with 40 terraces, descending the hillside below, one after the other. Rising high in the distance, the summits of Annapurna and Machhapuchhre (Fish Tail Mountain) mark the parameters of our adventure; our constant companions on the trail, the objects of our pilgrimage.

For now, the atmosphere is relaxed. We sit outside the hotel in warm sunshine surrounded by all the trappings of an English country garden: thickets of marigold, chrysanthemum and nasturtium, butterflies fluttering round hydrangea bushes. The trail up to Annapurna runs through the hotel and a steady stream of walkers comes by. Three Israeli students tell us they have been approached by Maoists and asked for 1000 rupees (about £7) each. They pleaded student poverty but the Maoists were insistent, and, as one was armed, they thought it best not to argue. They were dealt with very courteously and issued with receipts. An English hiker we talk to later said that he and his party were asked for 2000 each. The Maoists justified the price hike because the British, and the American, government supplies arms to Nepal (the very arms which the Maoists are probably using).

The guerillas don't like the Annapurna Conservation Area, presumably because it's a government initiative, and recently forced six of the checkpoints on the trail to close. The 1000 rupee fee that was levied to pay for conservation work they now take for themselves.

Nevertheless, Wongchu, so nervy yesterday, doesn't think we'll have trouble with the Maoists, who he refers to, dismissively, as 'Jungle Army' and, even more derisively, Long Noses.

There seem to be plenty of other things to worry about, if a large sign just outside the hotel is to be believed.

We are, apparently, in an Avalanche Risk Area. 'Cross the Risk Area before 10 am', the sign warns. If you avoid the avalanche, you could still fall victim to Acute Mountain Sickness.

Symptoms are divided into 'Early', which include, 'Headache, Loss of Appetite, Dizziness, Fatigue on Minimal Exertion' (I had three of these four in Ladakh), and 'Worsening', characterized by 'Increasing Tiredness, Severe Headache, Walking Like Drunk and Vomitting' (sic).

'What To Do?' asks the big metal signboard. The answer is unequivocal.

'Descend! Descend! Descend!'

The accommodation, on two floors, is clean and basic, with a bed and pillow and a lavatory and washroom at the end of the block. There is electricity but it only manifests itself in one dim bulb per room. As a result of strict anti-litter controls, all drinking water is boiled, instead of bottled. The chicken at supper is, well, muscular.

Day Fifty : Chomrung to Dovan

We set off about eight. Our 35 porters, though expertly marshalled by our 13 Sherpas, are not used to the stop-start interruptions of filming, and by 9.30 we have reached only

BELOW

Chomrung. Where, disconcertingly, our ascent of Annapurna (on the left of the horizon) begins with a steep descent into the village.

as far as the Chomrung General Store. More worryingly, our progress up to Annapurna has been entirely downhill. We'll surely have to pay for this.

The store, crowded with schoolchildren buying sweets before climbing up to their school in Chomrung, is our last chance to buy what J-P calls 'sophisticated provisions'.

The range of goods on the shelves gives a foretaste of the weapons we might need should we ever have to touch the void: Pringles, porridge oats, toilet paper, vodka, 'Man's Briefs', chocolate, 'Bandage for Knee Caps', nail clippers, Chinese playing cards and rum.

Once outside the village we continue down on paths occasionally stepped with wide stone slabs (mostly laid by women of the local Gurung tribe) until we cross the Modi Khola (the River Modi) and at last the ascent begins. The porters bend to their work. As I watch their rubber sandals nimbly negotiate the rocks ahead of me I'm ashamed to think how long I spent deciding which kind of boots to wear. And some of them are carrying 40 kilograms in their wicker backpacks.

For a while it's idyllic. Prayer flags festoon the trees at intervals, fat bees feed off the cornflowers, lizards sprint across the mica-sparkling rock.

'Namaste,' I say cheerfully to everyone we pass.

On one particularly steep section we're overtaken by a mule train, the animals sashaying nimbly past and shoving me sideways into the bushes with their panniers.

'Namaste!'

Wongchu sticks fairly close to me. He's been given the impression that I'm someone of consequence, though he's not absolutely sure why. He's in his late thirties, solidly built with the broad features and high cheekbones of a northern Nepali or a Red Indian chief. He's horrendously over-qualified for this sort of work, having twice summitted Everest. On one of those occasions he arrived at the top at 5.30 in the morning, so far ahead of the rest of the party that he lay down on top of Everest and fell asleep until they arrived. Now that is cool.

He talks in staccato bursts of heavily compressed English, a lot of which I miss.

'Bondo. They call me Bondo.'

I nod and smile, vaguely.

'Bondo,' he repeats, smiling broadly. 'The Gun.'

'Ah, yes.'

'Ask anyone on Everest for Wongchu, they may be confused. Bondo Wongchu everybody know.'

He drops bits of information at regular intervals, as if I need food for the mind as well as the body. Did I know that the tip of Everest is limestone, a seabed pushed five and a half miles into the sky.

I ask him what he thinks about the situation in Nepal.

He looks around with a shrug and an expansive sweep of the arm.

'Nobody in charge of the country anymore.'

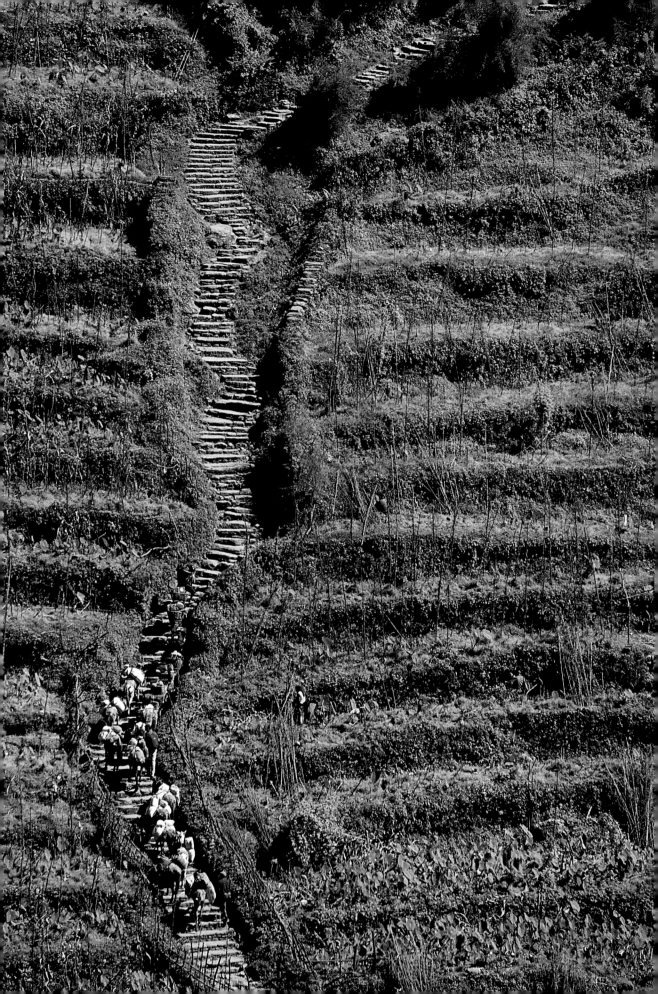

We climb over a spur and begin moving down through thick rhododendron and then bamboo forest. The way becomes increasingly dark, overgrown and claustrophobic. The sun has disappeared behind the mountains and a white mist is descending over the forest as we reach our overnight stop at Dovan. There are three of the long, grey, stone buildings with their blue, painted, tin roofs to choose from: The Dovan Guest House, the Annapurna Approach Lodge and Restaurant Hotel Tip Top. All are identical and all are full. In the courtyards a largely Western crowd of trekkers is resting, washing, snacking, lolling and generally looking knackered.

'Tourism,' mutters Wongchu, contemptuously. Though of course he makes his living from it.

The Sherpas set up camp. We've had a long, hard day's walk and only about 1000 feet (300 m) to show for it.

Basil is in a bad way. He doesn't like trekking – 'the longest walk I do is from the bar to the table' – and seems to have been cursed with a cold and a knife-like sore throat.

The talk at supper is not uplifting, turning mainly around the choice of our next camping spot, bearing in mind the risk of avalanche further up the mountain.

As we sit at the table after supper, Wongchu, unbidden, comes round and massages shoulders, arms, heads. A good massage too. He has fingers like steel.

'Sleep well, now,' he assures me.

How wrong he was.

Day Fifty One : Dovan to Derali

Temperatures fell sharply in the night and when I push back the flap of my tent it's ice cold with condensation. As we approach the toughest part of the trek, I can no longer ignore the inconvenient fact that I am feeling pretty lousy, and, if I'm about to get what Basil is already suffering from, things could get a lot worse.

He sits at breakfast with a pile of tissues beside him, dressed all in black and looking like death warmed up. In between painful coughs and raucous nose-blowings he delivers sharp and pithy observations on the joys of trekking, most of which seem to be eluding him.

French toast and boiled eggs are barely digested before the Sherpas set about striking camp with military precision. They like to keep moving. Or do they know something about avalanches we don't?

I stubbornly resist offers from Nawang and Wongchu to carry my backpack for me. It's become a matter of pride for me to carry it, a defiant attempt to show that there is still something I can do for myself.

We set out at half-past seven, climbing up steep stone staircases through a tangle of semi-tropical woodland, with wispy lengths of Spanish moss trailing from the branches of the trees like a trail of feather boas. When we emerge from the trees the sunshine is still way up in the mountain tops but the air is cool and fresh.

I feel a sudden surge of joie de vivre and ask Wongchu if he thought I could climb Everest. Flattered that he says yes with barely a pause I ask how long it would take.

'You must do training. Get used to altitude. Climb other mountains first.' He looks me up and down. 'I get you up there in maybe 75, maybe 100 days.'

I was thinking about a week.

'No time on this schedule, then.'

He grins and indicates my backpack.

'You want me take that?'

The distance between us and the tantalizing ceiling of sunlight high above us is gradually decreasing, but it's not until 10.15 that it tips over the rim of the mountains and spills into the valley. The temperature change is instant and dramatic. Off with fleece and on with 35 factor sun cream.

The scenery change is equally dramatic. After 24 hours of sometimes oppressive forest, the valley now opens and widens out and for the first time I have a sense of the monumental scale of what we are heading into. The 40-mile-long wall that stretches from Annapurna I in the west to Annapurna II in the east has no less than nine summits above 23,000 feet (7010 m). Even closer to us are Annapurna South at 23,678 feet (7200 m), Hiunchuli, over 21,000 feet (6400 m) and, barely five miles due east, the mesmerically eye-catching Machhapuchhre, the highest of its two pinnacles rising just short of 23,000 feet (7010 m).

This is sublime mountain scenery. Only Concordia in Pakistan, on the threshold of K2, reduced me to the same sense of inarticulate wonder.

Not much time for wonder, inarticulate or otherwise, as we have to keep moving, stopping, filming, moving and eventual stopping for a more substantial breather beneath a soaring overhang called the Hinko Rocks.

Animism preceded and has survived the religions that came to Nepal and it doesn't surprise me to hear that this conspicuous rocky cave is a sacred place. Talking of myths and legends, I ask Wongchu about the yeti.

He says that like everyone else round here he believes it exists.

OPPOSITE

The double whammy. Altitude and a sudden sharp, sore throat begin to compromise my appreciation of the beauties of the Annapurna Trail.

ABOVE

Crossing a stream in
yeti territory.

'I saw some yeti in the mountain.'

'What did it look like?'

'Look like monkey, it look like people like us.'

Wongchu rolls off a list of unlikely but intriguing facts. The best way to catch a yeti is to get him drunk. He likes tea and he likes alcohol, and people used to trap yetis by putting out a dead dog full of alcohol. It's the people who have hunted the creatures down.

'And now, one only left yeti.'

Beyond Hinko a sheer rock face rises to one side of the path, steep, smooth and sheer. A thin, white plume of a waterfall drops from way above, glancing off the rock and ricocheting down towards us in slow motion, it seems.

When the snow comes these rocks turn lethal. This is the high-risk avalanche area and Wongchu has seen people killed here. The only possible chance you have to avoid a fall is to have a sense of hearing acute enough to pick up the very first sound. The avalanche sound, Wongchu calls it. Then, as he puts it, 'Quick run.'

We reach the Sangri-La (sic) guesthouse at lunchtime and decide to go no further today. It turns out to be a good decision. By 2.30 swirling, vaporous cloud has descended, bringing the temperature down with it. Out of T-shirts and shorts and into scarves, hats, gloves and eventually thermals. We have a grandstand view of Machhapuchhre, revealing itself in tantalizing Garboesque glimpses between the drifting cloud.

It's a holy mountain. It is forbidden to slaughter any animal within its sacred valley, and Wongchu says his attempts to obtain permission to climb it have always been refused.

As the conditions become increasingly cold and inhospitable, the only members of our expedition who look at all cheerful are the porters. Released from their loads half a day early, they spend the afternoon noisily gambling away their take-home pay. A coin is thrown on the ground and where it lands it's replaced with a stone. Players then have to hit the stone with their coins. If you hit the stone, you pocket all the coins that have missed. It's a game that has apparently come down from Mongolia and is played throughout the Himalaya.

It's very much a participation game and the porters come alive, greeting every move with raucous shouts, jeers, groans and laughter. I've rarely seen so many people having such a good time for so long. It's quite depressing really, and brings on a prolonged bout of coughing.

We eat early, sitting on wool-covered benches round a rectangular table that is usually heated from beneath by a kerosene stove, but it isn't working tonight. Freshly made Gurung bread, thick, yet light and filling, then anodyne vegetable noodle soup and fried rice. The staple diet of the mountains is *dal baht*, lentils and rice, but our cooks seem unwilling to offer us this and instead try manfully to provide us with what they think Westerners want.

The night is cold. I take Nurofen and hope that it will help me sleep. It knocks me out for two-hour periods, tames the coughing but provides little relief from an increasingly angry, sore throat. One word repeats itself in my disordered dreams. Descend! Descend! Descend!

Day Fifty Two: Derali to Machhapuchhre Base Camp

At breakfast Wongchu asks me how I am. I give him quite a detailed progress report on cold, cough, sandpaper-like throat and general collapse of system.

He ponders this in a Harley Street sort of way, before narrowing his eyes like Sherlock Holmes confronted with a new and unexpected clue.

'You have beer last night?'

I try to cast my mind back.

'A little.'

Wongchu nods gravely.

'No beer.'

The sun is still out of reach, setting fire to the crests of the mountains, but still a long way from delivering us from this bitter morning chill. We fall to reminiscing about the good old days

LEFT

Machhapuchhre, 'Fish Tail Mountain', is looking in much better shape than I am, as Wongchu (who has twice climbed Everest) hangs patiently behind me.

in the heart of the Sahara desert.

The porters, so ebulliently happy yesterday afternoon, are quiet and subdued. They crouch, huddled together for warmth, waiting to be called out, helped on with their baskets and sent on their way. They're Tamang people from Loswa district close to Kathmandu, all of them slight and wiry, as if honed down to the lowest body weight for the work they have to do. They will be paid $8 for each day on the mountain.

Though we have only about 1000 feet (300 m) to climb today, the path rises and falls in a frustrating switchback.

I've given up saying 'Namaste' to everyone who passes, but I'm momentarily cheered when I plod up to the top of yet another stone staircase and come level with two middle-aged American ladies. I see a look of recognition on one of their faces and hear a gasp of excitement as I pass.

'Oh, my God!'

I nod appreciatively, straighten my back and move on.

'It's *Eric Idle*!'

This precipitates serious psychological collapse. A half-hour later, exhausted by the pain of swallowing and the increasing effort required to pull in oxygen at this height, I finally yield my backpack to Wongchu. He takes it with a quiet smile, as if accepting the surrender of a garrison after a long siege.

Shedding the weight doesn't make things any better. Whereas I was out in front with the leaders yesterday, I can only watch the gap between us widen as they disappear ahead and leave me leaning on my climbing pole, heaving for breath, Nawang and Wongchu standing solicitously by.

Stagger into Machhapuchhre Base Camp around lunchtime. It's a much more open, jollier place than last night's guesthouse, full of infuriatingly happy campers sitting outside their tents, spraying each other with a water hose, hanging clothes on washing lines and generally having the time of their lives.

Even the majestic scenery – shapely Fish Tail and chunky Annapurna – fails to lift my spirits. I feel completely busted. The merest movement, to take food, to peel off a coat, to unpack an overnight bag, requires major physical effort. After a cup of garlic soup I decide there is nothing to do but take to my bed. Because of my condition, I'm upgraded from tent to room. It's standard mountain lodge accommodation, a stone-walled cell, eight foot by ten foot, with a flagged floor that traps the cold and damp like a cheese store, and a wooden bed frame on which is a thin mattress and a pillow. There is not much else to do but turn my back on one of the finest mountain panoramas in the world and climb, fully dressed, into my sleeping bag until whatever it is passes.

'You eat,' orders Wongchu when I surface a few hours later. 'Need food.'

No-one else says anything. I think I must frighten the crew a bit. They've never seen me quite like this: glum and unresponsive.

Force down some garlic soup, enlivened with shards of spring onion and green pepper. My neck and forehead are feverishly hot, and once I've finished, all I want to do is to go back to bed. Wongchu and Nawang deal with me most tenderly. Despite all my protestations, they prepare a bowl of steaming inhalant and insist I use it. Nawang gets fresh hot water from the cooks and helps me bathe my feet.

OPPOSITE

Sublime landscape. Our tiny band dwarfed by Annapurna.

BELOW

The worst night of the entire journey was spent here at Machhapuchhre Base Camp.

PREVIOUS PAGES

*A mug of garlic soup
as the afternoon mist
comes down over
Machhapuchhre, the
sacred mountain that
has never been
climbed.*

Then they guide me into my sleeping bag, with Wongchu applying massage as I go. I feel rather as if I'm being laid out, and I must say at this moment the Grim Reaper would not be an unwelcome visitor.

Wongchu wants one of the Sherpas to come and sit with me through the night, but I dissuade him, and, watched over by an inanimate but impressive array of tablets, tissues, ointments, creams and sprays, I close my eyes and wait.

Day Fifty Three : to Annapurna Base Camp

I wake up, wrenched from sleep by some chest-wracking cough, and am seized by near panic. Everything is pitch black, silent and cold as ice. I have no sensation of where I am. Perhaps Nawang and Wongchu have found me a flotation tank. I scrabble around for my head-torch, sending a bottle of pills clattering across the hard stone floor. For a few minutes I simply lie there, staring up at a circle of slatted, paint peeling board above me and waiting for my heart to slow down.

All sorts of things go through my mind. The one thing I can't dismiss is that I might have to think the unthinkable. That, for the first time in any of my journeys, I may have to face the possibility of failure. I'm sixty, after all, and there has to be a point at which the body puts its foot down, as it were.

For a depressing hour or so I can't escape this profound feeling of being defeated, physically and mentally, by the Himalaya.

When I next wake, though there is absolutely no physical sign of time passing, I know, even before I search for my torch, that I've been out for a while. And in that time some sea change has taken place. I'm no longer hot and feverish, and the sense of survival seems stronger than the sense of doom.

With some effort I pull myself up and take sips of hot water from the thermos Nawang insisted I keep beside me. It's four o'clock in the morning and as sure as I was three hours ago that I wouldn't make it, I know now that there can be no question of turning back.

This morning, I feel I'm emerging from hibernation. Last night was winter and this is spring.

I leave the camp, with Nawang and Wongchu, climbing due west. The snowfields of the Annapurna Himal lie dead ahead, shining and brilliant in the rising sun. It's an adventurous morning's filming too, off the main track and clambering very slowly through the thick grass, with the camera catching our silhouettes against the hard glare of the mountains.

Nawang stays beside me all the way, making sure I take regular slugs of water. Wongchu, who, reassuringly, seems to think I no longer need his personal supervision, walks ahead, looking like Geronimo and pausing occasionally to chat to some descending female trekker, preferably Swiss or Austrian. These encounters really seem to cheer him up, as well as making up for my dawdling.

So it is a tired but unrecognizably happier band that pulls itself up the last, agonizingly long and steep flight of steps to Annapurna Base Camp.

Appropriately enough for Annapurna, the Hindu goddess of fertility, a *dal baht* lunch is waiting, and on the sun-filled terrace I can sit and enjoy a combination of relief and release. For the time being, at least, I don't need to go any higher.

There's quite a crowd of trekkers already at the camp and, with a captive audience, Wongchu is in his element. Like many climbers I know, he has an inexhaustible supply of disaster stories. He points out a small Buddhist shrine just outside the camp, which marks the spot where

ABOVE

The view that makes it all worthwhile. The Annapurna Sanctuary, a 360-degree panorama with nine summits reaching 23,000 feet (7000 m).

Anatoly Boukreev, a Russian climber, was killed by an avalanche. Annapurna I has taken the lives of some 15 people. Some, he adds mysteriously, have died because they offended the mountain gods.

'By eating meat?'

'Eating meat, yes. But also having sex.'

'Having sex?'

He nods knowingly. It happened to a climber he knew on one of his Everest expeditions.

'He had sex with many different kind of women in the Himalaya.'

He pauses until all heads are turned in his direction.

'He was the one who died on that expedition.'

As there has been absolutely no question of my having sex on Annapurna, the gods seem to be positively smiling. For once the sunset is not lost in the mist, and at six o'clock, 40 or 50 people from all over the world gather to watch the light show on the peaks of Machhapuchhre. A small act of homage to the Himalaya.

Day Fifty Four : Annapurna Base Camp to Pokhara

Last night my chest and lungs were better behaved but I was kept from deep sleep by an avalanche of images that roared through my brain, unbidden and unstoppable, for most of the night, making it feel like a video stuck on fast forward. At least I had no recurrence of the sensory deprivations of the night before. My room has two windows and I can see the cold mountainside in the moonlight. I can hear my neighbour through the wall. It's Basil, with a cough so fierce and bronchial that it sounds dangerous.

We're due to be taken off by helicopter some time this morning. I must be honest and say that, for me, it's not a moment too soon.

I think back to the enthralled group silent in the face of the majestic beauty of Machhapuchhre last night and I wonder if we aren't all in danger of falling into the romantic delusion that by staring at these great massifs of rock and ice we achieve some form of communication with them, as if something so forbiddingly colossal must somehow be friendly.

The mountains are far more likely to be enemies than friends. We take them on at our peril and, despite all nature's warnings, long to go higher. And the higher we go the more the mountains tighten their grip, squeezing the life out of most people, gently in some cases, more severely in others. The locals who see the mountains as gods to be appeased are only translating pragmatic experience. Human beings are not meant to live at these heights and they should expect trouble if they do.

If there is a reward for reaching this height (13,400 feet (4080 m)) it is the exhilaration of the immense. Because we're that much closer to the top of the peaks, the sunlight reaches us earlier than it did below and the dazzling clarity of the light sharpens and intensifies every detail of this mighty bowl of mountains. My scepticism thaws a little with the sun and as we walk beyond the camp and look out over the monumental sweep of the glacier that unwinds from the Annapurna Ridge, gouging a valley from the sheer rock, I realize how extraordinarily lucky I am to have seen all this.

And how much luckier to have a helicopter to take me away from it.

Our magic carpet arrives on time and, anxious not to hang around in these unpredictable conditions, takes off as soon as we've strapped ourselves in. Below us, in the slipstream, our porters spread-eagle themselves on their tents to stop them blowing away. I feel embarrassed and a little ashamed. We could have got down without a helicopter, but we certainly couldn't have made it up the Annapurna trek without our porters.

After circling the massif, we turn due south, following coiling glaciers, until they melt into streams that cross the spiky grassland and grow into small rivers, which disappear first into coniferous then tropical rain forest, re-emerging where the trees have been cut back to make room for cultivated clearings. Then the first isolated settlements appear and the clearings grow into terraces and the settlements grow into mountain villages with marked tracks, and the terraces become rice paddies in all shades of green and yellow and the marked tracks become paved roads, with power lines running beside them through the tin-shack slums around the airport. And the rivers become a lake.

The evolution of human settlement in 22 minutes. At Pokhara, the joys of hot water, shower, bed and the excellent news that Adrian Griffith and his fellow Gurkha officers were released, unharmed, after 48 hours in the forest.

Day Fifty Six : Kathmandu

Post-Annapurna elation will be short-lived. Higher mountains and tougher conditions are forecast for the crossing into Tibet, but for now we have breathing space in one of the most intriguing cities of the Himalaya.

My guide to the Nepali capital is Kunda Dixit, editor of the *Nepali Times*, an English weekly with a circulation of 8000. It's crisply laid out and well designed and has a sharp, well-informed, provocative style. The most recent edition carries the latest World Terrorism Index, which shows that, despite the Maoists, Nepal still comes below the UK.

So I'm not entirely surprised to find that Kunda Dixit is an urbane, elegant figure with a shock of prematurely silver hair, dressed immaculately in a pale grey *labada* and knitted tunic. I am surprised to hear that his real love is flying and his fantasy is that, with a pilot suddenly taken ill, Kunda takes control, lands the plane perfectly and is asked to take over the national airline.

We meet up in Patan, once one of three independent kingdoms in the Valley, and now almost a suburb of Kathmandu.

The jewel at the heart of Patan (pronounced Parton, as in Dolly) is Durbar Square, a dazzling collection of buildings dating back 350 to 500 years, to the days before Prithvi Naryan Shah, king of Ghorka, unified the kingdoms of the Valley in 1768 and created modern Nepal. There are temples, palaces with golden gates, a huge bell suspended between two pillars and a lion on a column. Nepal was never colonized, so the architecture has no Western derivative and its distinctive fusion of Indian and Tibetan

BELOW

A doorway in Patan shows the fine design and craftsmanship of the Newari people. As in most parts of the Himalaya, we are never far from men with guns.

influences was created by the Newars, the people of the Valley, and craftsmen of the highest order.

As we wander through the colonnades of the Krishna Mandir, a stone-built Hindu temple topped with a *shikhara*, the characteristically Indian, curvilinear spire, we can look across to the Royal Palace, in a completely different style, refined by the Newari architect Arniko in the 14th century. It has powerful horizontals of brick and timber with deep, overhanging eaves, projecting balconies cantilevered out over finely carved, timber supports, and, inside, an elegantly proportioned *chowk*, or courtyard.

Kunda tells me that the Kathmandu Valley, once a lake, is rich in fertile, alluvial soil. The kingdoms, grown fat from consistently good harvests, ploughed their surpluses into religion, festivals and fine buildings, competing with each other for the tallest tower or the biggest bell.

'They used to say there were more temples in Kathmandu than houses and more gods than people.'

The buildings are not purely for show. A family arrives to do a *puja* at Krishna Mandir, unsettling a flock of pigeons, who create a sharp gust of wind as they take off, circle and descend en masse a few feet away.

The most dramatic building in the square is the five-storeyed pagoda of the Taleju Mandir, with a bronze stupa at its apex. The pagoda, a tapering succession of roofs symbolizing the various stages of enlightenment, was perfected here in Nepal, and it was Arniko who took the design to the Ming court at Peking.

One of the pleasures of meandering round Durbar Square is the immense amount of carved and sculpted detail. In the Royal Palace there are stone slabs called *shildayras* that carry historical records from the Lichavi period, 1800 years ago. On the beams in the *chowks* are intricately worked and painted lotus flowers, dragons and swastikas, and the stone walls of Krishna's temple are adorned with athletic, erotic couplings.

'Krishna is the God of Love,' explains Kunda. 'He's a young guy with a flute and girlfriends all over the world.'

I'm rather envious.

'Our gods don't tend to have girlfriends. It's something we've rather missed out on.'

The smallest of the old kingdoms was centred on Bhaktapur, seven miles east of Kathmandu. On our way out there we're waved past a police checkpoint set up since the Maoists recently brought their attacks to Kathmandu itself. They're searching all the buses that run out to the country areas in the east. According to Kunda, journeys that took 12 hours can now take 48.

Kunda's view is that the Maoists recent change of tactics, targeting civilians in the capital, has lost them support.

'It's not that the Maoists are terribly brilliant or strong, just that successive governments have been weak and fractious and corrupt, and they (the Maoists) have tapped into that bedrock of

neglect and apathy and frustration in the people. They've grown so fast precisely because everything else has been in such disarray.'

With an estimated 10,000 to 15,000 rebels, with looted arms from the police and the army, how does he see the future?

There can, he is sure, be no military solution. There has to be compromise. The institution of monarchy is quite strong and Nepalis identify their country with it, but the King can no longer be an absolute ruler. He must be firm but fair. (Which seems to suggest he's neither.)

He points to achievements brought about by strong policies resolutely applied.

Forestry conservation has been a big success since local people were given their own areas of forest to administer, the hydroelectric programme, building of roads, water improvement projects. All give him hope.

'And,' he concludes, 'Nepal's press has never been freer.'

We're turning into the bus park below the walls of Bhaktapur.

'The Prime Minister has been sacked, parliament is in limbo, but the press is free.'

The day that started promisingly is growing grey and gloomy as, having paid our $10 fee to enter the city, we climb up the steps and in through a narrow, rose-brick gateway.

For Basil it's a nostalgic return. Much of Bertolucci's *Little Buddha*, on which he worked as both actor and stills photographer, was shot in Bhaktapur. Though smaller than Kathmandu or Patan, Bhaktapur, whose name means 'city of devotees', once boasted 99 separate *chowks*. A powerful earthquake in 1934 did serious damage and now only five of these grand courtyards are left. That they are here at all is largely due to a German-sponsored reconstruction programme. The connection with Nepal seems a curious one, but it goes back a long way. A German Jesuit sent one of the Malla kings of Nepal a telescope as early as 1655. Hitler sent a later king a Mercedes.

As in Patan and, indeed, old Kathmandu itself, there is some glorious work in Bhaktapur. The Sun Dhoka (Golden Gateway) is an arched entrance surrounded by richly ornamented deities covered in gilded, embossed copper. The figures of the gods are still worshipped and I see young Nepalis touching them and then their foreheads as they pass. All over the temple area there are statues and carvings worn shiny by touch. We clamber up into a small, octagonal, carved timber gem called Chyasin Mandap, the Pavilion of the Eight Corners, an 18th-century original, meticulously restored around an earthquake-proof, steel shell. A much grander building stands nearby: Nyatapola, the tallest pagoda in Nepal. Five-tiered and standing 100 feet high, it somehow survived the 1934 earthquake quite unscathed. One might imagine this would increase its attraction for devotees, but when I climb up the long, steep staircase past sculpted ranks of temple guardians – wrestlers, elephants, lions, griffins – I find only dust and a group of street children. Apparently, this magnificent building is dedicated to an obscure Tantric goddess, Siddhi Lakshmi, who very few people have heard of, let alone worship. As the temples rely on

ABOVE

Slices of life in Durbar Square, Patan. (left to right) Hindu temples side by side with pagodas (which the Newars introduced to China); a man does puja, *a ritual offering to the gods at Krishna Mandir; the pagoda style was developed here; Kunder Dixit, urbane, resourceful editor of the* Nepali Times.

rich patrons for their upkeep, Nyatapola remains neglected.

There is hope. Kunda is generally optimistic about the way the old city centres are looked after (all three are UNESCO sites). He's much less happy about the way modern development is going. The urban sprawl around Kathmandu is, he feels, destroying the identities of the three cities. They are becoming part of a Kathmandu conurbation, which is bad for Nepal. It increases the centralization of wealth and government in the Valley, further alienating the country areas, and puts great pressure on limited resources. Water supply is becoming a major problem. The latest proposal is to bring water in direct from a glacier, 15 miles away. It will be the biggest engineering project in Nepal's history, and if it works it will only bring more people and more money to the central Valley, further dividing the country. And it would not go unopposed. Only yesterday, Kunda reminds me, the Maoists destroyed a hydroelectric plant.

On our way back, the insalubrious suburbs, and the congested roads that take us through them, seem to bear out Kunda's darker prophecies, but life is not all gloom.

He tells the story of sitting next to Prince Charles (of whom he has a very high opinion) at a Nepali banquet. Halfway through the meal Charles upended a full portion of rice wine into his lap.

'Great embarrassment all round?'

'No, everything was fine.' Kunda smiles at the recollection. 'I told him that was the way we do our dry cleaning here.'

Day Fifty Seven : Kathmandu

To a high-walled, heavily gated, but otherwise reassuringly normal home near the Gurkha headquarters for a reunion with Adrian Griffith, the British Gurkha officer sent to look after us who ended up being abducted himself.

A relief to find him in good health and good spirits. We drink tea in his garden with his admirably phlegmatic wife, who claims never to have worried that he wouldn't come back. Adrian, whilst refusing to answer what he calls 'operational questions', gives us a little more

RIGHT
*With Pratima on a
bridge over the
Bagmati River at
Pashupatinath, the
most important Hindu
temple complex in
Nepal.*

background to what happened that evening when the Maoists called him away from his whisky.

They were taken to an empty house an hour from Lekhani and about five hours later, about midnight, were led deeper into the forest. His escort were not angry but they were insistent, and they had weapons concealed in their shoulder bags.

'Pistols?'

'Yes, pistols.'

'I went to sleep in a very filthy bed from which I received a lot of flea bites.' (His only injuries, fortunately.)

All the next day was spent talking, or rather, being talked at, by his abductors. On the second day of their captivity, by which time the story was all across the world's newspapers, word came down from the Maoist high command that Adrian and the others should be released. He feels pretty sure that the local commanders had been reprimanded by their superiors for taking him in the first place.

I asked if he ever felt in real danger. He said his two worries were of the danger of being caught in crossfire if the security forces mounted an operation to free him and the knowledge that a Nepali member of the Gurkha staff, abducted a year before, had been held for seven weeks.

'I think we were an opportunity target. They came down in order to disrupt the recruiting, realized there was someone more senior from the British Gurkhas there and saw it as a chance to publicize their cause.'

What of the recruits who'd sweated and strained their way through a day of tests?

Well, they would be given the chance to try again. This was the only time Adrian sounded less than convincing.

Before we leave Kathmandu, I meet up once again with the redoubtable Pratima Pande, who insists that I should see one of the great sights of Kathmandu, the temple complex at Pashupatinath, the holiest Hindu site outside India. Pashupati is one of the many names (around a thousand in all) of Shiva, the most revered god in the Hindu pantheon. So sacred is this site that non-Hindus are not allowed inside the temple at the heart of it. If they were, they would be able to see one of its great attractions, a ten-foot-high male member, or *linga*, which, and I rely on my *Rough Guide* for this, refers to a myth whereby 'Shiva transformed his phallus into an

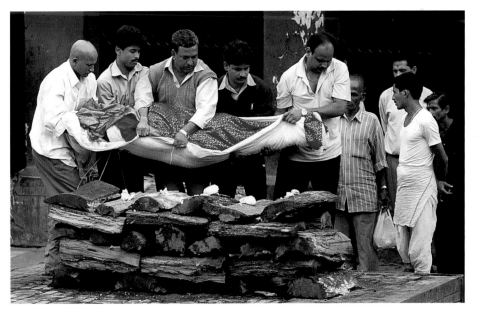

LEFT

Male members of the family lay a deceased relative on the funeral pyre at the cremation ghats at Pashupatinath. Ghee (clarified butter) is laid on the logs to help them burn. The man on the left has just had his head shaved in mourning.

infinite pillar of light and challenged Brahma and Vishnu – the other members of the Hindu trinity – to find the ends of it. Both were forced to abandon the search.'

Below the temple and flanked by the burning ghats runs the River Bagmati, which, despite carrying the effluent of 1.5 million people, is a holy river, and eventually joins the Ganges. Monkeys scuttle along the parapet ahead of us as we pause on one of two stone and brick bridges and look down on a sight I've heard about but never witnessed. A number of platforms, sort of jetties for the soul, are built on the river bank and on these the dead are cremated on wood pyres. One or two have bodies burning on them already, others are being cleared after a cremation. Attendants, brisk and businesslike in white aprons and cotton vests, are brushing the platforms clean, sending burning embers flying into the river, where they hit the water with a hiss and bob off down the Bagmati, trailing plumes of smoke like so many miniature steamships.

As we watch, a corpse is carried down past the temple and onto the bridge. Six members of the family are in attendance. They turn off and lay the body down beside a pyre already decorated with garlands of marigold.

Pratima explains that in Hindu culture it is very important that people do not die in their house, or that on death they are removed as soon as possible, so that the spirits captured there can be released. Indeed, there are those who, thinking their time is up, ask to be brought down to this holy place to die, only to recover and get up and go home at the end of the day.

The family we were watching have taken up their litter and moved across to the other side of the bridge, having strayed inadvertently onto the ghats reserved for upper-class Brahmins. This, Pratima tells me, is where the various members of the Nepali royal family were brought after the massacre two and a half years ago. Five of them, including the King and Queen, their younger son, and two princesses were cremated the same day they were murdered.

The family have now found the pyre reserved for them. To aid combustion, an attendant inserts slices of ghee (clarified butter) between the split logs. The mourners, all men (no women mourners are allowed to attend a cremation), are preparing themselves. The eldest son is sitting on the steps of the ghat having his head shaved by a priest, a *pandit*, with a cut-throat razor. He wears a plain white robe, white being the Hindu colour of mourning. There is something quite affecting about seeing the way he submits to this very simple, very public act of obsequy, in full view of any who happen to be passing.

The priest then talks to the family, presumably instructing them as to how it's all done, and they then lift the body from its bamboo stretcher, carry it, a little awkwardly, three times round the pyre, before laying it down, the head exposed. It's the body of a woman, younger than I expected, maybe not his mother or grandmother but his wife.

Basil leaves and water are placed in the dead woman's mouth as *prasad*, food consecrated and blessed by the gods.

Ghee is then placed on her body, with sandalwood to add a sweet-smelling incense, and the oldest male heir then walks around the pyre three times more. Then it is he who applies a lighted taper to the body, always near the mouth.

Shaking with emotion, he then bows, walks to the end of the pyre and buries his head on her feet. I feel I should look away, but I can't. I know nothing about these people yet, in this

brief ceremony, I feel a wave of empathy, not just for them, but for loss, for the end of a life. I come from somewhere where death is kept private, almost as if it's an embarrassment. We send our loved ones away hidden in a box, into a hidden fire. We don't even press the button that sends the coffin sliding into that fire. It's all at arm's length. Here in Pashupatinath it's very much hands on. The reality of death, the fact of death, is confronted, not avoided.

We walk on across the bridge, to the east bank of the river. Everything here is odd and unfamiliar. There are animals everywhere: dogs, cows and some of the 400 monkeys who scamper over roofs and walls, eyes and little pink hands out for any offering left unattended. Along the side of the hill is a series of small, stone shrines, each one containing a stone phallus, dedicated to Shiva. They were built to commemorate those women who came here to commit *sati,* to be burned alive beside their husbands, as was the custom before the British made it illegal. Among the temples and terraces higher up we come upon an enclosure where sadhus, flamboyant ascetics as I suppose you might describe them, gather. The holy men, who call themselves *babas,* are not at all averse to posing for the tourists. I rather like the idea of exhibitionist hermits and particularly enjoy the milk *baba*, who lives solely on milk, and an 87-year-old with six-foot-long tresses, who obligingly puts his leg behind his head for me.

Bearing in mind that I shall be in Tibet tomorrow night, it seems suitable that we end the day at the biggest Buddhist temple in Kathmandu, built for those who for thousands of years

have come through here on the road to and from the lands to the north.

Boudhanath stupa is immense, some 130 feet (38 m) high, and it squats like some great white spaceship, surrounded by shops, hotels and houses, off one of the busiest streets of the city. A pair of painted eyes looks down from the wall, serenely surveying the flock of birds, spread across the dome like stubble on a huge bald head, the shopkeepers and the crowd of pilgrims walking round and round in a clockwise direction, gaining more merit for each circuit they make. A web of colourful flags flaps from the highest point of the stupa, sending their prayers out to the gods. To my classically conditioned mind, all this display seems excessive and garish, like wrapping St Paul's Cathedral in Christmas paper.

Pratima invites us to a very smart party this evening. Lots of important foreign diplomats being introduced. I'm tired and just want to go to bed, but I do treasure one bit of polite conversation.

I'm introduced to an immaculately dressed man who takes a slightly pained glance at my appearance. I don't catch his name and grabbing a passing glass of wine, I hear myself asking, 'I'm sorry, ambassador of where?'

'France.'

It's time to move on.

ABOVE

Prayer flags flutter from the huge stupa at Boudhanath, the most important Buddhist site in Kathmandu and heart of the city's Tibetan community.

Day Fifty Eight : Kathmandu to the Chinese Border

The road that winds its way northeast from Kathmandu is called the Arniko Highway. It's appropriately named, for Arniko was the Nepali architect credited with introducing the pagoda to China and the road that bears his name leads to the only crossing point between the two countries.

It is quite likely that there was more contact between Nepal and China 600 years ago than there is today. The road route from Kathmandu to Lhasa has only been open since the 1980s.

The landscape at first is unsensational, the highway rising and falling over undulating, terraced foothills. A string of tourist hotels with names like Snow View Resort and Himalaya Lookout carry the promise of great things to come, but sadly fail to deliver. The mountains ahead of us remain undetectable behind a layer of sluggish low cloud.

This concentrates the eye on more intimate views: villages of brick and thatch houses and tiny plots of land, ploughed by hand, with nothing much to suggest anything has changed in the last few hundred years. Verdant, fertile country, but rural life is still on an intimate scale. At the bend of a river a mixed team of cows and donkeys is being turned in tight circles to thresh the freshly cut wheat. Milk churns are carried on bent backs.

The only significant modern intrusions are regular police checkpoints (not a purely Nepali phenomenon, we've learnt to expect men with guns everywhere in the Himalaya) and the bizarrely large number of whisky adverts on the side of the houses. Names like Matador, Pied Paper and Bond are so ubiquitous they give the impression that much of rural Nepal must be on the bottle.

The only other product that is so obviously trumpeted is education. They're proud of their schools here and it's common to see crocodiles of young children, in matching uniforms, ties and backpacks, emerging from establishments like The Golden Future High School or The Wisdom Academy.

After lunch at Barabhise in the valley of the fast-flowing Bhote Koshi (Tibet River), the

OPPOSITE AND LEFT

*Women are prominent
in Nepali rural life.
(opposite) In the
Himalyan foothills, a
woman carries home
scrub for cattle feed.
(left) Shopkeeper in
crimson sari on the
road to the border.*

countryside narrows into a deep, forested gorge. A bridge with a bungee jump incongruously attached rises high above us and a little further on we pass a heavily guarded hydroelectric power station. Just as everything seems to be getting steep and claustrophobic, the walls of the gorge widen, quite abruptly, to reveal, high above us across the end of the valley, the white-stacked rectangles of a mountain city. My first glimpse of Tibet.

Nepali immigration is in a large bare room decorated with three framed pictures of King Gyanendra, his queen and Ganesh, the elephant god. Having had our names laboriously entered on a Departure Record, we walk up a dirty muddy road towards the border crossing on Friendship Bridge.

As we have all our gear to transfer, we cautiously back our vehicles into the middle of the 200-foot bridge to the exact point where Nepal ends and China begins. I don't think anyone's ever done this before, and there is much shouting from both ends. In the mayhem we say our farewells to Wongchu and Nawang and Mingmar, the trio of Sherpas who have looked after us so magnificently, while at the same time keeping an eye out for our Chinese escort.

He turns out to be a slim, young man in a sky-blue fleece, holding some papers and looking extremely anxious. So preoccupied is he with this unorthodox crossing that he doesn't introduce himself for another two hours. Only then do I learn he's a Tibetan, by the name of Migmar.

Anything in the Himalaya with the word 'friendship' attached is bound to be Chinese, and, sure enough, they built Friendship Bridge across this gorge in 1985. It's a grim and deeply confusing place to be and we are pretty soon ordered to stop filming. As Wongchu and Nawang wave one last time before disappearing into the crowd behind a 'Welcome to the Kingdom of Nepal' sign, I experience an emotion not dissimilar to that of seeing my mother wave goodbye to me on my first day at school.

We're now in the hands of unsmiling Chinese border guards in uniforms that seem to have been specifically designed to be too big. With the SARS epidemic so recently over, I first have to fill in a Quarantine Form. I then take it to a booth where a man in a white coat checks it, produces a gun, points it right between my eyes and pulls the trigger. He then peers at the gun,

notes down my temperature and motions me into China.

The disorientation continues. Not only does the traffic drive halfway across the bridge on the left (Nepal) and the other half on the right (China) but, because of time changes, one end of Friendship Bridge (China) is two hours and fifteen minutes ahead of the other (Nepal). Propelled suddenly from mid-afternoon to early evening, we load up and drive as fast as we can, which means extremely slowly, up the six miles of slippery, winding track between the bridge and the Chinese immigration and customs post. Across the valley I can see Kodari, the last town in Nepal, receding below us. The gorge is steep and very beautiful but scarred with piles of rubbish, regurgitated from the backs of the buildings and spilling down to form scummy, foaming pools at the water's edge. In every country we've been so far private cleanliness and public squalor seem to quite happily co-exist and I've never really been able to work out why.

We arrive at Chinese immigration as it is about to close, and it's only pressure from our local hosts that stop us having to spend the night in the vehicles. We're allowed to take an overnight bag and walk up to the hotel, but everything else must be locked in the cars overnight.

Later: Room 505 of the Bai Ma Hotel, Xangmu. TV but no heating. Communal lavatory and bathroom down the passage. Single strip light, thin, inadequate curtains that are no match for the street lamps outside, and windows that seem specifically designed to funnel jets of cold air into the room.

This basic hotel, which we're assured is the best in town, is saved by its small, warm and cheerful dining room. Over *momos* (traditional Tibetan shell-shaped dumplings), stir-fry and Budweiser brewed in Wuhan, we meet up with Nina Huang Fan, our Chinese production assistant from Beijing, Mr Yang, the man the Chinese have sent to keep an eye on us, and Migmar, the soft-spoken young Tibetan, who still seems traumatized by the events on Friendship Bridge.

We're joined by Mr Tse Xiu, who is someone high up in the Foreign Relations Ministry of the Tibetan Autonomous Republic. He speaks with quiet authority, but not in English, unfortunately. When his message is relayed to us it's not exactly heartening. Everest Base Camp, which we are scheduled to reach in 48 hours, is presently suffering from strong winds and temperatures down to -25°C (-13°F) at night. He advises us to make the best of a hot shower tonight, as there will be no more creature comforts for a while.

Have showered in a trickle of tepid water and am writing this with a blanket around me and wondering just how much colder it's going to get.

OPPOSITE
Pool at your peril. Two very common images of the central Himalaya: rock slides and outdoor snooker tables.

BELOW
(left) Friendship Bridge, Kodari. The frontier between Nepal and China (a red flag flies on the east end of the bridge). One of only two north-south road connections through the Himalaya (the other is Kunjerab Pass in Pakistan). (right) Porter with Sisyphean load pushes open the gate into Nepal.

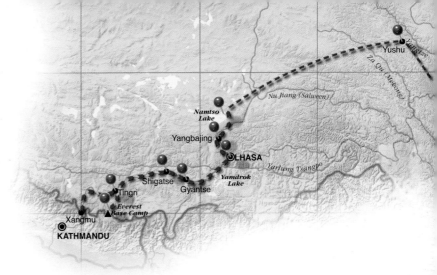

Tibet

Day Fifty Nine: Xangmu to Tingri

XANGMU HIGH STREET, quiet as the grave when we arrived, erupts into life at night. Sounds of shouting, drilling, thumping and banging drift, unhampered, through tightly closed windows and into my head. I pull all the blankets off the unoccupied bed next to me, curl up in a foetal ball and hope it will all just go away. It doesn't. It gets worse. The hissing, clunking, industrial sounds seem to be augmented by flashes and crackles. Can someone really be spot-welding out there at 12.15? The prospect of how exhausted I'll feel in the morning keeps me awake for at least another hour.

Wake at eight, but it's still pitch dark. In fact, it doesn't begin to get light for another half-hour. The government of China, in their wisdom, decreed that the whole country, wider than the United States, should have only one time zone. The further west you are the later daybreak comes.

The street outside, apart from the frequent clearing of throats and whistling of spittle, is quiet again this morning. I can find no satisfactory explanation for the nocturnal activity other than that Xangmu is a frontier town and frontier towns have a life of their own. We walk down the hill to resume the customs procedures.

A truck marked 'Four Friends Transport. Live Long Friendship Nepal, India, China, Bhutan' is at the head of a long queue of vehicles heading towards Nepal. There isn't much room at the customs, and trucks, individuals, a bewildered looking tour group and a flock of sheep are all trying to get through at the same time. Young, officious border guards in slack uniforms either push people around or ignore them completely. High up on the wall, and conveniently inaccessible, is a small box marked 'Complaints about Immigration'.

By the time all the formalities have been completed – and to be fair, a British film crew is a very rare sight in Tibet – it's early afternoon. Our final departure is marked by a small ceremony at which the manager of the Bai Ma Hotel gives us each a white scarf to bring us good luck on our journey. He seems a decent man, doing his best, though I notice he doesn't have a complaints box.

As we drive out of Xangmu (with few regrets, in my case) the squash of white-tiled buildings eases and we can see the wooded gorge we climbed yesterday, plunging picturesquely down to Nepal. The road to Lhasa (now, inevitably, re-christened the Friendship Highway) continues

RIGHT

First glimpse of the high peaks on the road to Tingri. Gaurishankar on the right, Cho Oyu on the left and Menlungtse centre. The height of the mountains shields Tibet from rain clouds, creating the arid wilderness in the middle ground.

OPPOSITE

Road-sweeping gang takes a breather in Nyalam.

to climb steeply, through forested slopes and past tumbling waterfalls, until it brings us at last to the edge of the Tibetan plateau. The Roof of the World was once a seabed. What lay beneath the ancient Sea of Tethys was heaved up onto the top of the world by the same collision of the Indian and Eurasian plates that built the Himalaya. It now rests at an average height of 13,100 feet (4000 m) and from its steep sides stream some of the world's greatest rivers: the Indus, Salween, Yangtze, Irrawaddy, Yellow River and Brahmaputra.

In the relatively short distance from Xangmu, we've made dramatic progress, vertically, if not horizontally. We're only 20 miles from the Bai Ma Hotel, but 5000 feet (1520 m) above it. Apart from a few poplar groves, the tree cover has gone and on the mountainsides bare rock shows through tight, tussocky cover. At a cold, exposed little town called Nyalam we stop to have papers checked before entering a new administrative zone. Women in masks sweep the street, outside a modern building a prosperous-looking man makes two of his employees unroll a length of carpet, which he proceeds to examine with great care. Recently completed terraced housing runs along the side of the road, an early indication of Beijing's plans to make Tibet a new frontier. This is a cheerless place, though J-P, never daunted, manages to find a shop selling wine and we roll across the River Matsang two bottles of Dynasty Red to the better.

The road continues upwards, over long, undulating, brown hills, until we reach the prayer flag-bedecked pass of Tong La, over 17,000 feet (5180 m) above sea level and the highest place I've ever been on earth (coming in well ahead of my previous record, the hot springs in San Pedro de Atacama in Chile at 14,700 feet (4480 m)).

Everything is bewildering, strange and wonderful. Running the length of the southern horizon is a chain of towering, white peaks and on the grassland below us a herd of yak, short-legged creatures, bodies close to the ground, their thick, black hair standing out against greeny-brown hills behind them.

We stop and walk a little way from the car, every step feeling like 20 at this altitude.

But that doesn't dampen the exhilaration.

It's dark when we reach the town of Tingri and, after some initial confusion, find our way off

the highway and into a capacious courtyard, which looks like that of a monastery, but in fact belongs to the Snow Leopard Hotel. Life centres around a big, low, woody room with painted beams and a brick parqueted floor, largely lit by the glow from a stove of burning yak dung in the centre of the room. This is what was lacking in those inhospitable Annapurna cabins: a fire, so simple and so intensely welcoming. We cluster round it and a lady with braided hair and rubicund, muddied face offers us yak butter tea. Nigel describes the taste as 'liquid gorgonzola', which is absolutely spot on. The rancid smell of the tea and the sharp aroma of yak dung smoke is not as horrible as it sounds. I find it odd, yes, but interestingly strange and unfamiliar, quintessentially Tibetan and proof that north of the Himalaya everything is very different.

In the dim recesses of the room we're served a very good meal of noodles with mushroom, pork, green peppers and lumps of soft, white, doughy Tibetan bread.

We're advised to break out the sleeping bags tonight. It will be below zero in our un-heated rooms.

Leaving the fire is the hardest thing, but once across the yard, beneath a bracingly clear night sky, I'm into a pretty little room, so different from last night. Proper curtains, a colourful wall with a frieze of painted flowers. Beside the bed I have a wooden cabinet, also very charmingly painted. By the light of a very dim bulb I can make out leering gods, dragons, clouds, waves and what look very much like flying teeth.

The only setback tonight is that the bottles of wine from Nyalam proved undrinkable.

Day Sixty : Tingri to Rongbuk

Though perfectly comfortable in my congenial little room, sleep was light and fleeting and broken by twinges of headache and nausea. The zero temperatures with which Mr Tse Xiu threatened us didn't materialize and when I should have been sleeping I was engaged in an energy-consuming nocturnal striptease, peeling off the various layers of clothing I'd gone to bed in and dropping them out of my sleeping bag one by one.

Open the curtains to find a yak calf helping itself to a bowl of water which has been put outside my room.

Wash in what's left of it and join the others for breakfast. On the way there I notice a big satellite dish in one corner of the courtyard. There's no evidence of a television anywhere about the place.

This is my first chance to have some time with Migmar, who has so far been preoccupied with getting us into China. He's 27, the son of Tibetan nomads who were enlightened enough to send him to school, from where he won a place at Lhasa University. He read Chinese (the Dalai Lama would have approved) and English, which, despite the fact he's never left Tibet, he speaks pretty well.

I'm impressed by the richness of the decoration on almost every inch of the timber columns, beams and ceiling boards, and Migmar explains that in the 9th century a Tibetan warlord tried to eradicate Buddhism and the only way that the culture survived was through a pictorial code. The Buddhist heroes were depicted as animals: dragons, tigers, even sheep. What began as a cipher developed into a rich tradition of imaginative painting, a particular target during the Cultural Revolution, when a renewed and virulent attempt was made to destroy Tibet's Buddhist past.

Instead of continuing along the Friendship Highway to Lhasa, we turn south on a dirt road, towards the heart of the Himalaya. Apart from the occasional four-wheel drives like our own, traffic consists of horses and carts trotting between isolated settlements, usually of low,

whitewashed houses with prayer flags fluttering from poles at each corner of the roof. The harshness of life up here in this dry and windy rain shadow of the Himalaya is etched on the faces of the farmers and their families. Skin is weathered and faces prematurely aged. The children, noses running and cheeks red and rough from the sun, cluster round as soon as we stop, asking us to give them something.

At one stop the villagers are celebrating with music and dancing. Music seems to lighten the load, and getting out the three-string guitars is a popular move. Soon a circle is formed and the dancers are moving slowly round with a step that doesn't seem to vary, though judging by reactions, the words they sing have been brought up to date. The women wear big, coral earrings, flower pattern shirts and the traditional Tibetan *chuba*, a long, sleeveless dress tied with a sash at the waist. Some of the men wear their version of the *chuba*, big, wide-sleeved coats, and one or two are in sheepskin jackets, leggings and heavy boots of the kind I haven't really seen since the pop festivals of the late sixties.

Migmar says that at times like New Year dances like this can be spun out for several days.

We move on, through desert scenery, with minimal vegetation but every kind of eye-catching rock formation: deep gullies, bluffs with soaring, scree-covered slopes, exposed synclines and anticlines, red and angry, as if freshly split from the cliffs around them. A brisk wind creates the only movement in this dead landscape, sending dust devils spiralling across the track in front of us.

A military checkpoint, beside a big, modern PLA (People's Liberation Army) barracks with a red-tiled roof, stands at the entrance to the Qomolangma National Park, and a metalled road, recently upgraded, leads us smoothly up to the next big pass, Pang La. This is the high point of our day's journey, in every respect. At the summit, a smooth, wide hill at 17,000 feet (5180 m), one of the finest views in the world is suddenly, almost abruptly, revealed. The full, majestic spread of the central Himalaya is laid out before us, like white-topped waves in a frozen ocean. It's an horizon full of giants: Cho Oyu, a huge massif that peaks at 26,928 feet (8210 m), Makalu 1 at 27,594 feet (8410 m), Lhotse 1 at 27,883 feet (8500 m) and the monumental pyramid of Everest, rising serenely above them all at 29,021 feet (8850 m).

The highest point of the earth's surface, which I am seeing today for the first time with my own eyes, is known to the Tibetans as Qomolangma (pronounced 'Chomolungma'), Goddess Mother of the Earth, to the Sherpas as Sagamartha and when the Imperial Survey of India first

ABOVE

(left) A circle dance takes shape in a village on the way to Everest Base Camp. There'll be much yodelling and foot-stamping, probably after we've gone. (right) These folk get-togethers are an important time for matchmaking.

143

determined the mountain's precise height it was known on British maps as Peak XV. It was given the name Everest in 1865, in recognition of Sir George Everest, the man who pioneered the mapping of India. (To add to the confusion, what we call Everest should really be called Eev-rest, which was the way Sir George's name was pronounced.)

None of these things goes through my head as I stand at the top of the pass, unable to take my eyes off this stupendous panorama.

Like K2, the world's second highest mountain, which straddles China and Pakistan, Everest is divided between two countries, China and Nepal. In the 1920s and 1930s Nepal was a closed country and the pioneering expeditions of George Mallory all came in from Tibet and concentrated on the North Face.

When expeditions resumed after the Second World War, it was Tibet's turn to be closed off, after the Chinese Communist invasion of 1949, whilst Nepal opened up around at the same time.

The main bulk of Everest ascents, now running at around 100 a year, are made via the South East Ridge from which Hillary and Sherpa Tenzing had conquered the mountain in 1953. The North Face remains the more mysterious; aloof, daunting and much more dangerous. It was first climbed by a Chinese expedition in 1960. They laid a dirt road to transport their equipment up here, which is why we are able to drive up to Base Camp. The track bounces over impacted, corrugated earth strewn with small boulders, but the four-wheel drives don't find it too difficult, and by late afternoon, after winding our way through valleys fed by glacial melt from the slopes of Everest, we turn past the Rongbuk *gompa*, the highest monastery in the world, and in to the walled courtyard of the guesthouse, administered by the monastery.

It looks, for a moment, like the most wonderful place in the world. The same long, low, Tibetan-style layout as the Snow Leopard in Tingri, but with a hugely more spectacular location. This turns out to be its only redeeming feature. From the filthy, littered courtyard to the soulless concrete rooms with broken windows and the foul, doorless lavatories, Rongbuk Guest House is pretty much a hell hole.

The redeeming feature, however, is not to be underestimated. There is only one mountain to

be seen from here and that is Everest. It stands, massive, grand and solitary, only a few miles away across the end of the valley. It is the horizon.

Day Sixty One : Rongbuk

Last night was desperately uncomfortable. A fierce wind blew, occasionally gusting with such ferocity that I feared it might tear the windows out. I lay awake, mouth dry despite regular swigs of water, listening to the village dogs fighting and detritus in the yard being flung about by the wind. As soon as I drifted off to sleep my breathing slowed and within moments I was wide awake, gasping for breath. I need the sleep so much, but I find myself fighting it, forcing myself to stay awake and breathe slow and deep.

The latrine is almost subhuman. It's hard enough to aim through a hole reduced to a slit by the calcified accretions of many previous visitors, without at the same time having to flash a torch to warn other guests and extract thin sheets of Boots travel tissue in a freezing, force 8 gale. Many years ago, encountering similarly appalling conditions in a boat on Lake Tanganyika, I took Imodium to prevent me having to go to the toilet ever again. As I squat in this howling tempest three miles up in the sky, I think cyanide might be the better option.

One advantage of this fierce wind is that when daylight comes it is clear and pristine. The summit of Everest trails a plume of spindrift, blown off the mountain by winds which, at that height, must be in excess of 100 miles an hour. The rest of the mountain, including the long, flanking shoulders below the arrow-head peak, is crystal clear.

The remainder of the guests who were here last night – Spaniards, Norwegians and a group of Australians – all leave today. They can't believe we're here for three nights, and whoop with joy as they're driven away.

Our cooks are making yak butter tea, which the Tibetans call Bo Cha, in the traditional, long, thin, cylindrical churn. It's a mixture of yak butter and tea leaves, with salt and milk added, and is a taste I've yet to acquire, and I'm sure I shall have plenty of opportunity to do so.

We had hoped to move up to Base Camp today, but with the wind still strengthening the decision is taken to stay down here and acclimatize. With atmospheric pressure about half that at sea level, everyone is suffering to some degree and Mr Yang, our minder, and John Pritchard, our sound recordist, are particularly uncomfortable.

Apart from the guesthouse and a new, red-brick hotel nearby, ready but tantalizingly un-opened, Rongbuk consists of a line of low cottages and the monastery, which looks old but was built less than 20 years ago to replace the one destroyed, along with thousands of others in Tibet, by fanatical Red Guards in the 1960s. Outside it stands a sizeable *chorten* topped with a small, black pyramid and hung with prayer flags like ribbons on a maypole. I walk into a courtyard of two-storey buildings with a painted balcony running round for access, and I follow the sound of chanting up a flight of steps on the far side of the square and into the temple. There are 60 monks here at the world's highest monastery, 30 men and 30 women. With their shaven heads and loose robes, it's difficult to tell them apart.

After prayers they gather outside and I present them with a *thangka* (from Kathmandu). It's accepted by the abbot, a big, amiable man with a very dirty, cherry-red duvet jacket over his robes. The monks gather round and study it with great interest.

By evening the wind has dropped as forecast. I sit in the room I share with Basil and make my notes as Everest, now completely clear of the cloud, turns pink in the dying sunlight. Apart from the very top, Everest is not one single, symmetrical shape like a Kilimanjaro or a Machhapuchhre, its outline being composed of a series of huge blocks.

Suddenly my view is obscured by two women banging on the window, staring in at me and holding their hands out. They're some of the saddest people I've seen and for a moment I feel a sense of frustration that the monastery can do so little for them.

Getting in and out of my sleeping bag are the most uncomfortable moments of the day. The cold snaps at my heels and yet dressing and undressing cannot be hurried at this altitude.

Day Sixty Two : Rongbuk to Everest Base Camp

Last night I slept. Indeed, I slept so long and so deeply that Basil thought I might be dead.

What a difference it makes to everything. The sky looks bluer, the food tastes better, the yak butter tea is like nectar and the prospect of a trek beyond Everest Base Camp and up towards the Rongbuk Glacier is the only thing I want to do with the rest of my life.

It takes us 20 minutes to drive the eight miles from Rongbuk to Base Camp, passing on the way the remains of the old monastery.

Some of the walls still stand, but it's little more than a skeleton, barely distinguishable from the rubble-covered slopes on which it stands. Above these desiccated ruins a flock of blue sheep are nosing some nourishment out of the rocks.

Everest Base Camp is nowhere near as romantic as it sounds. Part of it is protected by a 100-foot-high moraine, a wall of stone and shale, carried down and dumped by the glacier that has gouged out the valley. A stream trickles through but any standing water is frozen solid. In high season, between June and August, this area and the rock-strewn valley floor beyond are packed with mountaineers and trekkers. This year there were 32 separate expeditions.

Now, in early November, the camp is all but deserted though the legacy of the summer lies around: discarded brandy bottles, playing cards, batteries and bits of sodden, scrumpled clothing.

OPPOSITE

Chomolungma, 'Goddess Mother of the Earth'. The best name westerners could come up with for the world's highest mountain was Everest. The north face was first climbed by a Chinese expedition in 1960 (seven years after Hilary and Tensing conquered the peak).

A couple of motorbikes are parked beside a caretaker's tent, outside which a young man sits in the sun, having his hair cut by two ladies. Nearby, the yak herders with whom we shall be walking up to the glacier have set up two or three small tents of their own, while the yaks graze nearby, nibbling at the scatterings of wheat and dry grass laid out for them. One has made a small hole in the ice and is drinking from it. Their hair is mostly black, though some have white faces. All have the soft eyes of cows and the same sad, long-suffering look, as if resigned to whatever's going to happen. Despite looking eminently embraceable, they don't seem at all interested in my friendly advances, and I'm warned that they can turn very truculent.

I learn, too, that though yak is their generic name, it refers only to the male; a female is called a *dri* and a yak crossed with a cow is a *dzo* (this is a useful word to know when playing Scrabble, as my ever helpful Bradt guide points out). They are the preferred carriers at this height, stoical and persistent, sure-footed on the rocks. They thrive at altitude, protected from the cold by a thick saddle of insulating fat across their backs, and the big expeditions rely on them to transport heavy equipment up as high as 21,500 feet (6550 m). It's on the lower slopes that the yaks suffer. Anything below 8000 feet (2440 m) can be very uncomfortable for them, as they tend to overheat.

Though the herders seem not the slightest bit sentimental about their furry charges, theirs is one of the most one-sidedly symbiotic relationships between man and beast. In return for some grass the yaks give their owners milk, cheese, butter, meat, fuel, building materials, clothes and transport.

I join the herders around a fire of brush wood and bamboo kindling, which they keep alive by tossing on the odd yak nugget and pumping hard with an ancient sheep's bladder bellows. Sitting in a circle, eating cake made from *tsampa*, the barley flour and tea mix, they're jolly company, naturally given to smiling and cracking jokes, most of which are at my expense.

Their clothes are made from skins and fur and look as if they have been part of their bodies since they were born. Their complexions, skin textures, their whole physiognomy is a reflection

148

of the life they lead. Coloured by the wind and rain, stunted by the bitter cold, their features sculpted in a craggy resemblance to the weird and wonderful landscape around them, they're elemental figures, created by and in the likeness of the mountains.

Maybe all this accounts for the ease of their manner. They know what to do here. They know what to expect and how to deal with it. They have slope cred.

This morning means having fun with foreigners, and being paid for it. First of all, it's tea, invigoratingly salty, with a knob of yak butter thrown in, then it's time to get out the *chang*, a fermented barley beer, for me to try. It's poured out of a stained, dusty container, the sort of thing you might find at the back of the shed ten years after you put it there. Before drinking, Migmar shows me the important procedure of giving thanks. I must dip my third finger into the brew, and, flicking it each time, give thanks first to the mountain, second to the Buddha and third to the assembled company. It's a pleasing taste, *chang*, like chilled ginger beer, with a hint of apples.

This is the start of one of those magical meals that may not win any gastronomic medals but are unique and unforgettable – a Sunday lunch 16,900 feet (5150 m) up in the heart of the Himalaya. The ingredients include perfect weather, cloudless blue sky, light breeze, generous sunshine, the comforting presence of the yaks and the cheeriness of their owners, the reassuring company of big black crows, and the presence, at our backs, of the highest mountain in the world.

The conquest of Everest in 1953 was one of the milestones of my childhood. I was ten at the time and, like every other Briton, bursting with national pride (we somehow dealt with fact that Everest had been conquered by a Tibetan and a New Zealander). What happened on the mountain behind me 50 years ago defined the heroic, and led to a fascination with exploration that I suppose has brought me here today, completing the circle.

Only later did I learn that Everest might have been conquered 29 years earlier, when George Mallory and Andrew Irvine disappeared into a cloud close to the summit and were never seen again.

As the years went by, this heroic failure came to fascinate me more than Hillary and Tenzing's success. The fact that Mallory and Irvine left from a base camp almost exactly where we are now and lost their lives on the face of the mountain I can see so clearly ahead of me makes this a very special place, somewhere that has been in my imagination for so long.

Lunch completed, the yaks are loaded up, the tents struck and we begin the walk up to the glacier.

The warmth of the sun and the gentle tinkle of yak bells makes up for the grimly lunar landscape of grey stones and boulders. The herders seem in no hurry, whistling every now and then to keep the yaks together and occasionally singing as we plod slowly upwards. As the afternoon wears on, and the snowdrifts become less avoidable, it becomes increasingly obvious that the requirements of filming are slowing us down and we shall not reach the glacier before the light goes. We've also lost Basil and John Pritchard, both of whom seemed fine at lunch but, unable to cope with the increased altitude, have had to turn back.

We carry on for as long as we can, past valley walls hung with rocks eroded into wonderful sculptural shapes: pinnacles of mud with enormous boulders poised on top of them and Stonehenge-like slabs teetering on the edge of mud cliffs. At just over 18,000 feet (5480 m), I get as close to Everest as I think I ever shall. A moment of regret as we turn back. The ribbed stone pyramid above looks daunting but beckoning at the same time. I can see why it makes people do crazy things. In the 1930s a man called Maurice Wilson planned to crash-land a plane on the side of Everest and climb on up to the summit. In 1980 Reinhold Messner made a successful ascent of the North Face, on his own, there and back, in four days, without oxygen.

As I take one last look, I put myself, as I have done so many times in the past, in Mallory and

FOLLOWING PAGES
Everest at its most majestic. In June 1924 Mallory and Irvine would have crossed this same field of glacial debris on their final journey to the Rongbuk Glacier, on the right, and the summit. No-one knows if they ever made it or not. The Palin expedition of 2003 can be seen on its way to 18,000 feet (5485 m).

Irvine's stout walking boots and tweed jackets and feel what it must have been like for them to stand here 80 years ago, knowing that only two miles separated them from the top of the world.

Day Sixty Three : Rongbuk to Shigatse

Howling packs of dogs, yelping and snarling in the village last night, and, closer to home, some angry argument in the passageway outside my room, hoarse shouting and a man being restrained.

The words of Captain Scott on arrival at the South Pole come to mind: 'My God, this is an awful place'.

Today, though, I wash in the metal bowl for the last time, pay my last visit to the stained, encrusted lavatory, and take my last look at Everest framed in one of the squares of my cracked and much-repaired windows.

A Dutchman and his wife who stayed here last night are on their way from Lhasa to Kathmandu, on bicycles. It's taken them a month to get this far. I never thought anyone would make me feel pampered in a place like this, but as they wobble off on their bicycles and I climb into my four-wheel drive, that's exactly how I feel. A sturdy, smiling nun in a maroon robe, with a milk churn strapped to her back, stands to one side as our convoy pulls out. I'm torn between admiration for her indomitable cheerfulness and indignation at the grinding poverty that is the way of life for her and the villagers of Rongbuk. This is a beautiful, bleak place.

We run down into the valley, stacked high with glacial rubble, then climb up through a

BELOW

Passing an abandoned fort on the way down from Everest.

landscape of bare, brown, undulating hills, over a couple of spectacular passes and down through villages with snooker tables in the streets and horses tethered up outside front doors. We've almost 200 miles (320 km) to go before Shigatse, Tibet's second biggest city.

By the time we've passed through the town of Lhatse we've dropped down to 13,500 feet (4110 m) and are running past ploughed fields. There's not much traffic on the Friendship Highway: a few trucks lumbering along, a lot of horse and carts but hardly a private vehicle to be seen. As dusk falls we're in wide, desolate country, with dust blowing and the setting sun catching the tops of the smooth, brown hills and turning them a rich, mournful maroon. As we get closer to Shigatse we pass brand new electric pylons, at first lying in the fields awaiting construction, then, a little later, upright but unconnected and finally cabled up and striding over the last hilltops into the city.

It's a major culture shock after Rongbuk. I really feel as if we've come in from the outback. With its red lanterns and gold and stainless steel trim, the Shigatse Hotel, in the heart of the Chinese-built new town, gleams and glitters like a Las Vegas gambling joint. As we wait to check in, three girls in white coats emerge from a door off the lobby, marked, in English, 'Beauty and Massage', and ask us, quite ingenuously, which one we would like to choose.

This is all too much for us to get our heads round and we politely decline their services and, joy of joys, are taken up to rooms with carpets, lights, double beds, hot running water, no dogs and, luxury of luxuries, a bedside table.

This has to be better than sex. Sorry, Beauty and Massage.

ABOVE

The children of the plateau are weathered by a cruel combination of glaring sun and dust from the relentless wind. There is little water for washing, so the dirt becomes ingrained.

Day Sixty Four : Shigatse to Lhasa

Shigatse, with a population of some 60,000, is the second city of Tibet, and boasts the second largest monastery in the country, the Tashilunpo, which is the seat of the second highest incarnation in Tibet, the Panchen Lama. In many ways, his recent history has been more interesting than that of his more illustrious superior, the Dalai Lama. In 1952, three years after the Chinese invaded Tibet, they brought the Panchen Lama to Shigatse and set him up, with his connivance, as their official choice of spiritual leader. After the Chinese had raided the Tashilunpo monastery in 1961, the Panchen Lama became increasingly critical. He sent a report to Chairman Mao calling for freedom of religion to be restored. Mao called the document a poisoned arrow and kept it secret. After a speech in Lhasa demanding Tibetan independence, the Chinese lost patience with their man and he was imprisoned for ten years in Beijing. His death, in Shigatse, at the early age of 50, created further confusion. The Dalai Lama and his advisers in Dharamsala found his reincarnation, a six-year-old boy from northern Tibet, and the Chinese promptly arrested him.

Tashilunpo once again became the centre of a power struggle, when, in 1995, Tibetan monks favourable to China came up with another candidate for Panchen Lama, and he was duly enthroned at the monastery.

No-one seems to know where the Dalai Lama's choice is at the moment. He's been kidnapped, and the Chinese-nominated Panchen Lama is rarely seen in Shigatse.

We drive to the monastery along modern, urban streets decked with ads for China Mobile. The temple, however, is resolutely Tibetan and mightily impressive. Its complex of buildings is laid out on a slope leading up to the row of tombs of the Panchen Lamas and a chapel that contains the tallest Buddha in the country.

A steady line of pilgrims, many in sheepskin coats and clutching prayer beads, are making

their way up the stone-flagged pathways, flanked by juniper trees, that lead between the low, long buildings housing the various living quarters (there are 800 monks here) and the colleges where they can study Tantric philosophy, astrology, Tibetan medicine and history. Inside the colleges, small courtyards and whitewashed walls give the whole place the look of a mediaeval Spanish village.

Migmar tells me that boys are sent away to monasteries from the age of six, and they're only allowed back home once a year. He admits that when he was young all he wanted to do was become a monk, but his family sent him to school.

I ask him if it's right to say that education at a monastery would be more exclusively Tibetan, and school would offer a more international approach.

He agrees but says things are slowly changing.

'Today, in a monastery most of the monks try to study other languages, something like English or Chinese. In the past it was only Tibetan.'

We join the crowd, who seem to be heading for the Maitreya chapel to see the Buddha. Migmar says that the majority of the pilgrims are from the rural east of Tibet and some may have travelled over 1000 miles to get here. Not only that, but they would try and make the journey once a year.

Everyone who goes into the chapel, man, woman and child, has to squeeze up one of three steep and narrow stairways, about as precipitous as ladders, that can barely take two people abreast. The steps on either side are for going up and coming down and the ones in the middle are reserved only for the Dalai Lama and the Panchen Lama. Everybody struggles up and down. Quite happily.

Once up the steps the familiar sour smell of hot yak butter suffuses the chapel. Many of the pilgrims have brought butter and knives with them to cut slices, which they then drop in the copper bowls that contain the lighted candles.

Migmar explains that in Tibetan Buddhism the spirit leaves the body when you die and the more you can help the burning of the butter lamps, the stronger will be the light that will guide your soul to its next body.

The chapel has a powerfully devotional atmosphere. The lower recesses are dark and smoky, but a shaft of sunlight catches the face of the Buddha, 80 feet (24 m) above us. The lines of the eyes, nose and lips are beautifully drawn and, with elegant simplicity, create an expression of profound compassion. Buddha statues are usually made of stone, but this one, commissioned by the 9th Panchen Lama in 1904, is made of copper, which enabled it to be such a great size. And the size works: the expression, the long fall of the robes and the lotus leaf base combine to convey a feeling of strength, serenity and immutability.

The new paved road from Shigatse south to Gyantse runs alongside streams and between pollarded willows. We pass through a village that has a big wheel made of wood with boxes fixed to it for local children to sit in and be hoisted aloft. In a field a road gang are having a picnic

lunch, shovels all neatly stacked to one side.

Gyantse was once a rich wool town, on the lucrative trade route between Lhasa and India. A huge fort (*dzong*) dominates the high ground to the south of the town. Migmar and I stand on the battlements and look out over a flat plain that belies the fact that we are at 13,000 feet (3960 m) and still way up in the mountains.

Migmar points out the plastic sheeted greenhouses and the modern housing blocks.

'This place has changed so much in last 20 years. Before, all houses were Tibetan.'

Whereas the Chinese seem to have invaded Tibet many times, the British largely left it alone, though in the mid 19th century they did train up Indian spies, known as pundits, to infiltrate this secretive land. In 1903, however, on a trumped-up pretext, an army, under Colonel Francis Younghusband, crossed over from India, fought a bloody battle not far from Gyantse, before storming the fort from which we're looking out and going on, unopposed, as far as Lhasa. The British left four years later, leaving behind in Gyantse a post office and a public school. All that remains now is the Anti-British Museum, housed in the *dzong*.

A smiling lady attendant gestures to me to go inside. She makes sure all the lights are switched on in the 'Memorial Hall of Anti-British', where murals depict the ghastly acts of Younghusband's army and the heroic resistance of the Tibetans. This is echoed on a TV screen on which runs a recently made Chinese epic called Red River Valley, which also deals with the British invasion. There is nothing here, of course, that deals with their own invasion of Tibet.

We have a cup of tea (black tea this time, not yak butter) in front of the ruins of a walled monastery that contains an enormous and very ancient *chorten*. According to Migmar, there were many such monasteries here. Now they have been cleared and in their place are wider roads, high-rise buildings of tinted blue glass, and, as we drive down from the fort, a concrete pleasure garden, half completed, with ragged grass, fountains that don't spout and twee, concrete bridges running over a stagnant pond.

The road from Gyantse to Lhasa runs through lonely and very wild landscape, first of all beside a rocky, steep-sided reservoir, then curling round the sinuous shoreline of Yamdrok Tso (Turquoise Lake), the biggest single stretch of water in land-locked Tibet.

Night falls and we're still hugging the lake. Eventually the road rises steeply and winds slowly over what seem interminable passes over interminable switchbacks. I must confess to being fast asleep as we roll across the Yarlung Tsangpo (the mighty Tibetan river that U-turns round the end of the Himalaya and enters India as the Brahmaputra) and when I wake we're on a fast dual carriageway that is the long, western approach into the world's highest capital. We've reached Lhasa, the Forbidden City where, judging from the rows of shining, gaudy, neon-encrusted buildings on either side of us, it doesn't look as if much is forbidden any longer.

I want Lhasa to be as dark and different as I'd long imagined it, a remote place of romance and possible menace, but the drive up the long approach road along West Dekyl Yam dispels illusions. The buildings we pass are more Las Vegas than Lhasa and to be welcomed into the world's highest capital by flashing neon palm trees suggests the Chinese have well and truly won aesthetic control of this ancient city.

I'm aware that the bludgeoning tiredness I feel after crossing the mountains may well be souring my judgement and that once we're bedded in at what is purportedly one of Lhasa's swankier hotels all will be well again.

The shining, recently built Himalaya Hotel rises portentously from lower buildings in a quiet but characterless side street. It's clad in glass and as we pile wearily from our vehicles we're greeted by smiling doormen protected from the cold by fur-trimmed greatcoats. Unfortunately, the staff at reception are also protected from the cold by fur-trimmed greatcoats, as are the waitresses who take our orders at the Yak Bar. The Himalaya Hotel may have glittering, gold-wrapped pillars, shiny mirrors and ceilings encrusted with every shape and size of light fitting, but it is the dazzling gloss of an ice castle.

I pile all the bedclothes onto one bed and, stripping down to a vest, sweater and thermal underwear, climb in. I feel desperately disappointed. This was to be our reward, a hotel in the heart of the capital, the Holy Grail after some pretty savage days on the road. As it is, the Himalaya Hotel seems to be everything its name might suggest.

Day Sixty Five : Lhasa

Though for a while suffocation seemed more likely than sleep, I actually pass a reasonable night beneath my sarcophagus of blankets and when I wake a pale morning light is leaking into the room. My bags, still packed, squat around the doorway where I dropped them last night, looking mournful and expectant, like neglected pets.

With an enormous effort of willpower I heave myself out of bed and across to the window. The curtain opens jerkily to reveal a mottled sky and an horizon of crumpled, grey mountains framing dusty, undistinguished, largely modern buildings.

A view that could only lower already jaded spirits, were it not for one thing. Away to the northeast, rising gracefully above the city, like a mountain in its own right, are the white walls, russet towers and gold-tipped roofs of one of the most dramatic and serenely powerful buildings in the world, the Potala Palace.

OPPOSITE

On the shores of the largest freshwater lake in Tibet – Yamdrok Tso, the 'Turquoise Lake'. The Chinese have had mixed success in tapping its hydroelectric potential.

It's probably a couple of miles away, but even at this distance and this oblique angle it is mesmerizing, especially to one brought up with its black and white likeness in a volume of *The Children's Encyclopaedia*. To be honest, I was never quite convinced of the existence of the Potala Palace. Because its size and shape was so unlike anything I'd ever seen in the West, I always assumed that it was something mythical, an ambitious piece of artistic licence.

But now I see it with my own eyes I realize it is everything it appeared to be: a great Buddha of a building, looking gravely out over the city that was for so long the heart and soul of the Buddhist religion. The only thing I can see that is taller than the Potala Palace is the flagpole at its eastern end, from which flies the red flag of China.

Shave, dress, wrap a scarf around me and head for the dining room. A rubber mat in the lift reads 'Wednesday'.

Bas and Nigel are already at breakfast, dressed like Tenzing and Hillary. The staff are apologetic. The hotel is about to close for the winter and the heating has all been turned off. They do have portable radiators and will try to find some for us.

The bad news is that John Pritchard, ace sound recordist, has been examined by a doctor and found to have pulmonary oedema, an accumulation of the fluid in the lung that normally occurs in small amounts at high altitude. He's also showing early indications of pneumonia and must be admitted to hospital at once.

Later in the day we go to visit him at the People's No. 1 Hospital, getting lost in a series of functional modern blocks separated by strips of lawn, which they've tried to cheer up with pagodas and play equipment.

Eventually find the Mountain Sickness Unit (largely financed by the Italians) and in a small, friendly ward John sits up in bed, a drip inserted into the vein in his right hand and an oxygen feed taped, rather ineffectively, to his left nostril. Even John, who suffers from almost terminal cheerfulness, cannot disguise the fact that he is in quite a bad way, though not as bad as the only other occupant of the six-bed ward, a young Korean with the much more serious cerebral oedema, or fluid in the brain. Both are casualties of the punishing pressure that the body progressively suffers as oxygen levels decrease. It can affect anyone who climbs above 8000 feet

RIGHT

The magnificent Potala Palace in Lhasa. The tallest building in the world before skyscrapers. It was the home of the Dalai Lama until he fled his country after the Chinese invaded in 1950.

(around 2500 m), and no-one really knows why some suffer more than others.

We find a more congenial place to eat tonight. A small, Western-style, climber's bar and restaurant called the Summit Camp a few doors down from the hotel, cold as the grave, but at least built of brick and wood rather than the self-important chrome and glass of the Himalaya.

Over a Tibetan pizza we have to face the reality that John will not be able to continue with the journey. A temporary replacement is coming in from Beijing, and until that time Pete will carry the tape recorder and microphone, as well as everything else.

Day Sixty Six : Lhasa

'Thursday', the mat in the lift reminds me, as I descend from my seventh-floor eyrie, in which a mobile radiator with one broken wheel is engaged in a life or death struggle with the air of the Tibetan plateau.

We make for the Barkor area in the heart of the old city, where a rabbit warren of side streets leads off a main square. In fact, the rabbit warren once included the square, which was cleared less than 20 years ago, ostensibly to celebrate the 20th anniversary of the Tibetan Autonomous Region (as the Chinese renamed central Tibet), but also, some think, to allow the army easier access to the potential trouble spots of the Old Quarter.

A wide, granite-paved approach now leads up to the Jokhang Temple, the most ancient and holiest site of Tibetan Buddhism. Some of its remarkably modest stone walls date back to the mid 7th century, when Queen Bhrikuti, the Nepali wife of Songtsen Gampo, the unifier of Tibet, set up

ABOVE

Walking with Migmar in the Barkor, one of the few areas of Lhasa where the traditional Tibetan houses are still preserved. In the foreground, a prost-rating pilgrim.

159

ABOVE

Lhasa. On the roof of the Jokhang, the most sacred temple in Tibet where the Dalai Lama took his final exams in 1959. Apart from the gilded statuary, there is a fine view of the Potala Palace (right, background).

the temple on what was considered to be a powerful geomantic point representing the heart of a supine ogress. Much changed over the years and in the 1960s it was commandeered as a barracks for the PLA. Today, the Jokhang is once again a religious building.

A low, piercing sunlight bounces back off the flagstones and at first it's difficult to see 30 or 40 figures, hidden in the deep shadow, prostrating themselves before the walls of the temple. Most have bed-rolls, on which they flatten themselves, using pieces of cloth or cardboard beneath their hands to push themselves forward. Then they stand, hands pressed together above their heads, in front of their faces and then in front of their chests, before prostrating themselves and beginning the whole process again. Many of them, Migmar tells me, will have begun their prostrations outside Lhasa, with some coming from up to 600 miles (960 km) away, and taking two or three years to get here.

They fight for space with pilgrims from out of town, with matted black hair and deeply grooved faces, who pause on their devotional walk around the temple to pull juniper branches from plastic bags and feed them into the two small kilns whose smoke drifts across the square. They believe the pillar of smoke that rises from these fires creates a conduit between the earth and the sky down which the Buddha can travel. A very old lady with prayer beads in one hand and a stick in the other inches painfully slowly past the temple entrance.

The Jokhang Square seems to be the social, as well as the religious, heart of Lhasa. There are Tibetans from the east with complexions like old, weathered wood, pale Chinese immigrants, Muslim stallholders in white skull caps and farmers wrapped up in greasy sheepskin coats, wearing Stetsons with curled-up brims, looking almost identical to the people of the high Andes. Bored soldiers sit at strategic points, supposedly keeping an eye on things. One is having his shoes shined while trying to figure out the controls on a new radio, another sits, with great concentration, picking hairs out of his chin with a pair of tweezers.

Migmar and I join the clockwise perambulation, which they call the *kora*, passing rows of stalls set in front of old houses with Spanish-style, wrought-iron balconies. We stop for coffee at one of them, the Makye Ame restaurant, hung with red, tasselled lanterns, which manages to feel very Tibetan whilst serving Jim Beam whisky, playing The Grateful Dead on its sound system and offering 'Chicken à la King' as Dish of the Day.

It was here, on the first floor of a corner house overlooking the Jokhang, that Tsangyang Gyatso, the sixth and naughtiest of all the Dalai Lamas, used to drink and entertain a succession of lovers. In his book *Tibet, Tibet*, Patrick French quotes a contemporary Jesuit priest's verdict on the sixth Dalai Lama: 'No girl, or married woman or good-looking person of either sex was safe from his unbridled licentiousness'.

As if that wasn't enough, he also wrote poetry. Such apparently unrestrained love of life is not as incompatible with Buddhism as it is with Christianity, and later in the day we climb up to Sera, one of the great monasteries of Lhasa, to witness an activity that would probably be classed as highly eccentric in any religion other than Buddhism. Around 100 young monks gather beneath the trees of a shady, walled garden to take part in ritual arguing, a sort of verbal martial art. The idea is that one of a group has to stand and defend a proposition, which can be as provocative as possible (Migmar says he heard one monk arguing that there is no such thing as water) and the sitting monks must debate with him. Possibly because Sera has a long tradition of supplying fighting monks, the whole thing is very physical. The arguer, arms flailing, thrusts aggressively at his opponent and each error in the opposing argument is marked by a wide swing of the arm and a ricocheting slap of one hand against the other.

Old Lhasa can still be found – the Sera monastery was established in 1419 and the Jokhang Temple long before that – but new Lhasa is growing with an overwhelming momentum, and it has nothing to do with religion. This is a secular, consumerist boom, and from the lingerie ads to the health clubs to the main street boutiques with names like Ku-La-La, Eastern Camel and Gay Mice, it's clear where the new influences are coming from. America, via China.

Take some food to John, as the hospital doesn't provide anything. He now has the ward to himself, as the young Korean with cerebral oedema checked himself out in the middle of last night. John thinks he simply couldn't afford to stay.

LEFT

Am I right? Monk makes his point in ritual debating at the Sera monastery.

Day Sixty Seven : Lhasa

Woken this morning by sound of soldiers being drilled in an army barracks somewhere below me.

Down to breakfast, all muffled up. The usual little awkwardnesses as we try to communicate the difference between toast and a heated slice of bread to a bemused Tibetan staff.

Why we persevere with these esoteric demands I don't know. Probably because Nigel has produced a pot of Cooper's Oxford Marmalade, and eating Cooper's Oxford from a limp patch of warm bread is like playing the Cup Final on tarmac.

We drive out to the west, passing the Golden Yak roundabout, where two of these great beasts are impressively mythologized, and a number of monumental government buildings. The six-lane highway is virtually empty, save for a rickshaw with a live pig sitting in the trailer behind it, and an official convoy of black limousines, which appears from nowhere and fades into the void ahead, sirens blaring and lights flashing as if it was trying to negotiate Fifth Avenue or the Champs Elysées.

Drepung Monastery, once the biggest in the world, with 10,000 monks living and studying here in the mid 17th century, stands slightly outside the city, overlooking Lhasa from high ground to the northwest.

We disembark and begin the long climb up to the heart of the complex (Buddhism is a very steep religion), until we reach the impressive portico of the Prayer Hall. Monks' shoes, most of them modern trainers, litter the ground outside. I remove my own shoes and, pushing aside a

heavy, patchwork curtain, its edges dirty black and waxy from continuous use, find myself in a candle-lit interior, the size of a small cathedral, with long lines of red-robed monks sitting cross-legged on their cushions, chanting prayers from small strips of text on boards in front of them. A number of novices race through the hall dispensing butter tea. One of them trips over Basil as he's photographing and both he and his load fly into the air and land with a resounding crash on the stone-flagged floor. No-one bats an eyelid.

At the back of the hall, behind the line of candles, is a chamber that contains huge plaster characters from the rich cosmology of Tibetan Buddhism. Incarnations of the Buddha and various Bodhisattvas (beings who have reached enlightenment but rather than enter nirvana have chosen to return to earth and help others) as well as fierce, snarling, pop-eyed, horned figures who are their protectors.

The Communists came close to expunging Buddhism from Tibet. Six thousand monasteries, 95 per cent of all those in the country, were destroyed. But Buddhism is 2000 years old and Chinese Communism was only 60 years old, so it was not a battle they could win. Now the Chinese, comfortably in control of the political and economic life of the country, have adopted a more pragmatic attitude to the old religion. Buddhism is seen as being good for tourism, and the revival of the monasteries has been accelerating, though possession of any image of the Dalai Lama is remains a political crime in China.

At Nechung, half a mile down the hill, there is a thorough restoration going on. In a courtyard some 200 feet square a small team, mostly of women, is working away. Two of them are smoothing and shaping the plaster over an incense-burning oven, others are slowly and meticulously restoring the superb 14th-century murals on the walls of the arcades. Graphic, Hieronymus Bosch-like motifs of human torment are a recurring theme. Faces and skulls alternate, bodies hang upside down from serpents like clothes on a washing line, entrails are ripped out by wolves and naked bodies sundered by leering devils.

The work force goes about its task with quiet application. The only noise comes when they get together for an *arka*, a song and dance routine that they use to help them flatten the newly laid clay floors. Holding long bamboo sticks with stone pads on the end, they go into a sort of builder's line dance, rhythmically thumping the clay into place.

Someone hands me a stick and asks me to join in. Though I find myself regularly facing the other way to everyone else, I can now add Temple Restoration to my CV.

Back in the Barkor, we take lunch at a cheery upstairs café called Petoc. It's shamelessly aimed at foreign travellers and our Tibetan drivers are frankly embarrassed at having to eat behind a yak-hair curtain in a recreation of a nomad's tent. We, on the other hand, love it for its eggs and bacon, yak burgers and espresso coffee machine.

Halfway through this intercontinental fry-up our new sound recordist, a tall, thin Chinese, arrives from Beijing. Though he's got here impressively quickly, his expression is apologetic and his face a ghostly shade of green. We later learn that he's suffering from altitude sickness and won't be able to work for the rest of the day.

Recount this story to John when we take him food and supplies at the hospital tonight. It cheers him up no end. He's a lot better generally and now has only one aim – to get out of the People's No. 1 Hospital by any means possible.

Day Sixty Eight : Lhasa

Potala Palace and Potala Square should never be confused. One is the greatest building in Tibet, and the other is a large open space created by filling in a lake and flattening a neighbourhood of old Tibetan houses in order to celebrate 20 years of the creation of the Tibet Autonomous Region.

The only use of one for the other is that the best view of the palace is from the bleak square, where the wind blows the water of the ornamental fountains into your face and tourists pose in the middle of the emptiness to have themselves associated with the now equally empty palace on the hill.

The Tibetans call the peak on which the palace is built Mount Marpori and the soaring upward curve of the Potala's walls, rising 13 storeys and nearly 400 feet (120 m) high, stirs memories of the Himalayan rock faces we've seen to the south. Until the first skyscrapers were built, the Potala Palace was believed to be the tallest building in the world.

The mighty edifice that swallows up the mountain top today was built on the foundations of the 7th-century original. The White Palace was completed by 1653, and the central block of upper storeys, known as the Red Palace, was added some 50 years later. The entire complex has 1000 rooms. Despite that, it wasn't considered sufficient for the Dalai Lama of the time and within 50 years another palace, Norbulingka, was constructed on a 40-hectare site, a couple of miles to the west, in which His Holiness could spend the summer months.

A series of perilous staircases, as thin as firemen's ladders, lead remorselessly up from level to level, through dim and dusty apartments, until we're on the roof of the White Palace next to a room with deep red walls labelled 'Eastern Sunshine Apartment'. This was the Dalai Lama's bedroom and a more magnificent position could hardly be imagined. If you want to feel the monarch of all you survey, then this is the place to be, and I can imagine the young Tenzin Gyatso, the present Dalai Lama, making his early prayers as the first rays of the sun reached these gold-tipped rooftops, well before they reached anywhere else in Lhasa.

It must be 45 years since he last looked out from here over his capital and his country.

From the sublime to the ridiculous. We end our last night in Lhasa at 'JJ's' nightclub, whose red neon strip lighting pierces the night air, down on the square in the shadow of the Potala Palace. Conspicuous consumption is evident. Cars, some substantial, are drawn up at the door,

BELOW

(left) Makeshift lutes. (right) Woman with public and private prayer wheels. These have mantras written and inserted inside and must always be turned clockwise.

while inside beers are ordered in 12-pack slabs and delivered by pretty hostesses to tables filled with anyone from Tibetan girls on a hen-night and Chinese businessmen entertaining clients to shifty groups of underworld heavies. It's a big place, dominated at one end by a deep stage on which, to the accompaniment of a bellowing, distorted soundtrack, a show erupts. Strobe lights, pulsating disco music and John Travolta lookalikes alternate with Tibetan folklorique in a raucous mish-mash of old and new. I suppose it represents what's happening in Lhasa now. The power, the technology and the marketing is all Chinese, the past that is thrown into this mix is Tibetan.

Day Sixty Nine : North from Lhasa

We check out of the Himalaya Hotel this morning. Last images: porters wrapped in greatcoats and looking as if they were in their third month at Stalingrad, cleaners moving three-foot-wide brushes soundlessly across a spotless marble floor, a girl at reception smiling as if it were Christmas as the doors swing shut behind us. Fond farewells to John P, released from the People's Hospital and due to fly out to Kunming, Hong Kong and London later today.

The drivers are late. Most of them stayed on at JJ's until the small hours. Migmar stamps his

ABOVE

Entering the Potala Palace by the back door. As with most Tibetan buildings, it is well-whitewashed, though the decorators of the Dalai Lama's old home seem to have adopted a scatter-gun approach.

ABOVE

*Getting into hot water.
This Olympic-size
geothermal pool in the
middle of nowhere was
the one place in Tibet I
ever felt truly warm.
Outside it was
freezing.*

feet against the cold.

'Tibetan people never tired,' he reassures us.

North of Lhasa, the trans-Tibetan Highway 109 runs alongside extensive railway construction. A billboard not far from the road depicts a speeding, white, high-speed train, the Potala Palace and a joyful group of ethnic minorities dancing and celebrating. Below runs the slogan, 'The Tibet-Qinghai railway benefits all the peoples of China'. It's a little disingenuous, as 91 per cent of the peoples of China are from the same ethnic group, the Han. But the fact remains that the railway is likely to change Tibet as much as anything in its history.

By 2008, the year of the Beijing Olympics, a 700-mile (1120 km) high-speed line across the Tibetan plateau will connect Lhasa, for the first time ever, to the Chinese rail network. It's a fair bet that farmers and nomads, who make up 80 per cent of the indigenous people of the TAR, will find this less useful than the millions living in overcrowded conditions in the heart of China, for whom it will offer the chance of a new life, out west.

We pass two prostrating pilgrims, pulling themselves along the side of the road towards Lhasa, from which they must be several weeks away. The railway taking shape beside them will cross the entire plateau, one quarter of the land area of China, in 15 hours.

At Yangbajing a side road leads to a hot springs complex, where, in addition to storage tanks and a treatment plant that converts the geothermal power into energy for Lhasa, there is a lido with an open-air, Olympic-size pool. Immersed in the sulphurous water at 14,104 feet (4300 m) above sea level, surrounded by tundra and gaunt, grey hills, my body is, for the first time since arriving in Tibet, truly, unequivocally and luxuriantly warm.

Seventy miles further on, a town springs out of nowhere. A casual mess of a place called Damxung, where rubbish blows round and round in tight circles and hard men with pinched faces and red braids in their hair squat on the steps and watch us go by. Turning off here, we follow an unmade road up to Lhachen La, a 16,700-foot (5090 m) pass where the wind tears at the prayer flags and the sky looks ready for a storm.

This is the last pass before Namtso Chukmo, a sacred saltwater lake with great significance for pilgrims from all over Tibet.

First views of Namtso are dramatic. It lies, gun-metal grey and fringed with snow-dusted mountains. On a day like today it seems to discourage company. Yet down by the lakeside, near a cave hermitage called Tashidor, is a small town of tents and vehicles. The cliffs and rocks are festooned with flags and white scarves cling to a tall promontory like candle wax. A pile of mani stones (stones with mantras on) rises at one end of the shingle beach and despite the appalling conditions, people are out walking their *koras* or *mini-koras*, and a number of people are not even walking, but dragging themselves face first through the grit and gravel.

There are men in balaclavas and women with babies on their backs and scarves tied tight across their faces against the penetrating dust. There are figures whose big fur hats and robes of leopard-skin trim show them to have come from Amdo in the east. There are young men who weigh down their *katags* (white scarves) with stones from the shore, swing them round their heads and send them sailing up onto the cliff. The higher they go and the more firmly they stick the more merit for the thrower.

The hundreds, no, probably thousands of pilgrims who have defied the elements to come here and worship a lake, are largely poor, rural people. I don't know quite what to make of their tenacious dedication. My rational, enlightened, Western self recoils from the tackiness of it all, the parade of plodding, vacant faces. Another, more instinctual side of me is fascinated by and even a little envious of the deep belief that can bring them all this way and turn this remote and unforgiving lakeshore into a sanctuary.

Day Seventy One : Near Yushu, Qinghai Province

Keep going due north from Lhasa, across the Tibetan plateau that makes up a quarter of the land area of China, and you will come to Qinghai, the largest of China's 22 provinces.

It is not one of the world's great tourist destinations. *The Rough Guide* is, uncharacteristically, lost for words: 'Qinghai for the most part comprises a great emptiness'. *The Penguin Encyclopaedia of Places* (which has 12 lines on Grantham alone) doesn't mention it at all. Even when it does rate a few lines, as in Jan Wong's *China*, there's little to set the pulses racing. 'Qinghai,' she writes, 'was the heart of China's notorious gulag. Mention the place to ordinary Chinese and they shuddered.'

BELOW

The essence of bleakness. The grey, windswept waters of holy Namtso Lake, 15,500 feet (4570 m) above sea level. Yet prayer flags show that pilgrims come from all over Tibet to make the 18-day walk around it, or shorter walks around these towering rocks at Tashidor.

This morning in Qinghai it's raining, but, aside from that, this land of prison camps and nuclear weapons laboratories looks dour, but not depressing. We're running along a road not far from the town of Yushu, in a glacial valley 14,500 feet (4420 m) above sea level, hoping to meet up with a yak farmer called Sonam.

A sulky, grey sky sits low on the surrounding mountain tops as we pull off the road and bounce across rutted meadowland dotted with horses and cattle. In the centre of the herd is a black yak-skin tent with a motorbike outside.

Sonam greets us and Duker Tsering, the young Tibetan fixer who's brought us here. Sonam is slim, around 30 I should think, and not at all what I'd expect a yak farmer to look like. His face is oval, quite unlike the broad, squarer features of Duker, and with soft, sleepy eyes and delicate, almost feminine features, he looks like the model for a Renaissance Madonna. He's turned out in a smart brown suit, with a designer label sewn on the outside of the sleeve, and a natty pair of imitation crocodile-skin shoes. It crosses my mind that he might not be a yak farmer at all but an actor brought in to play the part.

Giving him the benefit of the doubt I follow him into the tent. It's surprisingly spacious, some 30 by 20 feet inside. Sacks of grain and flour fill one corner, a milk churn and a pile of dried yak dung fill another. There are three beds, all piled with brightly patterned rugs, blankets and bolsters. The only light, spilling down from a hole in the roof, falls around the handsome head of Sonam's wife. Tall, with a straw hat, woollen shawl, striped belt with red tassels and a big sand-coloured sweater, she's stirring a bubbling bowl of yak cheese at a stove built from turf and topped with dried mud. Two of their three small children run in and out. The eldest girl, Sonam tells me, has just started school.

We sit down on one of the three beds. Salty tea is poured for me from a big, blackened kettle, and in lieu of sugar, a rarity on the plateau, Sonam adds a small slab of butter, which liquefies

LEFT

Yak husbandry continued. Milking a dri, *as the female yak is called. After ten minutes I have just enough to make a cappuccino.*

into a greasy scum across the top. It tastes, well, not bad, just different. As someone wisely said, if they called it soup rather than tea we'd have no trouble drinking it at all.

Sonam doesn't speak much English and I don't speak Tibetan but we sit there quite happily without saying much, listening to the spitting gurgle of the cheese and the yaks feeding outside. Not that yaks make much noise either, beyond the occasional low, respiratory grunt, like old men dozing in a library.

I offer to help Sonam's various relatives herd the yaks and I walk beside an old lady who moves them along with sharp, chirruping cries and the occasional clod of earth thrown in the direction of any that step out of line. A grid of woven yak-hair ropes is laid out by the tent, to which the animals are tethered for milking. With Sonam's encouragement I have a go, leaning in, head up against the rear quarters, catching the toasty smell of the thick fur, hands groping about wondering where the udders are and what I should do with them when I find them.

By the time Sonam returns to check on my progress I have coaxed out about enough milk for a cup of cappuccino. He's far too nice a man to tell me off, but his laugh says it all. I must be much firmer with the udders, he says. I shall remember that next time I milk a yak. Sorry, a *dri*. (See yak sexing notes, Day Sixty Two.)

When the time comes to move on into Yushu for the Summer Horse Festival, the reason for our coming here, Sonam offers me a ride on the back of his motorbike. No helmets or anything like that, just hang on and go. Bounce across the meadow, accelerate up a steep embankment and onto the road, then down the hills, offering silent tributes to Chinese road-building skills as we race past shrines, beneath garlands of prayer flags, through a shallow river and into town.

ABOVE

Sonam the yak farmer
prepares a calf for
shearing. Yaks provide
food, fuel, rope, tent
coverings and just
about everything,
apart from the natty
suit Sonam's wearing.

Day Seventy Two : Yushu

The Yushu Hotel, its entrance garishly painted with the usual conflation of ill-tempered dragons, snowy mountains, lions, tigers and minor devils, was noisy with pre-festival singing and shouting last night.

My room has the usual idiosyncrasies. In this case, a basin pointing downwards at an angle of 30 degrees, which I don't use, not because of its peculiar tilt, but because no water comes out of either of the taps. This is unimaginable luxury compared to the other rooms on my floor, which share a communal bathroom and a pungently malodorous lavatory, from which I can hear the sound of throats being graphically cleared. Nevertheless, this is the best hotel in Yushu, or Jyekundo as it's known in Tibetan. This morning the narrow driveway is an ill-tempered place as dignitaries from as far away as the provincial capital Xining wait to be collected by their shiny four-wheel drives and taken the mile or so out of town to the festival ground. I meet an American in the lobby. He's in water-management and is very excited.

'This is the water-tank of the world, Michael.'

For a moment I feel another plumbing story coming on, but then I see his gaze is directed out to the mountains.

'The Salween, Irrawaddy, Mekong, Yellow, Yangtze. They all start round here.'

He shakes his head reverentially.

'Water-tank of the world.'

We have taken a tent at the festival site. All around us people are getting ready for the parade. A man with bells around his short leather boots waves red and white scarves and tries out a few dance steps. The dancers' outfits look central Asian, even Cossack, with embroidered sashes across chests, baggy, peppermint green silk trousers, dark hair squeezed into nets and covered up

with fiery red headscarves.

The main stand is beginning to fill up. Men in suits are arriving, TV crews running backwards before them, to be greeted with white scarves and shown to their seats. The political officials are accompanied, more discreetly, by military top brass.

Around the other three sides of the parade ground is a vibrantly colourful crowd, dressed to the nines: women in long patterned dresses, hair carefully braided, ears, necks and hands adorned with coral and turquoise and men in calf-skin shoes, shades and imitation Armani suits, which I'm told can be picked up in town for about $7 each.

A sharp crackle of fireworks starts the parade, which is led by massed motorbikes, decorated with mountains of flowers and coloured sashes, followed by the massed blue trucks from local co-operatives, bearing politically sound placards lauding the policy of opening up and developing the wildernesses of the West.

Tub-thumping commentaries in Tibetan and Chinese evoke the spirit of the Soviet era, an impression re-enforced by the arrival of massed formation tractors, motors rumbling, exhausts belching. People have only good feelings towards tractors. They are the one symbol of progress that everyone approves of and they receive by far the biggest round of applause.

By now quite a head of traffic has built up at one end of the ground, with the massed tractors finding themselves banked up against the massed trucks, who are waiting for the massed motorbikes to clear. The result is an almighty fug-filled jam, a sort of pageant of pollution.

Once cleared, a po-faced detachment of the PLA enter the arena, take up position by the ceremonial flagpole and present arms to the dignitaries in the stand. No spontaneous round of applause here.

Then, by turns, the show-ring fills up with horsemen wearing cowboy hats and jingling bells, sword-brandishing dancers in red lamp-shade hats, monks sounding long curved trumpets,

ABOVE

Lady from the tent next to ours at the Yushu Horse Festival. She ran a small shop and showed a marked interest in our director's Cuban cigars, probably quite rare on the Tibetan plateau.

children in matching blue and white track-suits and Tibetan dancers in traditional double length sleeves, which they whirl around like windmills to a tempo as jaunty as an Irish jig.

Day Seventy Three : Yushu

Much jollier up at the parade ground today. The speeches are over, the big-wigs have gone and a holiday atmosphere prevails. Screeching disco music blares out from the PA system, boys race through on scooters with girls they've just met on the back, children are paddling in the river, horses are being washed, a lady wearing a post-SARS face mask sells fresh-made yogurt from a bamboo churn. Picnics are breaking out, an elderly monk is shouting into his mobile phone and horses are feeding from nosebags made from plastic footballs, cut in half.

We're quite an attraction. The children are particularly interested by my notebook and Nigel and Peter's arms, handwriting and bodily hair being an endless source of fascination.

Occasionally I look up and think what an English scene this is. Many of the women favour wide-brimmed straw hats, others carry parasols, making parts of the camp look like a sea of Eliza Doolittle's or Frith's painting of Derby Day, yet when I look on the map we're in the middle of

nowhere with nothing for 1000 miles around. I suppose that's why these festivals, especially one on this scale, are so important. They bring people in from their tough lives in inhospitable places to enjoy, fleetingly, the seduction and security of the crowd.

In the arena, meanwhile, dancers and feats of horsemanship alternate. The Khampa horsemen who perform with such panache are renowned for being the toughest and most warlike of the peoples of Tibet, and the only ones to offer any serious resistance to the Chinese 'liberation'. Spurring their mounts into a full gallop, they ride in with ancient rifles, which they twirl around their heads, bring down to a firing position and aim to blow a hole in a 9-inch square of white paper sticking out of the ground. Others do handstands, bareback and at full speed, or hanging head-first down from the saddle try to grab as many scarves off the ground as they can while racing past.

The junction opposite our hotel, where the Xining-Lhasa road meets the southeast turn-off to Sichuan, is a hive of activity. Shops and cafés line crowded pavements where it seems everything is traded. Women are selling butter and yak cheese, which is hardened, cut into small blocks and carried on a string round the neck. More conventional necklaces are also available. They're expensive too, made up of the highly sought-after amber and coral, as well as cowrie shells (exotic luxuries for people so far from the sea). More furtively traded, but fetching high prices, are withered black shoots called caterpillar fungus or *Cordyceps sinensis*.

Difficult to find, and detectable only by a thin shoot sticking above the ground, it is apparently a potent tonic highly prized by the Tibetans. A herbal cure says Duker.

BELOW

*Well-preserved
chortens at Gyanak
Mani. They are
symbolic of steps to
enlightenment. Always
constructed on five
levels, with square base
representing the earth
and the tip of the
pinnacle pointing to
the heavens.*

'What does it cure?'

'Everything.'

I buy five of the shrivelled pieces of grass for 50 yuan, nearly £4, and find them several weeks later down one of the seams of my bag.

Day Seventy Four : Yushu

Today we leave Yushu/Jyekundo, the northernmost point on our journey.

On our way out of town, Duker insists that we stop at Gyanak Mani, believed to be the largest collection of mani stones in Tibet. Mani stones are a prominent feature of any sacred Buddhist site, and this one is particularly blessed, as it's believed that Princess Wengcheng, the Chinese bride of King Songsten Gampo, spent time here, 1400 years ago. Mani stones usually have the mantra 'Om Mani Padme Hum' ('Hail to the Jewel in the Lotus') inscribed on them, but this stone field and accompanying walls are much richer, with some having carvings of gods and whole sections of the sutras (Buddha's sayings) carved on them.

Recently, and controversially, the Chinese authorities moved a lot of the stones to build lavatories, but I'm told there was such an outcry that the ground was reconsecrated after the work was done. This morning a regular stream of pilgrims walks, and in some cases crawls, around the temple, each circumambulation guaranteeing more merit points in the next life.

I buy a stone, make my prayer and place it in a wall.

Time to say farewell to Duker, a helpful and patient guide with a good sense of humour.

He's a true Tibetan. His father is a nomadic farmer 60 miles from here. An aunt helped educate him at a monastery school and as soon as he learnt English he knew he would never return to the nomad's life. He fled to India for a while and learnt more about Tibetan tradition and culture in Dharamsala then he ever did in Tibet. Now he recognizes the importance of learning Chinese and his great hope for his son is that he will be truly international.

'At home in Lhasa or Oxford or Beijing.'

The road accompanies a meandering stream through a pleasant tree-lined valley. About 20 miles (32 km) from Yushu, the bubbling, fresh flow is swept into a faster, darker river, which will carry it 3500 miles (5600 km) from here to the shores of the East China Sea. It will also take us back into the Himalaya. Its name here is Tongtian He, the 'River to Heaven', but we know it as the Yangtze-Kiang, the longest river in Asia.

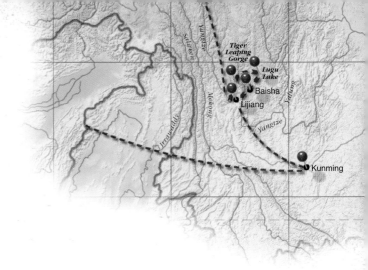

Yunnan, China

Day Seventy Six : Shigu to the Tiger Leaping Gorge

IN EASTERN TIBET and western Yunnan something quite dramatic happens to the Himalaya. They change direction. Crushed up against two unyielding plateaux, the world's mightiest mountain range meets its match and is turned inexorably southwards. The meltwaters of the Tibetan plateau, gratefully unleashed, pour south through a series of plunging, often impenetrable gorges, to spill into the Bay of Bengal or the South China Sea.

All except one.

At a small town called Shigu, some 100 miles into Yunnan, the Yangtze, like the Himalaya, changes direction, a quirk of geography that Simon Winchester, in his book *The River at the Centre of the World*, regards as being responsible for the very existence of what we know as China.

Having carved its way off the plateau and running hard alongside the Mekong, the Salween and the Irrawaddy, the Yangtze-Kiang, now called the Jinsha Jiang, River of Golden Sand, meets an obstruction. A thousand miles of tumbling water heading for Vietnam and the Gulf of Tonkin is, within a few hundred yards, spun round to the north and, though it twists and turns and tries to find its way south again, it is now effectively a Chinese river, heading east to create the enormous bowl of fertility and prosperity that is the heart and soul of the Middle Kingdom.

Such is the fame of the Great Bend at Shigu that I expect to see a battleground of the elements, some evidence of a cataclysmic confrontation between rock and water; but the Yangtze goes meekly, and Cloud Mountain, which blocks its way, is little more than a large hill. Sandbanks rise from the river and Shigu itself is a warm, sleepy little backwater.

Maybe it's worn out by its history. Shigu means 'Stone Drum', which refers to a marble tablet commemorating the epic defeat of Tibetan invaders that took place here in 1548. It describes 'heads heaped like grave mounds', 'blood like rain' and 'dykes choked with armour'. Another memorial reminds us that Mao's famous Long Marchers, pursued by the Nationalist army, crossed the Yangtze at Shigu in 1936. It took four days and nights to get all 18,000 of them across.

Popular legend believes that the limestone buttress of Cloud Mountain that turned the Yangtze north was put there by the Emperor Da Yu, with precisely that intention, some 4000 years ago.

There's a huge tourist car park by the river with restaurant attached. Early on this Monday

OPPOSITE

On the momentous Great Bend at Shigu, where the southerly-hurtling Yangtze River is turned around and sent east into the heartland of China.

morning it's quiet and there's only one bus parked up, but I'm told that the rest of the time Shigu makes a very good living from Da Yu and China's most famous U-turn.

No sooner has Da Yu's carefully placed mountain done its work than the river is flung into the thrashing, frothing, unbelievably turbulent passage of a 13,000-foot (3960 m) ravine known as Tiger Leaping Gorge. Despite the fact that the escaping tiger that gave it its name would have had to leap a half-mile or more to cross it, legend is as important as fact in China and this is the name by which it is known, loved and increasingly visited.

At Quiaotou, a few miles downstream from Shigu, they're pushing an ambitious new road through the gorge. This will be the easy option: the Low Road, but we're going to walk the High Road, a trekker's trail that clings to the sheer side of the mountain. Our guide, Li Yuan, is a tall, stooped figure with close-cropped, greying hair and a livid scar running down one side of his face. He has six horses to carry our equipment. They're waiting patiently on the edge of town, tiny specks beside an army of bulldozers and earth movers. Adding a touch of surreality, women of the local Yi minority step daintily through the rubble on their way to market, dressed in sweepingly long, bright dresses, huge silver earrings and square, black hats, perched, like mortarboards, on the back of their heads.

We purchase tickets for the two-day walk from a small tourist centre beside which is a map of where we're going and a warning in English that 'Tiger Leaping Gorge is one of the most dangerous gorges in the world which is not convenient to sail', before concluding poetically, 'However there is a kind of beauty making of magnificence tugging of people's heartstrings'.

Before we can have our heartstrings tugged, we have to survive a mile-long walk along the road out of town, as coaches swish by, stirring up clouds of dust. As we cough our way along in their wake, we can at least feel morally superior to the bus-bound tourist and soon we can feel physically superior as well, as our track winds up the hillside and the road slips out of sight below. We climb steadily upwards through scrubby woodland with big views of the southern end of the gorge unrolling below. Following a stone-built irrigation channel, we arrive at a farmhouse, in whose courtyard we loosen our boots and sit down at a table set with bowls of walnuts, sunflower seeds and crisp, delicious pears as round as apples.

The farm also has rooms and is run by Li Yuan's wife. Like him she is quietly efficient, attentive and smiles a lot. She's also a fine cook, providing us with a sumptuous lunch of rice, fresh mushrooms, liver and green chillies, kidney, pork, tomato and egg and a bowl full of quivering grey tubes that no-one touches.

They're both from the Naxi (pronounced Na-hee) people, one of the rich mix of ethnic minorities in Yunnan.

Lunch is easily walked off on a thigh-stretchingly steep climb known as the 28 Bends. Trudging upwards in a tight zigzag, I count off each one carefully and still find another 20 left at the end. The reward is a long, level pathway following an old trade route along which horses from Tibet were exchanged for tea from Yunnan. It leads through warm slopes of camphor, bamboo and pine, across a stream, then downhill through a grove of walnut trees. By now the valley has become a gorge, and I have to concentrate carefully on the increasingly narrow and precipitous trail. It's narrow and the drop precipitous. Far below are the angry, white-whipped waters of the Yangtze, dropping 700 feet (213 m) in a dozen miles. A lethal series of 21 rapids took many lives before two Chinese made the first passage of the river in 1986, entirely encased in a sealed rubber capsule. Sometimes the water is so far away and so hemmed in by mountainside that we can only guess at its ferocity from the distant roar.

As the evening light slants across the gorge a terrific panorama unfolds. On the other side of the gorge the Jade Dragon Snow Mountains, easternmost bastions of the Himalaya, rise in a series of smooth columns, sinuous ravines and needle-sharp pinnacles, their dark grey sides streaked with waterfalls. What makes this place different from Annapurna, Everest, even the Karakoram, is that the tremendous height is so close. When I stop on a narrow ledge to look around me, I find myself having to plant my feet very securely, for it feels as if the soaring vertical walls across the gorge are exerting some magnetic force, determined to tear me from my flimsy ledge.

No-one speaks now, and as we plod onwards round the mountainside, silenced by the sheer scale of the place, there is only the reassuring sound of the horse bells, and the distant hiss of the river unthinkably far below.

LEFT

Limbering up on the terrace at The Halfway House, proud home of the 'Number One Toilet in Heaven and Earth'.

It's dark by the time we reach Bendi Wan village and an overnight stop at a place called The Halfway House, run by the redoubtable Mr Feng De Fang. I've felt rather Hobbit-like for the past hour, as the scenery increasingly grew to resemble a Lord of the Rings backdrop, and the feeling that I might have morphed into Frodo Baggins is only increased as we pull the doorbell in the dim, lantern-lit entrance and are shown into a stone-flagged courtyard hung with gourds, pumpkins and stacks of drying corncobs.

Mr Feng is a slim to cadaverous young man, quietly busying round and making sure we have a warm fire to sit beside, and from his dark barn of a kitchen he and his wife produce an excellent meal of pork and fresh-picked wild mushrooms.

There's a small, very hot shower down below and the rooms are like those in an old Alpine chalet – cosy, cool and with very thin walls.

Kept awake by a noisy game of Chinese chequers on the balcony below, I bundle myself up in the duvet and tot up the day's work. A 12-mile walk, a 2500-foot climb and, apart from the quivering grey things, two of the best meals since we started out all those months ago.

Day Seventy Seven : Tiger Leaping Gorge

On the steps leading down to the lavatory of The Halfway House a wooden board is nailed up with a Chinese inscription that translates as 'Number One Toilet in Heaven and Earth'. As a bit of a connoisseur, I put this ambitious claim to the test. I can report a plain and simple squat toilet, in a room half open to the elements and cantilevered out over the mountainside, with a narrow, angled channel running away into the garden below. Once in the crouch position, however, the real beauty of this little facility becomes apparent. The land seems to fall away, and all that can be seen are the walls and saw-tooth peaks of Ha Ba Snow Mountain on the other side of the gorge. In normal circumstances I'm out of these places as fast as I can, but here, feeling myself suspended above the earth, halfway to the realm of the gods, I am tempted to linger long after my work is done.

ABOVE

Message in a bottle.
Mr Feng's connection
with the outside world.

This morning an ethereal mist lingers over the mountains, making breakfast on the terrace a chilly affair. Mr Feng De Fang produces coffee or green tea, walnuts, pancakes with smooth local honey, scrambled egg and fresh apple pie in a crisp batter.

We sit and eat too much and look out over the terraced fields below, where beans, sweet corn and wheat defy the forces of gravity and an odd mixture of walnut and palm trees cluster around farm buildings whose stone walls are set solid and sturdy against earthquake impact.

It's a serenely calming view, timeless save for a mobile phone inside a doctored mineral water bottle which hangs out over the balcony on the end of a stick. I ask Mr Feng if they keep it out there for security reasons but he says no, it's the only place they can get reception.

Mr Feng speaks good English, which he says he learnt from British hikers on their way through. Maybe this accounts for the fact that, as we have a group photo taken, he encourages us all with shouts of 'Lovely jubbly!'

The track continues north, clinging to the side of the rock face, the Yangtze a boiling froth 4000 feet (1220 m) below. At one point a sizeable waterfall comes bouncing off the rocks above us and we have to pick our way beneath it, over 50 yards of wet stones. I'm most concerned about the horses but they're a lot more sure-footed than I am, perhaps there isn't such a thing as equine vertigo.

The stony, slippery path reaches its narrowest point. The other side of the gorge looms so close that perhaps a tiger might just have made it after all.

Then we're descending fast on steep and potentially lethal tracks of crumbling, chalky rock past bulky rhododendron bushes.

An almost unstoppable momentum delivers us eventually to the river as it emerges from the gorge. It's 100 yards wide here and the jade green stream twists and turns and eddies and swirls between banks of bleached brown boulders. We've been told that a ferry crosses here but it seems highly unlikely. There are no moorings or jetties and the water looks decidedly tricky.

Then I make out some movement on the far bank and a small, steel-hulled boat emerges from beneath the shadow of a colossal overhang and, after taking the current in a wide arc, runs

RIGHT

Ferry Across the
Yangtze. Fighting the
whirlpools on one of
the world's mighty
rivers.

in towards us and docks by ramming its stern hard up between the rocks. Painted lettering on a metal arch at one end of the boat announces it to be the 'Tiger Leaping Gorge Ferry'. We clamber in and a man with a long bamboo pole and the looks and physique of a Spanish gymnast pushes us out onto the Yangtze with a flourish.

The boat seems very fragile all of a sudden. Its two outboard motors do their best but the current seems in control and swings us downstream beneath the overhang, where it's very hot and very quiet. For a moment I'm anxious. The power of the river and the power of the boat seem unfairly matched. The looming rock face above us offers no comfort.

The outboards surge, choke and surge again, but we hold our own against the current and soon we're grinding up onto a gritty beach.

An hour later we've climbed up to where the vehicles are waiting and I look back at the Yangtze, silvery in the twilight and calm and serene now after the trauma of the gorge, and I turn my back on it with a pang of regret.

ABOVE

The end of Tiger Leaping Gorge. The Yangtze below me has fallen 700 feet (213 m) in a series of 21 lethal rapids. I've walked 20 miles along the edge of a cliff and I'm going to bed.

Day Seventy Nine : Lugu Lake

There are 26 officially recognized nationalities within Yunnan, the most ethnically diverse province in China, and this morning, after a drive over the mountains and through gentle foothills spotted with Yi farms, we're entering the homeland of the Mosuo, who, like the Yi, are primarily Tibetan in origin. Their numbers are small, around 36,000, and are concentrated around a lake that straddles the border with Sichuan Province at a height of nearly 9000 feet (2740 m).

I'm going to meet Yang Erche Namu, known simply throughout China as Namu, a Mosuo woman who, after winning a national singing contest, ran away from home and found fame and fortune as a singer and later a model in China, Europe and America. Already I've had a glimpse

of what to expect at Lugu Lake. The tourist authorities, as anxious to bring people to these ethnic areas as they once were to keep them away, have made much of the matrilineal tradition of the Mosuo. A billboard on the way here showed inviting girls in local costume above the slogan 'Lugu Lake Women's Kingdom. God Living There'. They meant 'Good Living' but for the men who troop out to the lake in search of liberated ladies it comes to the same thing. The irony is that there aren't enough Mosuo women willing to live up to this hype and they have had to import Han Chinese sex workers masquerading as Mosuo to satisfy the demand.

It seems to be working. With 60,000 tourists visiting Lugu last year, the lakeside village of Luoshi has become a boom town, with property prices rising as fast as the multistorey, log cabin-style hotels.

Today the waterfront has an out-of-season feel to it as I set out to find a boat to take me to the hotel Namu has just opened on the other side of the lake. A few tourists are out photographing each other, an elderly Mosuo woman walks beside the water, spinning her prayer wheel, and a line of little black piglets trots out from beneath the timber-framed buildings. In almost every shop, whether it's selling groceries, Mosuo jewellery or tourist tat, there is a stack of Namu's books and CDs. She's prominent on all the covers, her trademark dark hair centre-parted and framing her face mysteriously, like a half-open curtain. She displays a range of personas: Namu looking ruminative, Namu looking beguiling, Namu looking distant, Namu showing a shapely, fish-netted thigh. She certainly looks like someone who's outgrown Lugu Lake.

A canoe paddles me across to a wooden jetty on which Namu is waiting to welcome me. Grabbing at the steps and clambering a little clumsily upwards, I already feel she has the advantage over me, and a kiss on the cheek followed instantly by the buzz of her mobile confirms that.

Her hotel, built on the site of an apple orchard, only opened four months ago. It resembles a Wild West fort. A walled outer yard leads to a pine log facade with tall double doors that open onto a courtyard, enclosed on all sides by two floors of accommodation. Between phone calls Namu escorts me, effusively, into a dimly lit room with a flagging wood fire at one end, a huge television at the other and, somewhere in the middle, the sewn-up, cured carcass of a pig. She insists on butter tea for us all, 'made by my mother', fiddles with the TV remote until she finds a pop video for us all to watch, then, with a lingering flutter of her big dark eyes, disappears to deal with a group of her fans who are staying here tonight.

My timber-clad room is draughty and bitterly cold, and Namu's fans are in celebratory mood, drinking down in the courtyard and committing Karaoke, very loudly, until the wee small hours. Eventually, they stagger to bed and I hear doors slamming shut. Unfortunately, they're noisier asleep than they ever were awake and snoring that must be seven or eight on the Richter scale shakes my pine-clad peace. Around dawn I fall into a deep sleep, from which I'm woken by the sound of fierce and powerful expectoration.

Day Eighty : Lugu Lake

I'm becoming quite endeared to Namu's superstar pretensions, partly because she's so unashamedly open about them and partly because I'm pretty sure that deep down she knows it's all a game.

Joshua, a Beijing-based American journalist, is following her around. She introduces him with an airy wave of the hand.

'He's doing a story on the real Namu,' she says, without much enthusiasm.

We talk at breakfast about the strength of superstition in modern China. Joshua lives on the fourth floor of his building in Beijing, because the number four is considered unlucky and so the apartment is correspondingly cheap. Eight, on the other hand, is auspicious, and mobile phone numbers with eight in them are only available at a premium.

He sees I'm reading Namu's book about her childhood, *Leaving Mother Lake*, and we talk about the world it describes: a society that has no words for husband, wife, marriage or virginity; in which women make all the decisions about who they go with and who they stay with. A man may be an *azhu*, a close male friend, but that's as close as they get to any form of marital obligation. They practice *Zouhun*, 'walking marriage', in which a man and a woman may spend the night together, but he walks back to his own home in the morning. Couples share neither ties nor possessions. Women inherit all the property and bring up the children.

We're interrupted by Namu's piercing voice, rising from the courtyard.

'It is my uncle's house, we have to bring something!'

J-P, who wants to film Namu at the childhood home where her uncle and aunt now live, suggests we take some Yunnan ham.

'No!' barks Namu. 'Not good enough.'

A little later, bearing Yunnan ham, augmented with cigarettes, sugar, a bottle of brandy and a bottle of whisky, we're picking our way across a ploughed field, over a suspicious-looking stream, past a sow with a gaggle of piglets in tow and into a dark, old, smoky, timber farmhouse. In a small courtyard chickens peck away around feeding troughs made from hollowed-out treetrunks. The main room has no windows, only a hole in the roof, whose rafters are coated with thick black grime from the fire. Chitterlings and pigs' bladders hang from the beams. Smoke-veneered, wooden panels around the sides of the room are hung with celebrity calendars, posters of pop stars, and cut-outs of glamorous ladies. While Nigel lights this atmospheric but gloomy interior, Namu preoccupies herself with her looks, holding up a hand mirror and adding a touch of make-up before producing a pair of clippers from somewhere and trimming her eyelashes. Her aunt, a good-looking woman with a black, turban-like coil on her head, whose sole concern seems to be to provide us with refreshment, puts three large lumps of pork fat in a bowl on the fire and drops tiny pancakes filled with wheat flour into the bubbling mix.

Luoshi, Sichuan. Out-of-season feel on the shores of Lugu Lake. (far right) The jetty of Namu's hotel. Reappearance of prayer flags shows Tibetan influence on this part of China.

ABOVE

*The courtyard at
Namu's family home,
where her uncle and
aunt now live.*

When we start filming, a black cat nestles down beside me, looking very sweet but tormenting our sound recordist with loud meows at unscheduled times.

Our talk turns to Namu's relationship with her mother, which is clearly at the heart of everything that's happened to her.

Not only was she not the boy her mother wanted, she was also what she calls 'a crying baby', to such an extent that her mother was driven to give her away and she was sent to live with an aunt. At the age of eight she was sent away again, this time to stay with an uncle who had lost his loved one in an accident and lived alone with his yaks up in the mountains.

Namu speaks of this with a nice touch of understatement.

'That was a very interesting time, and very hard. My uncle never speaks and the yak never speaks, so…' she gives a short, piercing laugh, '…so I had a really interesting childhood in the mountains.'

At 13 she went through the Mosuo woman's rite of passage, the traditional skirt ceremony.

'The *lamas* help you choose the day,' she recalls. 'And then in the morning, very early, mamma prepared the skirt, beautiful, long, long skirt, and beautiful jacket and hair things and flowers and the key. The key that is the power for you to continue to take care of this matriarchal family.'

The key fits what they call the Flower Room or Flower Chamber, which was Namu's first room of her own. From that time onwards she was entitled to choose who she wanted to share her room with.

Mosuo boys, on the other hand, have to wait until 18 for their freedom, which is marked by a ritual burning of their bed.

She describes the process of courtship.

'When a man come to your house, normally he leave three things, one belt, one knife, one piece of clothing. If the woman doesn't want him back any more she lays them outside the door as a sign.'

'What if she decides she's made a mistake and wants to see him again after all?' I ask.

Here it becomes wonderfully Victorian.

'She will ask her grandmother to go to tea with the boy's grandmother. They will bring like a bamboo box, some chicken meat, some Tibetan *momo*, some Tibetan wine, and when the lady receive all this she will tell the boy, why don't you go one more night there.'

The freedom of choice offered to the girls did not fool Namu. She recognized that it was another way of keeping her tied down, and all her instincts were to break out of the confines of the village and see the world.

'I want to go to Beijing, wear high-heeled shoes and pink lipstick, you know.'

So she ran off to Beijing and Shanghai and became a successful singer, until she damaged her hearing. Far from giving up, she turned to fashion and went to live and work in San Francisco, New York, Paris, Italy and Japan. She lived with a Norwegian diplomat but that now seems to be over and she's fallen for a Frenchman.

She tells me all this as the fire crackles and the smoke drifts lazily up into the rafters of what feels an essentially mediaeval cottage. Her aunt, thinking Namu is talking too much, tries to get at the fire to make us all a cup of salted butter tea.

The interesting thing about Namu is that she bothered to come back to Lugu Lake at all. Though she calls herself, wryly, 'a five-star gypsy', the claustrophobic world that drove her away still seems to have a hold on her.

I put it to her that she's still trying to win the approval of the mother who rejected her

LEFT

Namu's aunt is more concerned with hospitality than the interview.

and she nods. But it hasn't been easy for either of them. What Namu did, and how she did it, was in every way extraordinary, but it nearly severed her links with her mother for ever.

She also seems genuinely fond of her people, describing herself as a 'Mosuo cultural ambassador'. This seems to excite her and she leaps up. There is something we must see.

We're whisked away to a nearby promontory, rising a few hundred feet above the lake. Here, looking like a half-built millionaire's home in California, is Namu's latest contribution to the Lugu Lake property boom, her own half-built museum.

She talks vaguely in terms of some sort of Mosuo cultural centre, but as we step carefully over pipes and piles of dust and rubble I get the distinct impression that this is a museum of Namu.

She waves towards a substantial three-sided space.

'I'm going to put the translations of all my books from all over the world here.'

'That's huge, Namu. That makes the British Library look like a newspaper shop.'

But she has already moved on.

'And this is my kitchen.'

She enthuses about work spaces and artists in residence, and 'rooms for my best friends'. On a terrace outside we look down on the concrete shell of a swimming pool.

'That's the most beautiful view on the lake,' she says, and it certainly is a glorious position, out there with the mountains beyond and small, wooded islets rising out of shimmering, silver-blue waters.

There are problems, however. The architect backed out halfway through, she's had to sack the last lot of builders and is down to her last 5000 yuan (about £350).

She looks around at the mess, apparently unperturbed.

'My mamma think I'm crazy.'

I walk down some steps to a long, curving room with floor-to-ceiling window spaces, and there is the woman who so affected her life. There is Mamma, almost silhouetted against the declining sun. She's short and wiry, wears a Mao-style fur hat and is smoking a cigarette. A doughty little lady with shrewd, quick eyes. She sees me taking in the bare walls and empty sockets of the unfinished room and when I turn back to her I can see the ghost of a smile. A quiet smile of satisfaction. Or is it just the smile of experience, the smile of a mother who knows that she understands her daughter better than her daughter will ever understand herself.

On the way back to the hotel we pass by the local village, to which Namu donated a school for 60 children. We detour to look at it. It's run down and neglected. We can't get in but we circle it and try to peer inside. Namu mutters something. She looks puzzled and vaguely hurt by the state of it, but I have the feeling she's not surprised.

A little deflated, we return to the road. Namu dives into a car and heads back. Needing a bit of a breather, I walk back beside the lake, which is peaceful and unspoilt here.

ABOVE

Namu, the nicest narcissist.

Day Eighty One : Lugu Lake

The fans have gone and we have the 37-room hotel to ourselves. Well, ourselves and Namu. Namu, a little force-field of her own, is the centre of attention even when she's not around. She either retreats, with her mobile, to deal with her complicated international life, or sweeps out, usually in a different outfit, firing on all cylinders, organizing, cajoling and demanding.

Having talked about the importance of the Flower Chamber in her upbringing, she wants to recreate one for me. Orders are given and we all repair to the Karaoke room and watch pop videos until Namu, now in a long, black, satin dress with green silk lining, arrives, flicks off her mobile, then swings herself up on a raised platform before the fireplace and, with the relish of a natural actress, begins the half-interview, half-performance. I am expected to be both interviewer and supporting actor.

Though the Mosuo have this reputation for sexual generosity, the process she describes

RIGHT

With Namu, checking out lakeside property. The area is in the throes of a tourist boom, fed by belief that the Mosuo minority are much more free and easy about sex than the Han Chinese majority.

OPPOSITE

Last-night celebration dance in the hotel courtyard. The American West and the Chinese West seem to have a lot in common.

seems conventional enough. The first sign of attraction may well have taken place at one of the circle dances, a touch of pressure on the hand, a piece of skilful positioning. But the Mosuo girls are always in control, she says. Before anyone got as far as the Flower Chamber she would have been playing the field, asking one to prove his love by throwing a stone further than anyone else, or singing more sweetly, or riding a horse faster.

Once allowed in, the lucky man would be offered butter tea and little delicacies such as a potato, an orange or sunflower seeds. If things were going well, some wine might be offered as well.

'All this at 13?'

Namu shakes her head. At 13 they don't usually go with men, but they begin to learn about sex from cousins, sisters and, in her case from her mother, who, she says, gave her advice on 'how a woman should sit to show she had self-respect', and at the same time, 'how to walk to show herself off'.

Namu digs at the fire.

'The Chinese very secret, we're quite open about things,' she says, sliding a potato towards me.

'My mother told me sex is very good for the skin. You get good sex, you don't get pimples.'

I'm trying to find a polite way of asking how many men she slept with in her Flower Chamber, but she answers for me.

'In my Flower Room I was still virgin.'

I ask her if they used any form of birth control. She shakes her head. It's rather the opposite.

'Many Mosuo women want to get pregnant but can't,' she says. 'So they go to the Penis Cave on Gemu Goddess Mountain.'

'The Penis Cave?'

Namu's almond eyes widen.

'It's unbelievable. All stones look like a penis. They all different sizes.'

'Does it work?'

She nods.

'They go there to pray and normally after that they get pregnant.'

As a result of being allowed to choose their male partners and to have as many as they want without stigma, the Mosuo are seen in some way as less than civilized, but Namu sees it as quite the opposite. Theirs is a society that has no place for sexual jealousy and all the judgemental possessiveness that goes with it.

She says that her people are very like the native Americans she met in Albuquerque, New Mexico.

'I walk in there and feel that I'm like their sister.'

Tonight is our last night at Namu's and she has ordered a lamb to be grilled on the spit. First of all, though, there's entertainment around an open fire in the centre of the courtyard. Everyone's expected to sing. The crew is terrified and have been practising 'The Lumberjack Song' for days. The Mosuo women sing powerfully – hard, back-of-the-throat sounds that are often harsh and strident to our ears – but their range and control as they fly up and down the keys can be thrilling.

Then, with the men dressed like cowboys, they go into what they call Mosuo disco. Music thumps out from loudspeakers, but the movements owe more to line dancing than John Travolta. Namu talks often of East meeting West and Mosuo disco does seem to have brought Yunnan and Idaho a lot closer together.

Finally, a few rounds of circle dancing. Namu pulls me up and seems unfazed by my inability to get the footwork up to Fred Astaire or even Fred Flintstone standard.

'It's good exercise,' she says blithely, and suddenly I see the real Namu. She tries hard to be the vamp, but at heart she's the gym mistress. Must tell Joshua.

The drink flows and Namu's brother, who runs the hotel, is full of bonhomie. After bottles of Dynasty Red, gin and cognac have been passed round, he insists we have one last toast in the local corn wine.

'Tashi Delek!' we all shout, clinking our glasses and knocking back the smoothly fierce brew.

Namu is nowhere to be seen.

ABOVE

*Auto-rickshaw delivers
me to Dr Ho's clinic.
Man in white coat is
waiting for me. Turns
out to be the doctor's
son, business manager
and public relations
adviser, Ho Shulong.*

Day Eighty Two : Lugu Lake to Lijiang

There's a cockerel somewhere close by that wakes me every morning, long before it's light. Today I time its first call at 3.29. To make matters worse, it crows only on one note, a monotone cry like someone pretending to be a ghost.

It gives me plenty of time to get my head together and prepare for an early start. Breakfast is basic and heavy. Noodles, hot, spicy cabbage and coils of pudgy, white, steamed bread, washed down with butter tea, made, of course, by Namu's mother. Our drivers, like most other working people in China, carry plastic flasks of green tea at all times, wedging them perilously on the dashboard. Soon we're packed, have said our farewells and are making our way on a slow loop round the lake, passing the Coca Cola Hope School, proof that Namu is not the only philanthropist in Lugu Lake. The red soil has turned to mud with recent rain, and the 12,000-foot (3660 m) summit of the Gemu Goddess Peak is lost in the clouds. Compared to where we've been, Gemu seems no more than a foothill, but we are still above 8000 feet (2440 m) and, even here, the snow will soon come and shut the passes and Lugu Lake will be cut off for three months of the winter.

This has been the easternmost point of our journey. We are some 2000 miles (3200 km) from the Khyber Pass, as the crow flies, and now we must turn back toward the Himalaya and follow the mountains as they make their great southern arc towards India and Burma.

Within a few hours we are riding into the Yangtze gorges again, this time on the other side of the Jade Dragon Snow range from Tiger Leaping, but into canyons just as stomach-tighteningly spectacular.

Shanzidou, at 18,350 feet (5590 m) is the tallest of 13 limestone pinnacles that crown the summit of Jade Dragon Snow Mountain. With its brilliant white scarf of snow, this jagged diadem of ice and snow effortlessly dominates the northwestern horizon as we enter the village of Baisha.

Surrounded by a fertile plain, it's a quiet, attractive little place. Its main streets are more like lanes, with water rushing down open culverts, past houses of traditional mud-brick built on stone bases and topped with Alpine-style, wide-eaved roofs. Some of the buildings, including a fine stone gate-tower suggest grander times, and, indeed, Baisha was once the capital of the Naxi kingdom, before it was conquered by Kublai Khan 800 years ago.

In recent years it has rediscovered fame as the home of He Shixiu, known to the world as Dr Ho, one of the leading lights of Chinese traditional medicine. It's not hard to find his house, partly because the bus stops right outside and partly because of a battery of display boards leaning against the trees and covered with press headlines.

'The Famous Dr Ho', 'Dr Ho – He Has Many Friends', 'He Loves Open-Door Policy' and 'Bruce Chatwin – 17 Years Ago He Stayed Here for Two Weeks'.

His son, Ho Shulong, emerges from the front door of a modest, two-storey house to welcome us. For a moment, it's hard to get a word in edgeways, as he reels off details of his father's worldwide fame. Some 500 articles about him in 40 languages, 300,000 people treated in 40 countries. National Geographic Channel are here today to talk about making a film about him, as is a British woman who already has made a film about him, called *The Most Admired Man.*

The walls of the front room are adorned with hundreds of visiting cards as well as pictures of Mao, the Queen, Princess Di and Deng Xiaoping. Several of Bruce Chatwin's books, in plastic wrapping, hang from the ceiling like holy relics. My own visit has caused enormous excitement, for apparently I have been here before, with John Cleese, my fellow Monty Python.

Before I can clear this one up, Dr Ho appears, sidling diffidently into the room. He must be in his mid-seventies, and sports a black, knitted scarf and hat and a white lab coat. His face is that of the classic wise old Chinaman, thin, with a wispy white beard and moustache. His eyes are bright and responsive.

He clutches my hand and says how nice it is to see me again.

I'm aware of other visitors hovering – a French girl, two Japanese and two Australian doctors, who tell me they are here to discuss Dr Ho's treatment of prostate cancer. Ho Shulong, hearing our conversation, thrusts a sheaf of documents in front of me. They're from a physician at the Mayo Clinic in America, acknowledging the part that Dr Ho's herbal treatment played in the recovery of a patient from prostate cancer.

I'm taken through to Dr Ho's consulting room. It's modest, like the house itself, and a bit of a mess. The floor is covered with red plastic buckets and there are various preparations open on the shelves.

'So, old friend, nice to see you again,' he repeats.

I can't lie, but I don't want to spoil whatever game he's playing.

'You're looking well,' I offer, neutrally.

'I'm 80 years old and getting stronger,' he grins.

He sits me down on a lab stool and I tell him of the hard travelling I've been doing and the fatigue and all that.

He asks me about my lower back, then asks me to put out my tongue.

He nods.

'Take care of the food,' he advises. 'Eat simple food.'

'The pork is very good in Yunnan,' I suggest.

'I think pork not so good.'

He checks my pulse and nods reassuringly.

'Good pulse, no high blood pressure. No high cholesterol, no liver fat, no kidney stone, no gall bladder stone.'

I feel like someone who's just won a scholarship. And Dr Ho isn't through yet.

'This morning many French people come. Some have high cholesterol.'

'Yes?'

'Fat liver.'

'Ah.'

'Diabetes.'

'Really?'

'High blood pressure.'

'It's all that French food.'

'But your chi is weak.'

'Oh.'

'You know "chi"? It is your energy levels.'

I nod. Here comes the bad news.

'And your stomach. And you have a Chinese cold, a little Chinese cold. I see it from your lips.'

'Oh dear.'

'But be happy, happiness is best medicine you know.'

Happiness alone is clearly not going to be enough for me, and he sets to work preparing some of his herbal remedies. He will make something up for me. I glance at the labels as he measures out the powder. Fennel, Plantain, Wrinkled Giant Hyssop, Indian Madder, Chinese Sage, Nepal Geranium.

The slopes of Jade Dragon Mountain are famous throughout China as the Home of Medicinal Plants, with over 600 species available. Dr Ho takes pride in the fact that all the ingredients he uses are either grown here or collected from the surrounding hills by himself or members of his family. No outsiders involved, and nothing bought from markets.

Clutching my various powders in brown paper cones, I return to the now even more crowded front room to be met by Dr Ho's son with an open visitors' book bearing incontrovertible proof that Michael Palin and John Cleese did indeed come here some five years ago. Unfortunately, our names and comments are the work of a man from Woking who clearly thought he was being very funny.

I try to explain the error but Mr Ho Junior is not really interested. He's now jettisoned the visitors' book and is showing us out through a small back garden, where seeds are drying in wide, shallow baskets, and onto a wooden verandah where food is being set out. Dr Ho's wife, a beautiful woman, and a calming presence too, is supervising what turns out to be a wonderful meal, served in dishes that spread over the table and beyond: hyacinth, water-lily, anchovy, baby pig, Yunnan ham, tofu, broccoli and more.

She wears traditional Naxi costume: a blue bonnet and deep blue top with a white apron and a quilted cape tightly secured by two cross-ribbons and on its back a slip of white fur, representing the day, and above it a dark blue cloth representing the night.

Dr Ho joins us and I learn a little more about him.

Though he was always fascinated by herbal medicine, he was reviled by the Red Guards, who smashed his place up, and he was unable to get back his licence to practise until the start of the 'Open-Door' policy in 1985. Even then, he could practise only at public hospitals. Nowadays he

will see anyone and only asks people to pay what they can afford.

He was clearly inspired by the work of Dr Joseph Rock, an irascible, dedicated Austro-American botanist who lived and worked in southwest China for 27 years, until forced to leave after the Revolution in 1949. He admired the ethnic minorities and was apprehensive of their domination by the Han Chinese. He compiled an English-Naxi dictionary and sent back to the West a collection of 80,000 botanical specimens.

It was 'Rock's Kingdom', Bruce Chatwin's report for the *New York Times* in 1986, that brought Dr Ho to a world audience.

Which is why we're here today. And as far as everyone at Dr Ho's is concerned, I'm a regular visitor.

Day Eighty Three : Lijiang

From my hotel window two things compete for space in an otherwise clear blue sky. One is Jade Dragon Snow Mountain and the other is the great glass and steel tower of the China Construction Bank.

Lijiang is a tale of two cities: one a modern concoction of business district office blocks and shopping malls, the other an immaculately kept old town, with clay-tiled roofs, cobbled streets and a canal system that evokes Venice, Amsterdam or Bruges. Lijiang became rich and famous because of its key position the Tea-Horse Route from Tibet into China, but its idyllic situation, set comfortably in a shallow bowl of hills, is deceptive. A fault line at the edge of the Tibetan plateau runs below and the ripple effect of the tectonic collision that created the Himalaya has been responsible for over 50 strong earthquakes here in the last 130 years. The most recent, which registered over seven on the Richter scale, hit Lijiang in 1996, killing 300 and injuring 16,000. Many buildings were damaged or destroyed. The majority of them were in the new city.

The wood and stone houses of old Lijiang were built by people who knew about earthquakes and how to withstand them. They remain, thanks to UNESCO money, as an example of how to create harmony, line and proportion on a human scale. The result is a labyrinth of cobbled streets and squares, car free, perfect for walking, but also a victim of their own success. Large-scale preservation of the past is so rare in China that Lijiang has become a big draw, pulling upwards of 3 million tourists a year into an old town of 25,000 people.

It's around nine o'clock when I set out for breakfast. Wooden shutters are being taken down from shops and cafés. The first tour groups of the day have been disgorged from their coaches and totter awkwardly on the cobblestones behind the upraised yellow flags of their guides. Many of them already wear the dogged, mule-like expressions of those condemned to another day of organized enlightenment.

The agglomeration of gift shops that always accompanies a tourist boom has hit Lijiang like anywhere else, but the shops are small and well kept and the streets clean and sparkling. Feeling slightly ashamed of myself, I choose a café offering 'England Breakfast'. It's served with wall to wall Sting.

Gorged on egg, bacon, fried bread, toast and many other delights denied to me for several weeks, I finish my fresh-ground Yunnan coffee and explore the area around the main Sifang Square. There are no big vistas here. The streets twist and turn on each other, often running alongside or over the streams of clear, cooling water that flow from Black Dragon Pool at the foot of Elephant Mountain. No wonder that one of the most powerful Naxi deities, and the one they pray to for prosperity, is Shu, the water god.

In this morning of rediscovered pleasures I find a second-hand copy of a classic book on the city, *Forgotten Kingdom* by Peter Goullart, a Russian-born Frenchman who lived and worked in Lijiang in the 1940s until forced to leave by the zealous xenophobes of the Communist revolution. 'A book about paradise by a man who lived there for nine years', says a *Times* review of 1957.

It contains tantalizing snippets of information that you never find in the guide books; that the Naxi were born gossips and the despair of missionaries; that their preferred poison was black aconite boiled in oil, which was characterized by a paralysis of the larynx. 'In convulsions the victim could only stare frantically at his helpless friends without being able to utter a word.'

Goullart was particularly impressed by the Naxi women, who 'silently and persistently, like the roots of growing trees…evolved themselves into a powerful race until they utterly enslaved their men. To marry a Naxi woman was to acquire a life insurance and the ability to be idle for the rest of one's days.'

Echoes of Namu and the Mosuo women here, and once again evidence that Yunnan's ethnic minorities have more in common with each other than with the rest of China.

Day Eighty Five : Lijiang

I meet the most famous man in Lijiang outside the traditionally decorated, red lacquered portals of the Naxi Music Centre. 'Naxi Ancient Music' is written in English above this doorway, at which people are already gathering, asking when the ticket office opens. A man in his seventies,

quite trim, whose quick, lively, intelligent eyes dominate his face is dealing with fans. He's darker, darker than most Chinese, dark enough to remind me, with his impish smile, of Desmond Tutu. His hair is black (blacker than might be expected in a man of his age) and brushed forward quite self-consciously. He's dressed in jeans, smart leather shoes, two sweaters and a jacket. His name is Xuan Ke and he is the conductor of the Naxi Music Orchestra.

Last night he and his orchestra were playing for the Prime Minister of Singapore. In the foyer of the theatre is a photograph of Chinese President Jiang Zemin, with flute, playing with the orchestra on a visit here.

This morning the great man has agreed to show me Lijiang, but as soon as we start talking I know that his own story will be much more interesting. He was born in 1930 and received an early musical training from American Pentecostal missionaries. In 1949, after the victory of Chairman Mao, which he refers to, wryly, as 'something called liberation', he became a conductor in Kunming. He wasn't a Communist, he says, but in a group allied to the Communists. Mao's Hundred Flowers campaign, eight years later, initially seemed good news for people like himself. 'Let a hundred flowers bloom,' Mao declared, 'and a hundred schools of thought contend.'

It turned out to be a trap. Having encouraged intellectuals and artists to come out and help the party, Mao, fearing their criticism, turned on them and ordered them to undergo 're-education'. Xuan Ke was sent, at the age of 28, to forced labour in a tin mine.

'Animal living,' he says, unemotionally. 'No human rights at all. Animal food, animal living and working a lot, from daybreak to the midnight.'

He was nearly 50 when he was released.

With Deng Xiaoping as leader of China, tradition was no longer seen as a threat, and, while working as an English teacher in a local school, Xuan Ke slowly began to pick up the pieces of his musical career. Many of his friends had died and the most precious of their antique instruments had been hidden, some embedded in walls to prevent them being found and destroyed by the Red Guards.

In 1986 Lijiang was opened to foreigners for the first time since the revolution and, as the years went by, traditional Naxi music became a big draw. Now the rump of the old orchestra, invigorated by younger singers and musicians, plays every night, and the top people come along to hear them.

As we walk through Lijiang, Xuan Ke is frequently recognized and breaks off from his story to shake hands, exchange greetings, pose for photographs and tell jokes.

He takes it all in his stride, a man seemingly completely at ease with it all.

'This must be the best time of your life,' I ask him.

He smiles and shakes his head.

'Not yet.'

He has a big garden to look after in his house outside Lijiang, and an autobiography to complete. Most of all, I suspect, he relishes his role as satirist, court jester, respected subversive. All the things he was sent to the tin mines for are now not only expected of him, but officially sanctioned.

He chuckles as he tells me that he had 22 American congressmen at the show the other night. After the orchestra had played a particularly quiet and soothing number, he asked the audience if they'd thought that was peaceful.

There was general agreement and appreciative applause, to which he responded, 'Then why not play it on the border with Israel and Palestine?'

'Very big applause,' he says, 'but not from the congressmen.'

Before going to see his show in the evening, Basil and I eat a bowl of delicious pork crackling washed down with Mekong River Beer beneath the bending, canal-side willows at our new favourite eatery, Old Stone Bridge Snacks (Basil admits it loses a bit in translation). Tour groups are still out, plodding submissively over the bridge, eyes glazed and heads lolling. After we've eaten, I buy a collection of old photographs of Lijiang from a stall opposite and notice four of Namu's books on a lower shelf.

From the heroine of the Mosuo, to the hero of the Naxi. Xuan Ke and the orchestra are performing at eight and the queues are already forming. The narrow entrance of the Concert Hall leads to a courtyard converted into a galleried auditorium. Cherry-red lacquer dominates and Chinese lanterns are hung about. Baskets of carnations, dahlias and roses are set out along the front of the stage, and on the back wall there is a colourful mural of black-necked cranes in flight. Above the stage, and in sharp contrast to the swirls of red and gold decoration, is a sombre display of black and white photographs of faces, some blurred, some blank and expressionless like prison photos or police IDs.

Which is probably what they are, for these are all members of the original Naxi orchestra, who have either died or disappeared.

The present orchestra take their places, with the most elderly members, venerable and white-bearded like a troupe of former emperors, being led on by young women in Naxi costume. Xuan Ke makes an inconspicuous entrance, slipping quietly on from the wings to stand at a microphone at stage right. He's wearing a long blue robe, like a priest's soutane, whose simplicity makes him stand out from the dazzling brocades and silks of the older musicians behind him.

He clearly enjoys being at the microphone and addresses the audience in a mixture of Mandarin, Naxi and English, milking the laughs skilfully, in all three languages. I can see the schoolteacher in him as the orchestra sit patiently through a leisurely monologue that touches on all sorts of pet peeves. He makes sure we know that the Naxi Orchestra still needs help. It receives no financial support from the government. And he sounds a warning. Here on the Chinese borderlands, where Han and Tibetan meet, 'the music and musicians are in big danger.'

Young people change their minds faster and faster, going for Karaoke, rock 'n' roll and what he calls 'nonsense lyrics'.

At this point his voice rises and the teacher becomes preacher.

'The music,' he declaims, with arm raised heavenwards, 'is disappearing in the shadow of the Himalaya!'

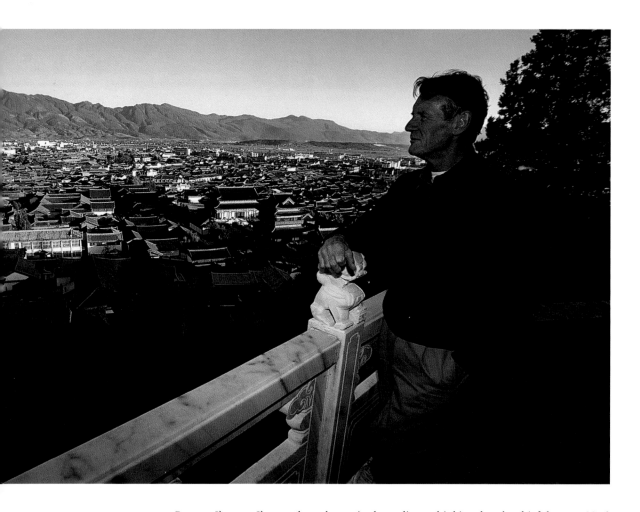

By now, I'm sure I'm not the only one in the audience thinking that the chief threat to Naxi music might be Xuan Ke's monologues. It's at least 15 minutes into the programme before bow is laid to string or stick to drum but, when it comes, the music, a piece written by the Tang Dynasty Emperor Li Hu over 1000 years ago, is fascinating and unusual, featuring early versions of familiar instruments, lutes, three-string violins and cymbals, accompanied by high soprano vocals.

The only wrong note is the jarring ring of a mobile behind me. Not only is it not turned off but the man proceeds to have a series of long conversations into it, quite oblivious to whatever's happening on stage.

The next song is 750 years old and was written, as Xuan Ke announces cheerfully, 'to express hatred of Kublai Khan'.

After this, he does a whacky impression of Pavarotti jerking manically about to reinforce a point about how even serious music in China has become infected with insidious pop star mannerisms.

The concert is brought to an end with a spare and soulful, if a little anti-climactic, bamboo flute solo, played by one of four young women who have also sung quite exquisitely.

At the end I try to get to Xuan Ke to congratulate him and thank him for our day together, but he's almost invisible between a wall of young female fans. And smiling happily.

Day Eighty Six : Lijiang

Our hotel is impressively located high up on the cusp of the new and old towns, a short, energetic walk from Lion Hill, which is considered the highest point in Lijiang. This is not strictly correct, as on the top of the hill stands a pagoda over 100 feet high, which claims to be the tallest wooden building in China. It's not old and has been put up to pull in the tourists, who, like us, feel duty-bound to walk up every one of the steps that climb steeply through five spacious floors. The view you expect to be rewarded with is quite disappointing, as someone's planted a girdle of conifers near the base of the pagoda that successfully masks much of the ink-black tiled rooftops of old Lijiang.

The designers have attempted to decorate the interior of the pagoda in local style, which includes several symbols in *dongba*, the old language of the Naxi.

Despite the best efforts to introduce a pan-Chinese orthodoxy during Mao's years, a rich and diverse cultural life has survived in the mountains of Yunnan. The Dongba, a Naxi word meaning not just 'the scriptures' but those who interpret them, are important guardians of the old traditions. They have their own cultural centre in Lijiang, where the 30 of them still alive work on translation of the old Naxi texts. Part shaman, part priest, the Dongbas also perform ceremonies and rituals based on the Bon religion, which pre-dated Buddhism in Tibet. In *Forgotten Kingdom* Peter Goullart describes his horrified fascination as he watched Dongbas dancing themselves into a semi-trance to reawaken the spirits of two young lovers who had killed themselves in a suicide pact.

'Just for an instant…we all felt that the lovers had returned… I thought at first the impression was entirely mine: but with a burst of weeping the two families prostrated themselves as one man before the little altar. The guests looked startled. Nothing was seen and the impression was gone in a flash. But they had been there and everyone knew it.'

Later in the day, we witness a Dongba at work a few miles outside Lijiang. When the last light of day has faded on the ice turrets of the Jade Dragon Snow Mountain behind him, he begins the ceremony. He's a sprightly old man, who I'm alarmed to find is only five years older than me, dressed in a long, mandarin-style, red robe and embroidered waistcoat with an amulet hanging from a cord around his neck. Wound round his head is a red cap with a headdress of five pointed leaves. He holds a drum in one hand and cymbals in the other, and, after striking the drum, he sets about purifying the area where the ceremony is to take place, which is unclean because of our presence here. With a handful of burning branches he moves around the courtyard and then the garden, chanting and passing the smoking branches over arches, walls and, finally, over all our equipment. Then, with ever-accelerating speed and more frenetic chanting, he races to the door of the building, runs out and with shouted imprecations hurls the branches away, casting out all the bad spirits he's collected from within the compound.

I must admit that there is an extra element of confusion, which is nothing to do with the

Dongba, for at precisely the same time that devils are being cast out in Yunnan, England are contesting the Rugby Union World Cup Final in Sydney. While working flat out to set up equipment, change film, filters and lights when necessary, Peter has his mobile phone on and progress of the game is being texted through to him from a pub in England.

Meanwhile, we turn our attention to the Dongba's young assistants, who are preparing to sacrifice two chickens.

The birds have their legs trussed and, after being anointed with water, their necks are cut and the blood drained into a bowl.

'14-5, England,' hisses Pete.

The chickens are dangled over the fire and the air fills with the smell of scorched feathers. The two assistants, one boy and one girl, seem uncertain what to do next and they lay down the blackened chickens and wait for the Dongba to help them out. Their confusion is hardly surprising. Tradition dictates that ancient scriptures are only communicated to males, and then not until the Dongba who communicates them is over 75 years old. So the chicken's fate is currently in the hands of a girl who can't know what to do, and a boy who won't know what to do for another ten years.

The ceremony now shifts inside to a room with a fire and a candlelit altar. As he makes various moves, the Dongba peers closely at an old book of pictographic texts, rather like someone following the instructions on a new video.

At one point he lays the book down and fumbles around. We watch in some suspense, as he reaches deep into his robes, only to produce a cigarette, which he lights up before carrying on reading.

For what seems like an interminable time he moves around the fire, passing chickens over the flame, before indicating to his assistants to fetch him a big black cooking bowl. The bowl is filled with water and the hapless, still-feathered chickens (which some of us think are not absolutely dead) are dropped in and imprecations muttered. At the edge of the firelight, behind the crouching Dongba, I can see Peter, face pale and eyes round as saucers.

As we come to the end of a roll of film he has time to get the news out.

'14-all! Extra time.'

What follows, as events in Lijiang and Sydney become inextricably entwined, are 20 of the more bizarre minutes of my life. Two rituals on continents thousands of miles from each other are approaching their climax, and as the Dongba becomes more agitated, Peter veers between ecstasy and anguish.

'17-14!'

It must be all over.

'17-17!'

It clearly isn't.

All I know is that the night air has turned very cold and the shaman, lit by a flickering firelight, is whirling around like a madman, eyes staring, sword in one hand and finger-cymbals in the other, as the news comes through.

'20-17! Whistle's gone!'

Our reactions have necessarily had to be whispered, like partisans in an occupied country, but now it's impossible not to let out a whoop of joy.

The Dongba finishing his dance, leaps in the air with the athleticism of a much younger man and comes to a standstill, acknowledging our appreciation with a broad smile.

Intense as the ceremony has been (for many reasons), I don't think any of us felt the sensation of the supernatural presence that Peter Goullart had described so vividly. But a week or so after we got back, Basil called me with his usual report on the photos he'd taken. No problems, except for all those taken with a flash at the Dongba's ceremony. Despite his camera being fully charged up, all the prints came back over-exposed and burnt out. It has happened to him once before, when photographing the Ghost Festival in Penang. All his shots were fine except those taken when the shaman entered a trance.

What's more, he knows colleagues who've experienced the same thing. Everything seems to point to some powerful force or energy current being emitted on the same frequency as the strobe of the flashlight.

Back in Lijiang, Nina, our hardworking Chinese assistant, orders the meal tonight. Something a bit different she says. I'm not so sure. One of the dishes, a chicken stew, has a claw rising from the middle of it.

Day Eighty Seven: Lijiang to Kunming

Goodbye to the friendly Qian Xue Lou Hotel, though I never found out what its name means. In Lijiang New Town, by contrast, English signs are quite prevalent. So it's farewell to the Finance Hotel, the Education Hotel, the Greatness Drugstore, the Belief Supermarket and a menswear store called 'Clench'. All slip away behind us as we head to the new highway that will convey us smoothly to the new airport.

The casualties of this rush to modernize are the remnants of old Lijiang. Those traditional wood and mud-brick houses that have the misfortune to lie outside UNESCO's protection can be seen like fish left behind by the tide, circled by the diggers and graders, waiting to be swept away.

Kunming, with a population just short of 4 million, is the biggest city we've seen since leaving Lahore. Armies of bicycles, traffic lights with numerical count-downs and paradoxical reminders everywhere that this burgeoning expanse of glass and concrete is a garden city, boasting one of the most generous climates in China.

For us, the City of Eternal Spring is another welcome step down from the high plateau. At a little over 6000 feet (1830 m), it's half as high as Lhasa and a third the height of Everest Base Camp. The air is positively balmy and a premature holiday mood grips us all as we put some distance between ourselves and the high mountains.

We lunch at a restaurant that serves Kunming's speciality, Across the Bridge Noodles. The story behind the name is both romantic and utilitarian. A scholar seeking peace and quiet retires to a cottage on an island. His wife brings him his food, but the bridge is so long it's cold by the time she gets across. She discovers one day that by pouring a layer of oil on top of the broth it would stay hot. So she poured on the oil, took the broth over the bridge, put in the various cuts of meat when she got there and a new dish was born. (I think the story says a lot about the importance of food to the Chinese. In England he'd have been lucky to get a sandwich.)

So we have set in front of us a bowl of very hot soup flavoured with chicken stock, duck and spare ribs and arrayed round it, with no regard for the size of the table, a multitude of side dishes including raw chicken and Yunnan ham, liver, fish, pork, spinach, onions and all sorts of other vegetables as well as chilli pepper to add to the fun.

It's a huge but quite delicate meal, with impeccably fresh ingredients.

Kunming is not only a floral showplace, still basking in the glow of having hosted Expo '99 Flower and Plant Festival, but the capital of a province with more ethnic minorities than any other. Gardens and ethnic diversity meet in a landscaped, 90-hectare site on the shores of Lake Dian, south of the city. Called the Yunnan Nationalities Villages, in essence it's an ethnic minorities theme park.

I'm taken round on a white golf buggy by an obliging, if a little brisk guide called Ms Mi, who is herself in minority national costume.

Rather like feeding times at the zoo, there is a strict schedule of which minority is 'performing' when, and we're swiftly off to the Dai village, where, in front of a tall, white, instant pagoda, men and women dance, the women conspicuous by dainty scarlet straps over their red schoolgirl shoes. Along with light blue and orange tunics they look rather odd, like a tribe of air hostesses. Then we're off to the Tibetans, who dance in front of an impressive reproduction of the Jokhang in Lhasa, incongruously set against a backdrop of banana trees and bougainvillea. A small crowd, watching without any apparent engagement, becomes even smaller as the show goes on, leaving only ourselves and an old sick man in a wheelchair, who stares mutely ahead, his grandson perched on his lap.

If it's four o'clock it must be the performing elephants, and soon Ms Mi, who is Yi, and me are at the back of a somewhat larger crowd, watching a group of rather dry elephants being led into position in a concreted performance area.

'Are elephants a minority in China?' I ask Ms Mi.

She looks at me with vague irritation.

'I'm sorry?'

'I wondered if elephants were a minority in China.'

She looks deeply concerned, more, I think, for my sanity, than anything else. After appearing to consider the question for a polite amount of time, she frowns and shakes her head.

The attempt to make elephants look cute by pumping disco music from the loudspeakers and then tugging at their legs is a most depressing spectacle and the jokey compere seems

thoroughly unpleasant. Maybe I'm just not getting the jokes, so I ask Basil, who confirms that he is indeed thoroughly unpleasant.

The weather's clouded over and the vast area of the park is almost empty, but the shows must go on and at five o'clock we're at the Mosuo stand. Their 'event' takes place in a smaller version of Namu's hotel, with log walls and lots of cowboy hats and line dancing. The audience walk in and walk out, talk and photograph each other as if the performers were invisible. There seems not the slightest respect, or, indeed, enthusiasm for the fact these are live performers.

This whole Yunnan Nationalities park has been like a weird, dreamlike playback of many of the places and the people we've met these past few weeks, and has the effect of making me feel enormously fortunate to have met our minorities in the wild, as it were.

Day Eighty Eight : Kunming

The first English-language newspapers since we left Kathmandu. It's not often I read the papers these days and feel cheered up, but *The China Daily*'s news of the first full ceasefire in Kashmir for 14 years is heartening. Kashmir was the most traumatized of all the areas we've been through on the Himalayan journey and its problems seemed insoluble. Now, President Musharraf has ordered a ceasefire along the Line of Control and there is a suggestion that he will allow talks to go ahead on the future of Kashmir without prior conditions. Previously, the Pakistan government has regarded a plebiscite in Kashmir as a *sine qua non* of any talks.

The Bank Hotel in Kunming is one of exceptional comfort but in the short time I've been here I've had to call someone to fix both the heating and the lights. Now I find that my bathroom scales don't function. This is not, I realize, a big deal, but we're paying for this little bit of luxury so we might as well get it right. I ring for assistance and have a not altogether satisfactory conversation with someone who seems unfamiliar with the word 'scales', but happier with 'bathroom'.

Within less than a minute the doorbell goes. Standing there is a hefty girl with a plastic cap on, flanked by two men in protective overalls, one holding a red rubber plunger and the other an enormous wrench. They stand there motionless for a moment, like figures on a coat of arms. I have the distinct feeling they would rather not be here.

It's quite a squeeze with all four of us in the bathroom, and, as we shuffle round, the man with the plunger gestures nervously towards the toilet bowl. When I shake my head and hand them the defective scales, their manner changes completely and, with lavatory-unclogging off the menu, we are one happy family, nodding and smiling and joking.

Taps are turned on and off as if to demonstrate something, but it's only after they've gone that I notice a small sign on the side of the shower apologizing for problems with the water supply.

'Please bare with us,' it reads.

Catch up with my notes, then walk into the central square of Kunming. The old city has been razed but the tall, arched West Gate has been rebuilt. This was once the Chinese end of one of the most famous highways in the world. Marco Polo knew it as the Southern Silk Road, an extension of the trade route that connected Asia with Europe, which we've touched on in several places on our journey. In the Second World War it was reopened as the Burma Road, a supply line that costs thousands of lives to build and extended through the appallingly difficult country of the eastern Himalaya to come out in Assam in north India.

Little is made now of its wartime connotations, but 100 yards away is the Hump Bar Café. The Hump in this case refers to the name given to the 500 miles of Himalaya between here and India by the AVG, American Volunteer Group, known as the Flying Tigers, who flew perilous supply flights across this towering mountain wilderness from 1941 until the end of the war. Six hundred and seven planes were lost crossing the Hump.

The walls of this comfortable, congenial old bar are covered in memorabilia of the period: maps and posters and black and white photos of the Flying Tigers standing beside planes with bared teeth painted on their sides.

The next port of call on our journey will be over the other side of the Himalaya, where the planes landed and the Burma Road broke out of the jungle.

Two last good memories of China, both meals. A lunch of fish in lemon grass, asparagus, chicken and delectable pork cooked beneath a vegetable crust, and a last evening thank you to our long-suffering Chinese fixers, minders and helpers in a chic restaurant, with photos of the old Kunming railway on the walls.

So I'm very happy tonight, and only wish John Pritchard were here to share our enormous sense of relief at having, in not much more than a month, crossed the hardest terrain we've ever travelled.

LEFT

The Hump Bar, Kunming. A small shrine to the Flying Tigers, Second World War airmen who kept supply lines between India and China open by flying across a 500-mile stretch of Himalayan peaks which they christened 'the Hump'. Photos, maps and a great place to drink.

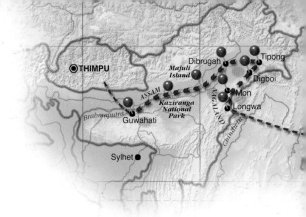

Nagaland and Assam

Day Ninety : Longwa

IN THE REMOTE hill village of Longwa I can stand with one leg in India and the other in Myanmar, or Burma, as it used to be known. (I like the word Burma and take heart from the fact that Myanmar's national anthem remains 'Gba mjay Bma' – 'We Shall Love Burma for Ever'.) Longwa, a collection of palm-thatched huts, a tin-roofed church and a huge satellite dish, isn't marked on any maps I have. It's at the end of the line, on the very edge of Indian administration.

It's also the home of the largest building made entirely from vegetation that I think I've ever seen. The chief's hut, or in this case, mega-hut, is some 200 feet long and covered with a striking roof of palm leaves that sweeps down from an apex of 50 feet or more to within 3 feet of the ground.

The hut occupies the highest point of a 4700-foot (1430 m) ridge, on either side of which the land falls away in a series of crinkly valleys. Along the top runs the India-Myanmar border. In fact, it slices right down the middle of the chief's hut, so he can walk between the two countries without ever leaving home.

Throughout the Himalaya, in Kashmir, on the North-West Frontier, in Tibet and Nepal, we've encountered a tension between the hill people, determined to preserve their customs and traditions, and the plains people wanting to build nations and impose control and conformity. It's no different here. There are a dozen different Naga tribes in these hills, who, until very recently fought each other and themselves, took heads as trophies and were generally left alone. From the middle of the 19th century, the British took an interest, but of an avuncular sort, never trying to subdue them but keeping them as a loose but friendly tribal area, which they called Nagaland. They were followed by American missionaries, who tried to persuade them to love God, grow crops and stop fighting.

When India was granted independence, the Nagas were not happy. Assimilation and domination by their Assamese lowland neighbours was seen as infinitely worse than staying with the British, and they made things difficult for India, boycotting general elections and fighting a fierce independence war against central government right up until the 1990s.

In January 2003, after 40 years of bloodshed, the NSCN, National Socialist Council of Nagaland, met in Delhi and announced that the war was over. Others are not so sure. They claim that the dream of an independent Nagaland will never go away.

OPPOSITE

Oh no! Three countries still to go! Palin feels the pinch in Assam.

The problem is that the Naga tribes remain essentially a trans-border people who don't fit neatly into any of the boxes that the politicians have created for them. This may vex central government but it also means I can stand astride this particular frontier without fear of being mined, electrocuted or shot.

The people of Longwa are Konyak Nagas, the most numerous of 16 sub-tribes. They used to be known as the Naked Nagas, the title of a book by an Austrian anthropologist who worked here in the 1930s, some of whose observations, such as 'Virginity wins no halo in the Naga heaven', suggest reasons for his fascination with them.

Today, things are very different. Such has been the success of the American Baptist Church that 99 per cent of the Naga have been converted to Christianity. Nakedness is a thing of the past, as is the once common custom of head-hunting. (Though a recent *National Geographic* article reported evidence of active head-hunters as recently as 1991.)

We have come here with Shingwong, whose official title is Extra Assistant to the Deputy District Commissioner. He's a soft-spoken Konyak, with square, grave features, more Tibetan than Indian. He wears a Western jacket and trousers. Tomorrow there will be a big spring festival here and the guest of honour will be the local MP.

The MP has asked to meet us and after our meal tonight Shingwong takes us to see him, in a small, dark barn, with a hard earth floor. By the looks of things the MP's had a few. His eyes are unfocussed and his mouth seems to have collapsed at one side, making him look not only unattractive, but dangerous.

Squatting on stools around him and lit only by flickering firelight is gathered a cross-section of mountain people, who seem to be from a completely different world. Most have red shawls thrown over bare shoulders and round their waists are aprons, held in place by belts made of bamboo cane. Some have bones in their hair and through their ears and small bronze skulls hanging from a necklace. These represent the heads that man has taken.

They grin vaguely at us as our purpose is explained.

'BBC. Journey round the Himalaya.'

But none of it's going in. They're all completely rat-arsed.

Day Ninety One : Longwa

The concrete walls of our rooms in the government guesthouse seem to attract and trap the cold. I get up early. Outside, the mist lies in the valleys, as thick as fresh snow. I walk around the chief's hut, in and out of India, measuring its circumference as 250 yards. I'm full of admiration that something on this scale is built entirely from leaf, stalk, bark, branch and trunk. Shingwong tells me the whole village helps in the construction of these longhouses.

A little further along the ridge, a cluster of tall stones rises from a grassy mound. It looks like a graveyard but is more of a trophy room. These stones represent the number of heads brought into the village.

A crudely dug, stone-stepped pathway runs down from the top of the ridge to a wide flat area with the white cross of a newly built church (by far the biggest building in Longwa) looming over the festival site. Stalls have been set out round the side of it, selling antique gongs, rattan umbrellas, wooden figurines as well as essentials like clothes, cooking pots and local medicines such as cinnamon sticks for toothache. Food ranges from lemon grass and betel leaves to porcupine, bred for eating. Its strong, tangy, venison-like flavour is considered a delicacy round here, and the quills are cut up and made into necklaces.

In fashion, the generational difference is marked. The young favour saris, jeans and T-shirts but the grannies and grandfathers still go barefoot, their thin, spindly legs often pocked with sores and unhealed grazes.

One very senior citizen leans proudly on an old flintlock rifle. Bamboo sticks have worn long,

LEFT

The past and the future in Longwa village. Local Nagas, squeezed in between barbed wire and satellite dishes, cluster over a meal.

ABOVE

Belly up. Konyak Naga head-hunter outdoes me in stomach decoration. Nor are my Paul Smith belt and Craghopper trousers any match for his hornbill feather, wild boar's teeth and neck-chain showing he's taken five heads.

OPPOSITE

Another old warrior, with fern accoutrements.

distended holes in his earlobes. He has skull medallions round his neck and is clearly very proud of his hunting past. He obligingly confirms that he has taken five heads.

His face, like those of many of the older generation, has what looks like a black stain running across it. On closer examination I see these are tattoos and not black but deep indigo, made of a number of very fine pin-prick marks. He pulls aside his shawl to show me that the tattoos extend across his chest and stomach and round onto his back. The old man knows Shingwong. He used to help his father, a surveyor working for the British on the first maps of Nagaland. He says he was ten years old when he first saw an Englishman. At first he had been frightened to go near them, they were so white he assumed they had no blood.

I ask if this old man with the skulls round his neck and headdress of boar's teeth and hornbill feathers is now a Christian and he nods emphatically.

Shingwong thinks that conversion was made easier among the Nagas because their belief system was always based around one invisible god, one creator, which made the transition to Christianity seem less drastic.

Despite the grip of the Baptist church, the Konyak culture is still taught in schools and pre-Christian dances form the highlight of today's festival.

Women process down from the ridge, four abreast, holding hands and wearing coral bead necklaces, headdresses, blue or black tunics and skirts with striped hoops. They form wide circles and move round infinitely slowly, chanting almost sotto voce. The slow, dirge-like pace is dictated by purely practical considerations. The jewellery of each dancer weighs 10 to 25 lb (5 to 10 kilos) alone.

The men then perform a war dance, which recreates the story of a head-hunting party. They appear, ironically enough, from behind the Baptist church, armed with machetes in one hand

and rifles or spears decorated with goats' fur in the other. On their heads are bear-skin caps and hornbill feathers, round their waists aprons and cane belts, squeezed tight to help puff out their chests, and on their feet incongruous black leather shoes of the sort you might wear to the office. On their backs are baskets in which to bring the heads home.

There follows a dramatic enactment of a raid on another village. Children cover their ears as the rifles are discharged, and the men end up with a celebratory python dance, in which their gyrations cause the sun to catch the glaze of their feathers and thus recreate the sinuous movement of the snake.

In the afternoon the arena is cleared and football posts are put up for a game between Longwa and Khemoi, a village in Myanmar. As there are no official games between the two countries, this is the closest there is to an India v Myanmar international. Despite a hard-fought first half, the Blues of India pip the Reds of Myanmar 8-2 and, to add insult to injury, the defeated team from Khemoi has a two and a half-hour walk home.

In the evening I have an opportunity to see inside the chief's house. He's agreed to be interviewed, and, armed with a bottle of rum as a present, I clamber through an entrance at one end. It is a cavernous space inside, like being in the upturned hull of some great ship. As there is hardly any natural light coming in, the soaring height of the roof is lost in gloom. I find myself in a long chamber, empty save for two huge, hollowed-out tree trunks, which Shingwong says are war-canoes, and an aircraft seat, which they say came from a bomber shot down in the war. The Nagas are proud of the fact that they saved nine Allied airmen.

In the heart of the house, the chief sits at the centre of a semicircle of elders, an impressive number of brass heads hanging on their chests. A fire blazes. Above it hang various trophies, animal skulls and horns, and a number of ceremonial gongs.

The chief doesn't look like a man who needs another bottle of rum at the moment. As I hand it over, his wide, bloodshot eyes meet mine for a moment, and I feel like someone who's arrived

very late at a party.

He has been the Ang, as they call the local headman here, for 25 years. It is an hereditary title, and will pass to his son, provided that son is by the daughter of a fellow Ang, and not by one of the chief's concubines. I ask how many concubines he has. Ten, comes the answer, after a longish pause for calculation.

He will probably be the last Ang for whom head-hunting was a condition of office. He has taken five heads, he claims. He is now a Christian and was baptized, by total immersion, in a nearby stream. When he was young, he says, the village was ruled by fear; now it's ruled by the fear of God.

I still can't get used to hearing such Sunday School sentiments from a group of people who, with their bleary eyes, boar-tusk headdresses and monkey-fur decorations, look like every missionary's idea of the unapologetic heathen.

Tonight a huge thunderstorm breaks over Longwa. Torrential rain rakes the tin roof like machine-gun fire and a mighty rushing wind sets doors banging, dogs howling and curtains blowing. Good weather to lie in bed to.

Day Ninety Two: Longwa to Digboi

After the rains, the dirt road out of Longwa is heavy-going. We're in reconditioned Second World War jeeps. Comfort is sacrificed for nimbleness and they're alarming but agile on the slippery stuff. Our driver puts on a dusty cassette of Beatles hits. 'Help!' could have been written for this trip.

Shingwong's daughter, Pang Nou, shares the car with me. She's just completed a Master's degree in English Literature at Delhi. Her theses were on Plato's Concept of Love and the Book

ABOVE

Shingwong translates the words of the chief, on my right, as we talk to him in his hut. This picture has a distinctly period flavour. Hard to believe from the look of the place that most of them here are baptized Christians.

of Job. She tells me that, though in Delhi she felt her homeland seemed unbelievably far away, the Indian government is taking Nagaland very seriously. The roads are free, they pay no tax and the benign attitude to local culture is all part of the greater worry that Nagaland might fall into the clutches of the hated enemy on the other side of the border. Not Myanmar, but China.

After some 40 miles, the town of Mon appears like the new Jerusalem on a hill ahead of us, its Baptist church perhaps the largest and longest of the great white mini-cathedrals that rise above the palm and thatched terraces of the Naga Hills.

Our jeep, which has skated through the mud so athletically up to now, slithers to a halt at the last quagmire and we take a while to get started again. Our driver, chewing on the betel with grim determination, does his best to make up time, narrowly avoiding an 'After Whiskey Driving Risky' sign, but by the time we reach the church, the service we've come to film has long begun.

The Konyak Baptist Church is as big as an aircraft hangar, and every seat in the gallery and the body of the church is taken. Shingwong estimates there are 2500 worshippers here. The church was built in 1952 and the services are invariably packed.

The preacher is a Konyak who has been working as a Baptist missionary in Bhutan for the last nine years. In that time he's made less than 100 converts, which, I must say, makes me want to go to Bhutan right away. He speaks at great length on this and related matters, then everyone stands to sing 'Onward Christian Soldiers' in Konyak, after which the congregation, largely passive up till now, is exhorted by the pastor to speak their minds and give thanks to the Lord.

A sedate, middle-aged lady next to me is transformed into a wailing ecstatic. As the prayers flow, her voice rises to a near scream. Stretching out her arm, she begins to rub her hand up and down my back.

'Hallelujah, Praise the Lord!' she screams.

The pressure from her hand increases and it moves up to my head, ruffling my hair one way and then the other.

'Halle-LU-JAH,' she crescendoes, leaping to her feet, arms flung wide above me, eyes tight shut.

'PRAISE…THE…LORD!'

OPPOSITE

*Full house in the
church at Mon. Later,
the congregation of
2500 sang 'Onward
Christian Soldiers' in
Konyak.*

Day Ninety Three : Digboi, Assam

Another night in a government guesthouse, this time on the plains of Northeastern Assam, a fertile salient pushing up into the tail of the Himalaya. The tropical lushness of these gently rolling hills is the work of the heavy monsoon rains that are channelled up the Brahmaputra valley. Overflowing flower beds almost reach up to the door and the guesthouse boasts the only 18-hole golf course in Assam.

The money in Digboi comes from oil, discovered here in 1889 and commemorated at the Digboi Centenary Museum of Oil, at which it is obligatory to remove your shoes before entering.

Also commemorated a few miles northeast of Digboi is the Indian end of the wartime Burma Road. Having so recently stood at the Chinese end, in Kunming, I'm interested to see what's left here.

There is very little. A strip of the old tarmac, which soon gets lost in the undergrowth, is all that remains of the road itself, and beside it is a patch of garden, complete with concrete furniture, that's called the Stilwell Information Park. The main feature of this display is a 20-foot high hoarding with a painted map of a section of the route, named after the American General 'Vinegar Joe' Stilwell, who pushed this supply line through.

On top of the map, an unequivocally modern message is delivered. 'Rejuvenate our Life Line, Revitalize our Relationship, Reach out Beyond the Borders,' it reads. A reminder that if you look at the geography of Assam you will see that its border with the rest of India is only a few miles wide, but her borders with China, Tibet, Burma, Bangladesh and Thailand run for 3700 miles (5900 km), and Beijing is as close to Assam as Delhi. But nothing much seems to be happening out to the east today. For now, it looks pretty much as if everything stops here.

An hour's drive from the oil town of Digboi there is a coal mine. This isn't itself surprising, given this fossil-rich little corner of India, but Tipong Mine is a singular place indeed. A red-brick Nottinghamshire pit village in the middle of a jungle.

It's a still morning and shreds of mist have not yet dispersed. A smell of sulphur hangs in the air and the jungle gently steams. Miners are arriving on Hercules and Hero bicycles for the first shift of the day. I join a group of them on a narrow, cable bridge, which bounces like a trampoline as we cross. Below is a 40-foot drop into a sluggish river, transformed from a mountain stream into an industrial sump, stained with oil streaks and oxides.

The men have lamps and hard hats but the rest of their clothes and equipment are flimsy. Sandals, flip-flops, old gym shoes, vests and torn trousers are the order of the day. Before going underground they gather round a brazier made from pipes and old railway parts. There seems no sense of urgency.

A priest in dhoti and thick, knitted sweater moves among them, offering a plate of sweets and a prayer. He gives me a *tika* mark on my forehead. I want to tell him that the last one I had was put on by the King of Nepal, but he'd only think I was mad.

The protection of the gods is taken very seriously. Built above one of the mine entrances is a

small, pink temple to the goddess Kali (alias Parvati, Sati, Uma and Durga), and as she is the consort of Siva the destroyer, she must be constantly propitiated. When the motley group of miners does eventually enter the mine shaft, I notice each one first touch the tunnel entrance, then his forehead and then his heart.

No sooner have they gone down than a greasy cable stiffens and begins to turn. Out of a second tunnel emerges a line of wagons filled with slack. As they reach the top of a low rise they're grabbed and pushed on by a work gang largely composed of elderly women in grimy saris. These ladies roll the narrow, coffin-like wagons down a short slope and assemble them into a train. When enough are ready they are collected by a very old saddle-tank steam engine called 'David', built in Lancashire in 1864. Its boiler is now so caked and encrusted with deposits that it resembles a moving fossil.

Our host, Mr Das from Coal India Ltd, won't allow us to film any of this until we have an armed police escort, and they haven't turned up yet.

We suggest doing a discreet wide shot while we're waiting but Mr Das shakes his head.

'This is a very disturbed place.'

He smiles tolerantly, like a teacher dealing with hyperactive pupils.

'It is our headache to look after you.'

He seems a decent man, around 40, a Bengali, with intense dark eyes, a thick moustache, brown bobble hat, a windcheater with 'Herod Active' written across it and an uncle who's an accountant in Guildford.

He invites us to his office. It's a low, brick building, painted pistachio green, inside and out. There is a concrete floor and a board on the wall with three columns marked 'Production Totals', 'Targets', 'Achievements'. A one-bar electric fire glows and two or three of his colleagues are introduced and sit at the table with us. Our two armed guards, thin men wrapped in headscarves, walk by outside the window.

Sidestepping any further questions about security with a brisk 'there is some insurgency', Mr Das clambers onto the safer ground of statistics. In quick succession, I learn that India is the fourth largest producer of coal in the world (after the USA, Russia and Australia) but the biggest

ABOVE

Safety is the big issue at Tipong. I suppose they could start by giving them overalls.

employer (600,000 people), that Tipong produces a particularly valuable high calorie coal, that they have had no fatal injuries of any kind since 1994, when nine were killed after an electrician tried to mend an electrical motor without turning the current off, that, instead of shafts and lifts, the miners here walk to work down inclined passageways that reach 1150 feet (350 m) below the surface. The only shadow over Tipong is that they only have technology to bring out 40 per cent of the coal deposits. The rest they have to leave in the ground.

What really animates him is an obvious and glowing pride in his labour relations. Tipong has a cosmopolitan workforce, from South India, Nepal, Orissa, Bihar, comprising Muslims, Christians and Hindus, but everyone looks after everyone else and they provide schools and communal activities for everyone equally. Women who are widows of company employees are offered surface jobs.

David's wheezy whistle announces that the 140-year-old tank engine is coupled up and ready to leave for the depot two miles down the line. I'm privileged to ride the footplate as we bowl gamely down the hill past lineside exhortations like 'All Time is Safety Time' and 'There is no Substitute for Hard Work and Sincerity'.

We cross the river on a girder bridge with elegantly functional red-brick piers bearing a construction date of 1923. The line levels out. Bicycles overtake us easily. Goats and chickens stroll by. The fireman doesn't so much toss coal into the boiler but places it there by hand, positioning each piece carefully before ramming it home with a metal rod. Once away from the cleared area of the mine, the jungle closes in and David has his work cut out to push us past overhanging branches and bushes. It's an enchanting run, a blend of *Thomas the Tank Engine* and *The Jungle Book*.

After lunch at the Tipong Mine Guest House, a once elegant, plantation-style building, now surrounded on all sides by coal heaps, Mr Das takes us up onto one of the hills overlooking the river to hear a selection of Safety Songs, specially written for Tipong. A five-man choir, accompanied by a harmonium and a tabla, a pain of small hand-drums is set up in the garden of a red-brick terraced house overlooking a hillside of mango, pineapple, jackfruit, guava, betel and banana trees. Across the river a slowly moving plume of white smoke rises above the trees,

tracing the progress of David back up the valley again. Against this background of an industrial Arcadia, Hahmid Rachmar and his group, all sweatered up like a glee club, perform the safety song they've written themselves. It's a catchy song, beautifully performed, and in the abundant goodwill afterwards Mr Das shyly reveals that he's learning the violin at home.

'Does your wife mind?' I joke.

His brow furrows. 'No, she is very helpful.'

I leave Tipong with some doubts as to whether there really is a mine here at all and thoughts that this grubby Garden of Eden might simply be kept going by Mr Das and his friends so that they can learn music and write hit songs.

The last thing I do is ask him to write down the words of the catchy Safety Song.

I try them at the guesthouse, in the bath.

'Safety First, Safety First

In every step of work, be it the rule,

It is for us to remain awake all the time, There's danger in every move.

If we obey the rules

There will be no sorrow for us,

Safety First, Safety First.'

Perhaps we should adopt it as the crew's anthem. On second thoughts, it's too late now.

Day Ninety Four : Digboi to Dibrugah

A pack of pye-dogs circles the entrance to Digboi station, backing away with wary reluctance at the approach of my cycle-rickshaw. I buy a ticket for Dibrugah, 52 miles (80 km) down the line, for 18 rupees, about 25 pence. I notice that a ticket on the sleeper service to Delhi, over 1000 miles (1600 km) away, would set me back £8.

That the railway extends here at all has everything to do with oil, tea and coal and very little to do with passengers. The wooden bench seats are functional rather than comfortable and progress is slow and punctuated every few hundred yards by a blast of the engine's horn to clear the railway line of all those who use it as a highway, meeting place, or just for grazing.

Fortunately, I have some good companions. Sitting opposite me are two women, one tall and slim with classic English features, the other a short, stout, bespectacled Indian lady whose face wears an expression of such serene good nature that it's impossible not to want to talk to her. The reason why they're travelling together is a remarkable story that unfolds as the train shrieks its way westwards.

Anne, the older of the two, is the daughter of an illicit relationship between an English tea-planter and one of the women from 'the lines' (i.e. a tea picker). Such liaisons were strictly forbidden and Anne's father could never publicly acknowledge his child. He went off to the Second World War and died in Singapore in 1942. Anne's mother, poor, uneducated and illiterate, had no idea how to find information about him. She didn't even know how he spelt his name.

Anne, neither English nor Indian, never really fitted in with the tea-planters, who, embarrassed at such situations, were unapproachable and unhelpful. Enquiries about her father were stonewalled.

Anne was sent to a convent school and later met and fell in love with an Indian fighter pilot, who wrote to her every day, and even once dropped a letter to her from his plane. They had a daughter together, but he was a married man and, in a mirror image of her mother's situation, they kept their relationship secret. He eventually returned to his wife. Anne got a job as a secretary in a tea company, where she saw a copy of the London *Daily Telegraph* in her office. She noted down the name of their defence correspondent and, on a whim, wrote and asked him how she might find out about a tea-planter called Stuart who went missing in 1942.

Thanks to his help, she eventually learnt her father's name, one of many on the wall of a mass grave in Singapore. Armed with this lead, and with some help from one of the tea company's directors, she finally made contact with her father's family in England, 47 years after his death. His sister Mary was still alive and asked to meet Anne. Mary's granddaughter Sarah is the girl travelling with Anne today.

The two women derive so much pleasure from each other's company, that one can only wonder what things might have been like if they'd known of each other's existence years earlier.

It seems years have passed since leaving Digboi when the train finally pulls into Tinsoukia, less than 30 miles down the track. As we approach Tinsoukia station the view on both sides is of decommissioned steam locomotives, row upon row of them in overgrown sidings. Some lie on their sides, some are hung around with vines and creeper and, as there seems to have been no attempt to strip them down, they remain intact, as if a spell had been put on them.

We move out of Tinsoukia at a pace that would make a snail seem nippy. Seeing our impatience, a jolly, bespectacled lady in a gold-trimmed sari smiles broadly across at us.

'This is a train for people who have no work.'

We talk about local things. She's a professor at Dibrugah University and has strong views on the need for India to look east. She is a firm believer in an economic development initiative, ungracefully mnemonicized as BIMSTEC, to encourage co-operation between Bangladesh, India, Myanmar, Singapore, Thailand and China. A recent meeting, however, was hobbled by the Indian government refusing visas to the Chinese delegation until the night before the conference. Understandably, they cancelled.

'The Indians don't really empathize with the Chinese then?' I ask.

'I don't think our mind-set is still yet fully open to Chinese co-operation,' she replies.

I take that as a no.

She agrees with Mr Das the coal-mine manager's point about the cosmopolitan make-up of

LEFT

Hearing Anne (holding the handbag) and Sarah's story on the world's noisiest train, from Digboi to Dibrugah, Assam.

OPPOSITE

*With elephant and
mahout (elephant
trainer) in the jungle
on the way to the tea
plantation.*

Assam, but has a different explanation for it. In 1823 a Scotsman called Robert Bruce first noted the commercial potential of the wild tea plant and within 20 years it had become a major and highly labour-intensive crop. The Assamese, being partial to opium at the time, were not good at hard labour, so it became necessary to look further afield for the workforce, hence the widening of the gene pool in Northeast India.

We stay tonight at a tea plantation house called a *changa*, which is in effect a bungalow on stilts. Beneath the extensive boughs and trailing tentacles of an old rain tree, we sit round a fire and watch a delicately energetic dance performed by girls who look more Thai or Burmese than Indian. Assamese specialities are brought round. Long, rolled rice-cakes called *bithas*, made with molasses and sesame seeds, a grilled root with tomato and aubergine dip, feather light *pooris*, chicken and fish from the Brahmaputra.

As night falls the handsome house behind us looks like an ocean liner, with its deep well-polished decks and white balustrade. It belongs to a local tea-planter called Manoj Jalan and his wife Vinita. His plantations employ 8000 people, and tomorrow he's going to show me round. On an elephant.

Day Ninety Five : Dibrugah

The first thing I notice about my elephant is that it has no howdah. A howdah is a seat to make riding more comfortable, and I don't have one. So I find myself being unceremoniously thrust up onto the elephant's back and ordered to move forward until I'm tight up behind the mahout, the elephant driver. The elephant's back is narrower here and there's less chance of my doing the splits. Once I'm in position, the elephant is given an order and I feel myself rearing skywards as it straightens first the front and then the back legs. I'm now some ten feet off the ground and hanging on for dear life to a thin piece of rope that runs across the its shoulder.

Manoj, a carefully turned-out, trim figure with boyish features, is next to me. He's riding his own elephant and doesn't look altogether happy.

My mahout shouts the order *'Agit!'* ('Forward!'), one of 20 words of command the elephant has to learn, and this, accompanied, I notice, by a sharp blow to the back of the ear, sets the animal moving slowly ahead. There are three females and three young in our procession. The young elephants are not particularly interested in anything other than getting in the way and practising their trumpeting.

Feeling more secure, I look around. The mahout uses his feet tight up behind the elephant's ear to control direction and, far too often it seems to me, strikes the animal with the blunt end of a machete. Elephants' ears, seen from behind, look surprisingly delicate and vulnerable. Pale, curled at the edges and marked with long purple veins, they're like giant leaves in autumn. I'm surprised, too, how much hair there is on an elephant's hide, short little shoots on the full-grown females, much longer and thicker on the young. The prehensile trunk is always working away; look out for a quick snack, a leaf or two, some shoots to strip and, if possible, an entire bush to uproot.

According to Manoj, the Assamese were the first to harness the natural skills of elephants to help with human activities, and their use became widespread in the logging industry when the railways were being pushed up into the plantations and oilfields. They showed the rest of India how to control and domesticate wild elephants but now, with logging drastically cut for environmental reasons, many of the mahouts and their elephants can no longer find work. A few, like these, are retained to clear bamboo cane or tidy up the tea plantations, but it's a dying art.

With Manoj Jalan (on leading elephant) in his Mancotta Estate. Elephants used to be used for logging. Now timber conservation has rendered many of them and their mahouts redundant. The lucky ones still get work clearing undergrowth in tea plantations.

Having overcome my fear of falling, I'm enjoying this slow, powerful progress through the undergrowth. I'm hardly aware I'm on a living creature. It's more like being on board ship on a gentle swell.

All of a sudden there is the most enormous blast of sound, not unlike a foghorn at full volume. We've emerged onto a metalled road into the path of a group of men on bicycles. The cyclists are laughing and ringing their bells, the elephants are frightened and the mahouts and Manoj are shouting frantically.

'*Ghat! Pich-oo!*' ('Stop! Go Back!'). My driver rains blows down on the back of his animal. It seems only to get her more distressed and she bellows again and starts off up the track at a canter, which for one stomach-tightening moment I think might turn into a full blooded charge.

The mahout brings her under control, but I've had a glimpse of the power of the beast and I'm not unhappy when, after two hours straddling its back, my elephant kneels once more and I can clamber off.

For a while I think I might never be able to close my legs again.

Among the many pleasures of Mancotta Bungalow is its collection of old books. I pick up a copy of *The Survey of Assam 1825–1828*. This was the first time this part of the world had been mapped and the provenance of the areas covered has a nice personal touch to it. We learn that the details of one large area of Himalayan foothill is 'based on information of a Persian sent by Mr Scott into Bhotan (sic)', and the entire map between Assam and China is 'from information collected by Lieutenant Wilcox'.

A survey of Bengali exploration published in Calcutta in 1998 intrigues me in a different way. The index at the back of this book appears to record every word mentioned. A random glance at the 'R' column lists not only 'Ranpur' but 'reached', 'reasonable', 'rather', and indeed 'random', as well.

Day Ninety Seven : Dibrugah to Majuli Island

After a restorative break, it's time to move on from the world of fresh bed linen every night, a whisky every evening and a copy of the *Assam Tribune* every afternoon. I think they used to call it the colonial life and I can feel myself slipping into it.

The danger is that in faithfully and tastefully recreating the colonial lifestyle you recreate colonial attitudes as well. There is no shortage of labour in India, and this, along with residual effects of the caste system and poor education, results in there being a lot of people happy to wait around and be told what to do. I look forward to my Scotch at sunset but I know that if I pour it myself, jobs might be at stake.

So servility is perpetuated.

The gates are unlocked for us and we leave Mancotta's past behind and drive west. For several miles a vast plain of small, trim bushes, all neatly clipped and standing at a uniform height of about 36 inches stretches away on either side. Tall trees rise from among the bushes to shield them from the full glare of the sun. In this quiet period before the new shoots start to appear women in brightly-coloured shawls and scarves move through the glades, grooming and trimming. It must have been a listless time for plantation managers. A time for chota pegs and perhaps a visit to the lines.

These great prairies of tea, still referred to as 'gardens', produce 340,000–390,000 tons (350–400 million kg) a year, half of India's total tea production.

The source of this bountiful fertility lies close to a snow-capped mountain in the arid desert of southwest Tibet. Mount Kailash is considered by Hindus, Buddhists and Jainists as one of the most sacred places on earth, the abode of their fiercest gods, the navel of the world from which life-giving rivers flow. The Indus and the Ganges both rise in its shadow, as does the Yarlung Tsangpo, which flows east through the length of Tibet, before entering the great bend of the Himalaya, plunging through a series of wild, barely accessible gorges and emerging in Assam, flowing due west and with a new name, Brahmaputra, 'Son of Brahma, the Creator'.

It is by now an immense river, with 1000 miles (1600 km) of water behind it, and it endows Assam with a rich alluvial flood plain, 445 miles (712 km) long and an average of 60 miles (96 km) wide.

It sustains not only the tea industry but a rice bowl too, as well as wheat, sugar cane, banana, tobacco, mustard, jute, silk and just about anything you care to put in the ground.

My first sight of the mighty Brahmaputra is from the ferry boat station at Neamati ghat, a few miles from the crowded town of Jorhat.

There is an air of lassitude to the place. A bus is drawn up, waiting to collect disembarking passengers. Dogs chase each other sporadically before curling up on one of several coal heaps. Tarpaulin-covered shacks offer tea and samosas.

The river seems very still and very silent. It's around 500 yards wide, I would guess, but it's difficult to tell, as it fills more than one channel. The land is endlessly flat. Out there all the lines are horizontals, subtle pastel shades fading into distant perspectives. The Brahmaputra is like an inland sea, as magnificent and implacable in its own way as the plateau where it was born.

Somewhere downstream is Majuli, the world's largest river island, and we're here to try and get ourselves aboard one of the embattled ferry boats that are the only means of reaching it.

The bank on which we're waiting will probably be submerged after the monsoon rains

swell the river, which might account for the lack of any jetty. When the boat arrives, embarking passengers have to slither down the bank as best they can and cross two wooden beams that serve as a gang-plank. The 100-foot-long flat-bottomed boats set no store by elegance. There is a basic cabin below, which is covered by a corrugated aluminium roof. Passengers pack in as best they can. From the anxious shouts and gesticulations you might think this was the first time a ferry had ever docked at Neamati but, as ever, remarkable order comes from the chaos, and by the time we cast off, every late-comer is aboard, as well as several bicycles, one or two motorbikes and a white Ambassador car. The women gather below and a mixture of men in Western and local dress sit, stand, squat and generally make themselves comfortable on the corrugated sheets above.

With a steady chug of diesel, we pull out into the wide brown stream, which, judging from the tree trunks, leaves and clumps of jungle scudding by, is not as lazy as it looked. We pick our way carefully among low sandbanks, some of which are cultivated. Ruddy shelducks sunbathe on the beaches. Cormorants perch on the fishing poles. Colours are soft and vaporous: muted greens, strips of golden sand and a huge haze-blue sky above.

My travelling companion is a well-informed young man called Maan Barua, whose father owns a resort hotel in nearby Kaziranga National Park. He's 20 years old and knows an awful lot more than I ever will. From him I learn the sex of the Brahmaputra, one of only two male rivers in India, and that ruddy shelducks mate for life. He's also promised to show me a river dolphin, if one passes.

After an hour and a half on the water the engine beat slows and the traditional man with a stick (in this case a bamboo pole) prods the shallow mud banks as we approach the island. As soon as the bank is within leaping distance, half the roof-class passengers fling themselves off and race up the hill to the bus. The bus driver, clearly enjoying his moment of power, sounds the horn again and again, prompting more and more people to death-defying leaps.

Majuli Island covers nearly 250 square miles (650 sq km), which, Maan tells me, is half as big as it was 50 years ago. It's been continuously settled for 3000 years, but since the arrival of

a saint, Shankara Deva, at the start of the 16th century it has become best known for its religious institutions, a form of monastery called *satras*. These differ from mainstream Hinduism by preaching devotion to only one god, Vishnu, and rejecting the use of icons or images.

The Uttar (meaning 'North') Kamalabari *satra* is in a peaceful rural setting among rice and mustard fields criss-crossed with well-trodden mud paths and dotted with small bonfires. We are required to remove our shoes and socks when we reach its arched gatehouse entrance, with the date of foundation, 1673, inscribed on it. Purity is a very important part of the tradition of the *satras*. The *bhakat*, the community of monks, has taken a vow of purity and if they prepare food or touch someone who is impure they must immediately wash.

In the centre of the monastery complex is an east-facing prayer hall called the Kirtanghar, some 200 feet long and surrounded by vegetable gardens and tropical fruit trees. The living accommodation is set round the perimeter of this intimate site in four residential terraces called *haatis*, which are themselves broken down into two storeys of rooms called *bohas*, lending the *satra* the air of an Oxbridge college marooned in the jungle.

The thing that strikes one most of all is the handsomeness of the monks. All look very healthy and lissom, with pale brown skin and hair worn either close-cropped or in long, lustrous black tresses, tied at the back.

Accompanied by an older monk called Dulal, dressed in a white robe and dhoti, we're shown preparations for a play called Rasa Lila, which involves many of the most beautiful boys transforming themselves into beautiful girls. In this particular celibate sect, all the women's parts are danced by men.

The whole play lasts five to six hours and they only perform it once a year, so they are doing an excerpt for us in which Krishna, a dashing romantic incarnation of the god Vishnu, appears to a group of milkmaids, who all fall in love with him.

Inside and outside the *bohas* the young men are wrapt in concentration, applying make-

up to each other, rubbing white base over leg hair, or in the case of the monk who is to play Krishna, covering himself with a mixture of calamine and indigo, blue being the traditional colour in which Krishna appears.

Dulal, who has spent 35 of his 41 years in the monastery, tells me that some of the young men are sent here by their parents because they can't afford to keep them at home. Families who have experienced pain or disease might send one of their children to the *satra* in the hope of improving the family fortunes. A ten-year-old was being offered for sale in a market in Uttar Pradesh when one of the monks heard about it and brought him here.

By now, some of the young monks are pulling on skirts and blouses and another is, with great concentration, strapping on a pair of small artificial breasts, which he then covers with a bra. Krishna is having trouble coping with two wigs and a crown.

The dance is accompanied by a flute, harmonium, finger cymbals and three drummers, each with a *kohl*, a cylindrical drum only found in Assam, about 20 inches long, made from jackfruit tree stems with leather at either end and carried round the neck and across the chest.

The dance, which involves Krishna, 14 milkmaids and a demon who Krishna fights off with a tree, takes place in the Kirtanghar. It's exquisitely executed, requiring the most concentrated co-ordination, as every tiniest body movement, of arms and legs and hands and feet, is precisely choreographed, and every facial expression has to be exactly in accordance with tradition. Fingers must always be turned up at the ends to resemble the lotus, and when they make their delicate curlicue movements the eyes of the dancer must always follow them, creating the effect of the whole body as a stream in motion. A white butterfly flutters across the room as if to set them an example.

The performance attracts a small audience, and I notice that women spectators who wish to watch these men dressed as women are not allowed inside the prayer hall, but have to watch from behind bars outside.

Day Ninety Eight : Majuli Island

The air is warm and the light soft as I cycle along the high track between the fields. The bike I've been given is enormous, but then the sandy roads of Majuli are full of people riding bicycles much bigger than themselves. Maan is with me and we stop to see flying foxes hanging from the branches of a capacious banyan tree. A well-placed missile lobbed at the tree wakes a few and sends them soaring into the air on wings over three foot wide. The banyan is intertwined with an equally magnificent bo tree, with a geometrically elegant rattan palm somehow squeezed in there too. The rank luxuriance of the island is the result of regular flooding, which probably accounts for the impermanence and adaptability of human settlement. Bridges are light and mainly bamboo, houses are on stilts with grain and hay stores well off the ground. Nothing looks as though it expects to last long.

One of the minority people on the island are the Mishing. There are an estimated 45,000 of them, believed to be the original lowland people, animists, believing in the Sun God, Donyi, and the Moon God, Polo. They took refuge on the island, where they could practise their unorthodox Hinduism without interference.

It's the custom throughout Indian villages that the men plough and carry, but the women are responsible for the more specialized tasks of cultivation and harvest. In one of the many small ponds left behind by the floodwaters I witness the extraordinary sight of Mishing women catching fish.

About 20 of them, dressed in off-the-shoulder saris, walk through the shallow water, leaning on upturned conical baskets held out in front of them, rather like Zimmer frames. As they move forward, they stamp the baskets up and down to flush the fish out of the mud. Once they have a fish trapped in the bottom of the rattan frame, they pick them out, still wriggling, and drop them down their cleavages. Pausing only to tighten the waist band on their saris, they move on, the odd tail flapping defiantly between their breasts.

The whole process is carried out with much singing, chanting, laughter and general exuberance, which only adds to the strangely erotic quality of this particular harvest.

Day Ninety Nine : Majuli to Kaziranga

At 6.30 in my monastic cell in the *satra*'s guesthouse in Kamalabari town, I'm woken with a cup of 'bed tea'. The tea, milk and sugar have been boiled up together in the Indian fashion. There are no windows in my room but I can tell the sun's up by the pattern cast on my wall from a ventilation grille. A cow moos brusquely, crows screech in the trees nearby.

A bucket of hot water is delivered next and I take it into my dark, stained cubicle of a bathroom, looking round rather hopefully for the giant spider with whom I shared it last night. He seemed a friendly sort. Unable to find him, I wash carefully, nose pursed against the reek of the drains.

I'm at the *satra* by seven. From inside the Kirtanghar comes the sound of ragas being practised, and outside a class of a dozen young boys are being taught the 64 exercise positions needed to learn dancing. They're pretty good at back rolls and walking on their hands but less deft at the *ora* position, which requires them to balance on one leg, with the other straight out, almost doing the splits.

A young monk who has just finished milking the cow is washing himself clean under one of the old handle pumps. There's no running water here.

*The monastery (satra)
on Majuli Island. With
Jadab Burah (right)
and his older
roommate Lila Ram.
Because of vows of
purity they would have
to wash themselves
completely after
touching anything in
the room that I'd
touched.*

Dulal has agreed to give me a lesson on the *kohl*. First, he ties a dhoti around me. Dhotis, a variation on the sarong, must be worn when playing. I sit cross-legged facing him on the smooth, mud-floored passage outside his room. The first surprise is the weight of the cigar-shaped drum. When I draw attention to this, Dulal, a man of supreme calm, whose brother is a taxi driver, smiles. He teaches children of seven on that same drum.

Dulal shows me three basic movements. *Tao*, a slap with open palm on the smaller end, *dhei*, the same on the wider side and *khit*, resonating then damping the sound with the fingers.

He nods generously and compliments me on having grasped the basic moves. I wipe a few beads of sweat from the brow and allow myself a moment of smugness, which is swiftly despatched.

'You will need another five years to get it right.'

Hearing that we're leaving today, Jadab Burah, who played a milkmaid yesterday, and Lila Ram, who played the devil, invite me to have a last tea in the room they share. Jadab is 18 and first came to the monastery when he was nine. His parents live less than a mile away and he still attends the local school and has friends, including girlfriends, outside the *satra*. He came here to learn dancing and is quite sure he'll stay for life. Lila Ram, who has been here for 16 years, is learning *gayan*, the art of cymbal playing.

They are delightful company, but when I leave they have to work out what I've touched in the room, as that object will now be impure and their vows require them to wash thoroughly should they come into contact with it.

All this is done with great ease and much laughter. In most institutions, however benevolent, you feel like an outsider looking in, but the special quality of Uttar Kamalabari is that everyone from the young boys to the grey-haired older monks, has gone out of their way to include us in the life of the *satra*.

It seems a place of rare and genuine happiness, where the hardest disciplines are artistic rather than religious and the goals are more concerned with fulfilment than denial. I catch myself thinking it's too good to be true, but maybe that just sums up the difference between our world and theirs.

Back on the river, the wide, open reaches of the Brahmaputra are as calming as the monastery. Most of the vast, impermanent mud flats are devoid of humans or livestock. A few other boats pass, including a travelling theatre group in a green barge, noisy and low in the water. Mobile theatre is highly popular in Assam.

Time drifts by. A flock of lapwings from the other side of the Himalaya wheels above us. A solitary vulture turns slowly over the southern bank. Maan takes my binoculars and has a closer look. He is searching for more vultures and their absence confirms his worries over their dramatic decline in numbers, thought to be largely the result of chemical pesticides.

Where we shall be tonight is considered a shining example of how environmental protection can work. Kaziranga, which boasts the disconcerting slogan 'Come. Get Lost', is a 293-square-mile (760 sq km) reserve on the banks of the Brahmaputra. It was the first wildlife sanctuary in India, set up 100 years ago, by the Viceroy, Lord Curzon, after his wife had gone to see the famed horned rhinos of the area and returned without encountering a single one. Since the Rhino Protection Act of 1913 the horned rhino has returned from the brink of extinction, and Maan tells me there are now 1500 to 1600 of them in the park, 70 per cent of the world's population, protected by 400 staff and 120 anti-poaching camps.

Not everyone sees this as a fairy tale. Serious concerns have been raised that animals matter more than people and that the local population has paid a high price for Kaziranga's 'success'.

We shall see.

Day One Hundred : Kaziranga

We're at the gates to Kaziranga National Park, awaiting the opening ceremonies of the much-publicized 2nd Elephant Festival. There could hardly be a greater contrast with the serenity of Majuli Island. Crowds are gathering on both sides of the road and, occasionally, a policeman will stride into the middle of them, waving his hands and blowing a whistle as if his life depended on it.

A constant blast of truck horns reminds us that the road we're standing beside is the NH 37, Assam's equivalent of the M1. Large signs call this stretch of it the Elephant Corridor, but it takes more than a sign or two to turn truck drivers into conservationists, and the presence of the crowd only seems to encourage them to drive faster.

The rich are here, men in suits and women in gorgeous saris, and the poor, in extended family groups, stand and watch them. A procession of elephants is gathered further up the main road, but nothing can begin until the local big-wigs are here.

Maan and I pass the time talking about Indian politics. He gets vociferously angry about the general level of corruption, but even more worried about the BJP, the right-wing Hindu nationalists currently in power. They're communalist, anti-Muslim and suspicious of ethnic minorities of any kind. A travesty, he thinks, of the principles of tolerance and diversity on which India was founded. He's about to tell me more when hysterical police whistle-blowing announces the arrival of a ministerial convoy accompanied by a jeep with a machine gun mounted on the back. This, it transpires, is only the Minister for Environment and Forests and it's a further hour before incandescent whistle-blowing and ferocious arm-waving narrowly avoid members of the public being mown down by the vehicles bearing Chief Minister of Assam and his party.

Priorities having been duly established, the long-suffering elephants begin to process down the road towards us. I count 41 of them, all colourfully attired in the national colours of red and green and carrying advertising for the Numaligarh Oil Refinery, whose tankers have

been scattering us to the sides of the road all morning, and who are, astutely, chief sponsors of the Elephant Festival.

The elephants walk slowly, silently, with expressions of infinite patience. Their mahouts, in freshly pressed brown overalls and matching safari hats, look solemnly ahead. The crowd streams after them along the avenue of rosewood trees that leads through the fields to the arena. Many of them are representing local groups and organizations. They carry their pro-conservation banners aloft, shouting, singing and sidestepping the increasingly generous piles of elephant dung.

Once in the arena, a short speech explains that the motivation behind the elephant festival is to encourage local people to see the elephant as their friend and not something that tramples through their villages, damages their crops and destroys their livelihood. Unfortunately, this is but the first of many speeches on the theme of elephants as our friends, which the elephants and ourselves have to stand and listen to for over an hour in the hot sunshine.

Once the long paeans to biological diversity and ecological integrity are over, the elephants can get on with what they're there for. Playing football. It didn't seem a very bright idea when I first saw it in Kunming and it doesn't seem so here. Elephants are not natural footballers. You might as well get the Arsenal squad to pick up tree trunks with their noses. It's just not their field of expertise. They do their best, of course, but their ball skills are painfully slow and their ponderous movements and the commentator's attempts to present this as the last few seconds of a World Cup Final hint at desperation.

The elephant tug of war, on the other hand, is much more promising. The point here is quite simple – to show how much bigger and stronger elephants are than humans. Not an oft-disputed fact, you might think, but the proof of it is wonderful to watch. No matter how many men rush out of the crowd to grab the rope, and I reckon there were at least 60 clinging on to it at one point, the elephant merely has to walk a couple of steps to have them tumbling after him like the tail of a kite.

Later in the day, when the elephants have been taken away from the arena to be fed and watered, I encounter them in a different and quite unforgettable light. We are allowed close to three elephants and a calf as they trundle down to a muddy creek for their evening ablutions. At first, like all of us, I'm a spectator, impressed by the rapport between the mahouts and

their charges, marvelling at the ease with which they persuade these colossal creatures to lie on their sides in the water. This is a rare thing to see, and can only happen if there is absolute trust between elephant and man and an environment with no outside threat.

Then they ask me in among them. At first I'm apprehensive. I have once in my life, in Africa, seen the seen the terrifying power that can be unleashed when an elephant takes a dislike to you, and I approach very warily, stepping gingerly into the ankle deep mud. As I do so, one of the elephants, a 55-year-old bull called Joiraj, decides to stand up. Like a small island coming to life, he rears up above me, stretching up to his full 14 feet and proceeding to fling water from his trunk over his back.

He's a magnificent animal with a proud set of long, curved tusks and not someone I'd mess with. The keeper, however, has no such qualms.

'*Boit!* (Sit!). *Tere!* (Lie On Side!)' he shouts and within a matter of seconds he has several tons of bull elephant crumpling down into the water and rolling over like a dog waiting to be scratched.

The mahout beckons me forward and indicates where Joiraj most likes to be washed.

So it is that at the age of 60 I find myself rubbing an elephant of 55, behind his ears and particularly at the point where the tusk disappears into the folds of his cheek. His eyes roll towards me, registering languid approval. I'm told that he likes nothing better than to be slapped quite hard on the bridge of his nose. Tentatively at first, then, at the mahout's urging, rather more powerfully, I strike the top of his trunk. But it's only when I give him a really good whack that he appears to enter elephant heaven, rolling his eyes, stretching out his legs and emitting an infinitely appreciative rumble. The sound of a contented elephant is a wonderful thing, and I'm amazed that this battleship-grey hide, and these hard, immemorially ancient flanks can be as sensitive as a cat's chin.

In the evening we're driven into the heart of the park for a barbecue organized by the Minister for Forests at one of the anti-poaching camps.

One of the guests is a fellow Englishman, Mark Shand, who knows about conservation and knows his Himalaya well too. We swap a few stories. He is very keen that we should film a man he's just met who claims he can call rhino.

'Looks a bit like Benny Hill, round glasses, big grin. And he's best after lunch, when he's had a bit to drink.'

ABOVE

Football at the 2nd Kaziranga Elephant Festival. Even Wednesday could beat this lot. But why should they have to play with a human-sized ball when they're ten times bigger than us?

Day One Hundred and One : Kaziranga to Guwahati

In the park at first light, a layer of mist draped like gauze across the cotton trees. Maan and I are climbing aboard for an elephant safari, getting on the easy way, up an access tower and then straight onto one of the wood-frame howdahs that can accommodate six people.

By happy coincidence we're aboard my new friend Joiraj, and as we step ponderously out into the park, I ask Maan about the future of the elephant in Kaziranga. He thinks that it's all part of a wider picture. Unlike in Africa, there has been a long tradition in India of domesticating and training elephant, primarily for the logging industry. Now the pendulum is swinging away from cutting down and more towards the preservation of forest, so a different role must be found if the elephant is not to return to its natural state, with all the damage that can cause to local inhabitants.

As far as Kaziranga is concerned, there is work for them, not only on tourist rides like these, but in patrolling the park itself. Wet, often swampy ground and stretches of thick grassland standing 15 feet high make large swathes of the park inaccessible by motor vehicle. For surveillance and accessibility elephant is still best. But they are expensive to run, in feed, maintenance and, believe it or not, elephant pensions, paid on retirement to the animal rather than his keeper, so some form of culling may have to be considered. Of course, as far as Joiraj is concerned, this is unthinkable and I might have to ship him back to London.

This morning, though, he earns his keep and from our perch we have a wide view over the tall *ikora* grass and the shorter grass in front, where beads of dew catch the morning sun and storks and pond heron strut about. We see swamp deer and hog deer, wild buffalo and a few energetically chomping wild boar, with their thin, bristly black hair parted across their backs like cheap toupees. A long-legged, duck-like bird flies by and Maan becomes very excited. It's a Bengal florican and there are only 400 to 500 left in the world. Which makes the rhinos of Kaziranga seem positively commonplace.

And at last we come across one, a greater one-horned rhino, with its wide lip and protruding upper jaw for better grazing, encased in almost colourless armour platelets, and standing still as a statue, like a great silver-grey rock. It measures about ten feet long and four high and Maan estimates it must weigh nearly a ton and a half, some 1500 kilograms.

Unruffled by our presence, the rhino lowers its head and carries on with breakfast.

By evening, we've left this expanse of unpolluted nature behind and are ensconced at the Dynasty Hotel in the Muslim quarter of Assam's capital, Guwahati. From my window I look out over an urban panorama, a mosque, a row of shop units, endless lines of mottled, blackened apartment buildings, offices and warehouses.

And not an animal in sight.

BELOW

With Maan, and well-scrubbed Joiraj, on early morning safari. The virtually impenetrable 15-foot (5 m) stands of thick ikora or elephant grass, in the background, provide a network of routes for the rhino.

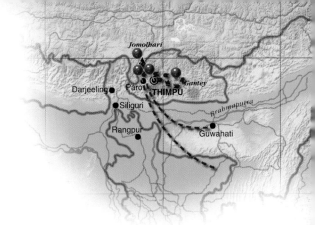

Bhutan

Day One Hundred and Three : Gantey

HAVING BEEN LULLED into lowland warmth and balminess in the Brahmaputra valley, I find myself tonight dressed in several layers of winter clothes, in a candle-lit room, hugging close to a wood-burning stove and gratefully accepting the offer of a hot-water bottle to relieve the icy chill of my bed. I'm a mere 140 miles (225 km) from steamy Guwahati but have forsaken the lazy horizontals of the Brahmaputra for a return to the rugged verticals of the Himalaya, and the bustle of the streets and markets for the silence of one of the most tranquil countries in the world.

Bhutan is the only independent Buddhist kingdom and one of only two remaining Himalayan kingdoms (Sikkim having gone to India and Tibet to China). It's a little larger than Switzerland, with a population less than the city of Birmingham, so there is room to swing cats. Add to this a deliberate government-imposed surcharge of $65 a day and you can begin to understand why we flew in to an airport that looked like a mediaeval palace on one of the only two planes that comprise the national fleet.

Bhutan (the name means the end of 'Bhot', the old name for Tibet) is a country of very strong character. The cultural confusion of East and West, of temples and shopping malls, robes and baseball hats, which marks so much of Southeast Asia, doesn't seem to have done much damage to a country where the official language is Dzongkha, the official currency is the *ngultrum* and the official policy is Gross National Happiness before Gross National Product.

Of course, there are telephones and cars and satellite dishes and laptop computers, but they are inside traditional buildings and used by people wearing traditional dress. Bhutan sees no contradiction between its past and its present. Its history is not to be found on display in tourist-friendly heritage parks, but on the street and in the countryside, as a part of everyday life. National costume is worn throughout the country, quite unselfconsciously, and very elegant it is too. The men wear the *kho*, pronounced 'go', an ankle-length robe with prominent white cuffs, pulled up to knee height and tucked into a belt. Women wear the *kira*, a length of silk or cotton wound around the body, and a short jacket called a *togo*. The fabrics are locally made and distinctive, varying from plain, utilitarian designs to complex weaves and intricate patterns.

Concrete has not yet rolled over Bhutan. Thanks to careful husbandry, over two-thirds of the country remains forested and the majority of the houses I've seen from the single-track main

OPPOSITE

Back to the mountains.
Snowed-in above
Phobjika Valley,
Central Bhutan.

road that runs east from the airport at Paro are combinations of colourfully decorated wood frames and rammed earth walls, reminding me of Alpine chalets and Tudor manor houses.

The village of Gantey, at which we arrived late in the day, is set in restful landscape in the central part of the country, on a hill overlooking the broad glacial valley of Phobjika. Surrounding and enclosing this peaceful place are the Black Mountains, which rising above 16,000 feet (5000 m).

As if to confirm this bewilderingly thorough and barely believable change in our circumstances, light snow is falling outside as I take one last look at the ghostly outlines of wide roofs around us and begin the delicate process of inserting myself, and hot-water bottle, into the narrow neck of my sleeping bag.

Day One Hundred and Four : Gantey

Breakfast conversation is dominated by wet bed stories. As the only one whose hot-water bottle didn't leak, I feel rather left out.

My Bhutanese host and guide has been up for some time doing crossword puzzles, to which he's addicted. Dasho Benji ('call me Benji') is what one might call a larger than life figure. A colourful character. He's the King's cousin, and, over a period of 30 years, has held positions of power in Bhutan from Home Affairs to Chief Justice to Minister of the Environment. No longer a member of the government, he uses his considerable influence to pursue the environmental causes that are his first love. He also likes to go to Calcutta for golf and horse racing and is generous with his drink. He makes no apologies for enjoying the fast life, but now, at the age of 60, he's having to move into the middle lane as his body registers the toll of many happily misspent years. His broad, ruddy face is dominated by a pair of deep-set, ever so slightly bloodshot eyes, which seem naturally attuned to merriment and give little indication of the hard times he has known. His father, who was Prime Minister of Bhutan, was assassinated while in office.

Today, though, he is in impatient mood. He wants to show me something of which he's intensely proud. A colony of black-necked cranes, one of the world's rarest birds, winters in this valley.

The black-necked crane was first identified in 1876, by one of the great explorers of the

RIGHT

Gantey village. With Dasho Benji, wearing traditional kho, *on the lookout for elusive black-necked cranes.*

LEFT

*Successful sighting.
Black-necked cranes
on the wing. They
have migrated from
the other side of the
Himalaya.*

Tibetan plateau, Count Nikolai Przhewalski of the Imperial Russian Army. Of the 16 species of crane, it was the last to be found.

Before 1990 the general estimate was that there were only 800 black-necked cranes in the world. Since China opened up and began to share information that estimate has risen to between 3000 and 5000. They fly down from Tibet and Ladakh every winter and gather here, attracted by the marshy wetland of the valley floor. But there is a complication. The Gantey valley recently discovered a potentially lucrative source of income from the raising of seed potatoes. The soil and air here are free of all the most common diseases from which potatoes suffer, so the seeds are much in demand, especially in India. Plans were afoot to drain the valley and build more farms. Benji fought to prevent the destruction of a unique habitat.

'The government said that, you know, we cannot stop the development of the country for 20 birds. But we found 80 of them.'

He gives a smile of satisfaction.

'And today there are 270.'

He is certain that his close relationship with the King helped. King Jigme Singye Wangchuck, educated in Britain, succeeded to the throne after the death of his father in 1972. He was 27. Before that, I get the impression that he and Benji had some pretty good times together, a sort of Falstaff-Prince Hal relationship. As Benji puts it to me.

'I was his court jester. I used to make him laugh.'

'So saving the cranes was a payback for the times you've cheered him up?'

Benji nods.'I believe that. I believe that very strongly.'

We aren't far from the village when we have our first sight of them. In the brilliant morning sun, some 30 or 40 birds are pecking around for grain and insects in a recently ploughed field. They stand about three feet tall (1m) and look to me like a cross between a goose and a heron, with slender, pale grey bodies, black tails and, of course, black necks. The only splash of colour is a tiny red cap. They aren't arrestingly beautiful by any means, and I suppose I'm a little disappointed that rare doesn't necessarily mean resplendent. Indeed, Benji, in his red and green check *kho* with black, knee-length stockings and pristine white trainers, is a lot more exotic than the birds we've come so far to see. But their rarity has won them respect and the black-necked crane is thought to have great religious significance, proven by the fact that when they first arrive in the valley they always circle the monastery on the hill three times.

Benji takes me up a of past timbered houses, fenced green paddocks and piles of fresh-cut wood, which looks like Switzerland in old photographs. He points out darting finches and snow pigeons with fawn backs and black and white tails, which, he says, are usually to be found much higher up.

At the end of the lane, beside a tumbling stream, is a modern, well-equipped, decagonal building, which houses the Black-Necked Crane Information Centre. Here I learn a little more about these celebrated creatures. Like the shelducks of the Brahmaputra, they mate for life (which adds to religious status, I'm told). They can live for 30 or 40 years.

Two or three mounted telescopes are trained on the swampy valley floor below us. A river dawdles through it, full of brown trout that are never fished, it being against the Buddhist religion to take life. A number of black-necked cranes are already gathered, and more fly in, until there must be 150 birds down there. J-P and Nigel become very excited and discreetly move the camera into a closer position. It's very hard to catch the birds in flight and it's not until Peter walks right round the far side of them (ruining a pair of trousers in the process) that they take, languidly, elegantly and prematurely, to the air.

'I didn't see you do that,' says Benji in his capacity as founder of the Black-Necked Crane Preservation Programme.

In the afternoon we ride a pair of small and very truculent horses up the hill to get a wider view of the valley. Last night's snow lies crisp and even up here, and we unpack our lunch and make a fire.

Benji, once again, didn't see us do this. So strict are the environmental laws in Bhutan's national parks that timber and branches must be left where they fall, and cannot be moved by anyone without special permission. As 28 per cent of Bhutan is designated national park, there's a lot of firewood going begging.

Benji points above us, to the hanging lichens that cover the trees like dust sheets in a shuttered-up house.

'This is an indicator of good-quality air, you know. Shows the air is very good up here.'

In the afternoon we return the horses to the park-keeper and walk back through the village. The houses are good-looking, rectangular in plan and usually of two storeys, the lower one for livestock, the upper for the family, with an open loggia below the roof, not for cocktails or deck chairs at sunset, but for drying crops and storing wood and cattle fodder.

As in Tibet, decoration of the houses is of great importance. In Bhutan an added refinement are the finely drawn paintings on the white, half-timbered walls, some of which are not for the prudish.

I counted about half a dozen painted penises in Gantey village, erect and beribboned, and often emitting a thin trail of cosmic sperm. They seem to be as unremarkable here as a box hedge in Dorking. Françoise Pommaret's *Odyssey Guide to Bhutan* explains that they were inspired by the teachings of one of the country's most popular religious figures, Drupka Kunley, who lived around the turn of the 16th century and was known as the 'divine madman'. He was from a distinguished family and, though he refused to take holy orders, he wandered the country with his own brand of Buddhism, which put the sexual act at the centre of religious experience, and from what we know, he practised what he preached. The fact that his phallocentric ideas are still celebrated says a lot for Bhutan's relaxed attitudes to sex. If you painted a penis on your house in Dorking, you'd probably be arrested.

Benji's enthusiasm for the rural way of life – and over 80 per cent of Bhutanese still work on

the land – seems to be greater than his powers of mobility, but he insists in clambering up steps cut out of a tree trunk to show me the interior of one of the village houses.

A bright girl called Dawa Zangma, which means 'moon', lives here and helps the family income by weaving. She can make a *kira*, with all its complicated colours and patterns, in eight days.

Dawa Zangma is 13, apple cheeked with straight, thick, dark hair. She's about to leave the home and the loom to go to boarding school.

She lays aside her work and helps her mother prepare butter tea, which we drink sitting cross-legged on a small carpet, which is rolled out specially for us. There are, as far as I can see, no chairs in the house, which she shares with her mother, father and two sisters. Benji confirms that in a traditional Bhutanese house where there is little money around life is lived on the floor (which is why they move with much more agility than myself). There is no cutlery and no glass in the windows, which are covered at night by sliding bamboo shutters. Everyone eats or sleeps in the one big room, dominated by the stove at its centre.

The attractive appearance of the houses belies the condition of the villagers. We are still in the Bhutanese winter and those inhabitants who can afford it will have packed up everything and moved to lower slopes with their livestock. Those who stay on may be employed in the reconstruction work at the monastery, but that's about it. A woman, well wrapped up, sits behind the counter of the single local store. On display is a pretty meagre selection of chillies (the *sine qua non* of Bhutanese cuisine), cabbage, cauliflower, beans, potatoes and dried fish from Bangladesh. Though they seem to enjoy eating meat and fish, the Buddhist prohibition on taking life means that it all has to be killed by designated butchers within the country or brought in from outside.

As night falls and the warm sun is replaced by steadily falling snow, we sit around the stove, eating red rice and yak stew and a fierce plateful of what must be one of the oddest national dishes in the world, *hemadatsi*, chillies in a cheese sauce.

Bhutan, which has only had a king since 1907, must now rank as one of the most successful

ABOVE

Evidence of the cult of Drupka Kunley, the 'divine madman', on a house in Gantey village. More common in East Bhutan, these painted penises are believed to ward off evil spirits.

BELOW

Workmen take a tea-break at the Gantey gompa (monastery), which is being refitted. Quite slowly.

monarchies in the world. The current ruler is a widely respected, modest man who prefers to live, not in his palace, but in a log cabin in the grounds.

He tours the country regularly, consulting local people and hosting big meals at which he himself serves the food.

'He's not a king who goes on European holidays,' says Benji.

He is, nevertheless, an absolute ruler. Though he himself is working on a constitution that will limit his power, King Jigme, is to all intents and purposes, free to do as he likes. Benji sees no problem with this.

'It's very important to have an absolute monarch, a guy who cares for the country, who knows where he's taking us. Left to ourselves…we'd be squabbling.'

His policies are all geared to the preservation of Bhutan's cultural identity, and this has led to allegations that outsiders, particularly Nepalese immigrants in the south of the country, are not allowed the same rights as the Bhutanese. Benji sees this as justifiable.

'Small countries like Bhutan, surrounded by larger countries with fast-growing populations looking for land…have to be on the lookout. We don't want the Sikkim syndrome, where Sikkim was just overpopulated by Nepalese. The original people of Sikkim became a minority in their country…they got voted out of power, and then they all voted to become a state of India.'

Bhutan's survival after the war was a triumph of diplomacy and timing. Independence from India was agreed in 1950, just before the Chinese invasion of Tibet. If it had been after the invasion, Benji thinks India might well have wanted to keep control of Bhutan. As it is, the two countries have maintained good relations. Bhutan's biggest export is hydroelectric power, all of which goes to India, and recently the Bhutanese army flushed out insurgents who were using the country as a base for operations into north India.

Benji positively glows with pride.

'Led by our King…we took these terrorists on and in one swift fall knocked them all out in two days. It's amazing how we did it.'

The question is how much longer Bhutan will be able to walk this tightrope between the feudal system (officially abolished in 1953) and a forward-looking future. The King knows what he wants. In May 2004, he announced 'Bhutan and its people are ready to have a democratic political system.'

Day One Hundred and Five : Gantey to Thinpu

The Gantey valley has turned grey overnight. A fresh coating of snow has picked out the field boundaries and transformed the gently sloping, treeless slopes from straw brown to light silver, making this beautiful corner of Bhutan look like the Yorkshire Dales.

From my window I can see a woman from the house behind, in a blouse and long pink skirt, stepping gingerly across the ice to the public water pipe. She brushes a white cap of snow off the top of the tap and starts to wash. The flying droplets of water, back-lit by the morning sun, splash round her face like particles of gold.

Before we leave, we pay a visit to the monastery, or *gompa*, at the far end of the ridge above the valley.

ABOVE

Retail opportunities on the road out of the Phobjika valley. This lady yak herder who so successfully waylaid us made the yak-hair bags herself.

Benji explains that Bhutan may be a Buddhist kingdom, but the sects here are different from those in Tibet. The Galupka school, the Yellow Hats, dominate in Tibet and the Drukpa Kagyu school, the Red Hats, in Bhutan. The Je Khenpo, head of the Drukpa school, is the religious authority here. The Dalai Lama has no jurisdiction in Bhutan and has never visited the country.

The monastery has been undergoing renovation for two years and outside the main door a temporary roof has been erected to shelter a timber yard and workshop. Four craftsmen are at work carving a complex decorative motif on a 50-foot-long, blue-pine beam. One man is using a dagger to carve out a *dorje*, a diamond thunderbolt motif that is a recurrent theme in Bhutan. It's all done by hand, and each has a line of wood-handled tools and a portable radio laid out beside him.

An ancient gateway leads to a big courtyard, in the middle of which, in the Bhutanese style, is the impressive main temple, with the monks' accommodation surrounding it, in single-storey cells with painted lintels, door frames and eaves. It's a building site and looks as though it will be for some time to come.

Over the barking of a pack of dogs I can hear prayers are being chanted from somewhere. The restoration work is largely being done by gomchens, lay monks who don't have to be celibate or live in the monastery. The monks who remain here support themselves by offering their services out for family occasions, providing blessings for births, marriages, deaths, new houses and performing any ceremonies these innately religious people require.

On our way out a dishevelled, tousle-headed young man who can barely walk, approaches us and shows us a deep and nasty gash low on his right leg. Pete, who is a saint in these matters, washes the wound and advises him to go to hospital before it turns gangrenous, but the man says it's been like that for four years. He then starts to sing a love song to me. Benji shakes his head disapprovingly. He says the man's obviously mad. I try not to take this personally.

We head back towards Thimpu, but conditions on the road are much worse than when we came in. Stopping to take a shot of a herd of yaks against the snow, we find ourselves victims of an admirable piece of retail opportunism. A small, doughty lady races out of her tent and sprints a couple of hundred yards through the deep snow up towards us. For a moment, we imagine she's come to shoo us away, or demand a BBC contract, but nothing of the kind. Scrambling up onto the road, she produces a range of yak-hair tote bags and sells all three of them more or less instantly.

Once over the 11,000-foot (3350 m) pass out of the valley, we expect things to get better. Quite the opposite. The snow is deeper and the road icier and much more treacherous. Lichen-clad conifers plunge steeply down on one side of us, disappearing into a cold shroud of mist, so it's hard to tell just how far we might fall if, as seems all too likely, the minibus slides off the road. From marvelling at the delicate beauty of the snowbound forest, thoughts turn swiftly to problems of survival. The normally nerveless Nigel, who, not long ago, was in a serious accident on the ice in Alaska, has the window open on the other side of the bus, ready for a quick exit. We negotiate a score of steep hairpin bends at a snail's pace. The snow is falling more thickly now, and every now and then the wheels slide and we prepare for the worst. After almost an hour of hearts in mouths the snow turns to sleet and the conifers turn to rhododendrons and the dirt track to paved road and we can at last breathe normally again.

The Central Road, which is the only road connecting east and west Bhutan, is less than 20 years old, an indication of the government's ambivalent attitude to the opening up of the country. It twists and turns dizzily around the spurs and shoulders of the mountains. They say the longest stretch of straight road in Bhutan is the runway at Paro airport.

Nevertheless, journeys that took two days now take two hours, and we are in Thimpu by afternoon, and the near white-out on the pass already seems a distant memory.

So too is the gentle timelessness of the Gantey valley.

Thimpu, the capital of Bhutan, is no rip-roaring metropolis, but it has roads and roundabouts (where policemen direct traffic with wonderfully flowing arm movements, as if they're doing t'ai chi) and car parks and cosmopolitan restaurants and banks and hotels and, according to Benji, its very own property boom.

When Thimpu was chosen to be the capital in 1952, it was little more than a few houses clustered around the majestic Tashioedzong, and it grew slowly until 1974, when Bhutan was opened to foreigners for the first time. Since then it has mushroomed and has a current population of 50,000. To accommodate everyone, the rules on traditional house-building seem more liberally applied here and the streets of boringly respectable four- or five-storey blocks look more Mitteleuropean than Bhutanese.

At the Arts Café I meet Tsewang, a young actor and film maker, recently returned from showing his new film 'Travellers and Magicians' at the Deauville Film Festival. It's set in the Bhutanese countryside and in it he plays a man trying to get away from the restrictive world of the village.

He himself was the son of farmers and recognizes that, by many international standards, Bhutan remains backward. Literacy is a little over 50 per cent and television only came here five years ago. But though life is hard, he doesn't think this is a bad thing. Unemployment is quite high here and this worries him more than lack of money.

'The Buddhist version of poverty is a situation where you have nothing to contribute.'

He feels that in Bhutan there is still a strong sense of, as he puts it, 'unison with the earth'.

'In San Francisco I felt lost. Everywhere you go you have billboards telling you that you need to buy this or that, or the latest Cherokee four-wheel drive, but here we have different kind of billboards.'

A coach pulls up and a line of docile tourists file past us into the café.

'We have the prayer flags, we have the temples. These are our markers, you know, reminding you, in the Buddhist way, that you are not here for ever.'

Bearing this in mind, I end the day sampling one of the night-spots of Thimpu, a decorous, well-behaved snooker bar called Rumours. Pretty girls smash balls around the table like old pros and a television set is tuned to live coverage of England's cricket match with the West Indies in Barbados.

Benji, who doesn't like to miss a get-together is sitting at the bar with me and his attractive and urbane cousin Khendum. The talk meanders round to reincarnation. Khendum admits she has 'a little problem with reincarnation'.

She doesn't believe in it.

'I can't reconcile my practising of Buddhism with that aspect of it,' she says with an admirable directness.

Benji has definite preferences.

'I'd like to be reborn as a black 7 foot 6 basketball player who earns a lot of money.'

Khendum gives me a wry smile.

'He'll be a cockroach.'

'Thank you. Thank you very much,' says Benji courteously.

She and Benji are both part of Bhutan's privileged, wealthy, cosmopolitan elite. Like Tsewang, they're outward-looking and internationalist, and though they are fiercely proud of their country's cultural protectionism, all of them accept that change is accelerating and inevitable. As Khendum says, 'We're not romantic or idealistic enough to think that things will always be the way they are now, but we'd like to slow the development process up to a degree that we can handle change when it comes.'

Realistic, sensible and a trifle wistful at the same time.

Day One Hundred and Six : Thimpu to Takstang

The slopes of the Himalaya are rich in plants that have medicinal properties. Used for thousands of years by rural, mountain people, they are now increasingly attractive to an international market seeking an alternative to chemical drugs. The canny Bhutanese government, together with the World Health Organization, recognized this demand and in 1979 set up an Institute of Traditional Medicine, which researches, catalogues and produces herbal remedies. Recent newspaper reports suggest that they might have hit pay dirt, with a product already being tipped as the first 'herbal Viagra'.

The word 'Institute' fills me with ominous images of two-headed dogs and white-coated men with small spectacles, so, as we approach the heart of Bhutan's traditional medicine establishment on a hill above Thimpu, I'm much relieved to find that it's a colourfully decorated, half-timbered building that looks like a well-preserved Elizabethan manor house.

We're welcomed by three serious men, two of whom are called Dorje. They show us around an immaculately laid out display of traditional medicines in a long, library-like room with beamed ceiling and glass cabinets. The debt to Tibetan medicine is acknowledged in the old anatomical charts showing the five wheels or *chakras*, the centres of spiritual power that control

ABOVE

*Khendum waits for
me to explode after a
generous helping of
betel nut.*

all our bodily systems. Traditional Bhutanese medicine also borrowed from the Indian idea that the balance of the Three Humours, bile, wind and phlegm, dictates the state of our physical and spiritual health.

Of their prize discovery they are as bashful and cautious as you would expect government scientists to be. They admit that they are working hard to produce products that will have a commercial application, as it brings in the money to keep the Institute going, and that they have recently concocted a mix of five herbs that 'could possess spermogenetic powers'.

'Increase virility,' adds one of the Dorjes, helpfully.

Their mixture is currently on a two-year test, after which conclusions will be examined. When I enquire about its constituents, glances are exchanged and there are mutterings about bio-piracy and international property rights, but it seems the key ingredient is none other than our old friend *Cordyceps sinensis*, or caterpillar fungus, five pieces of which I bought off the street in Yushu for £4, and which are currently stuck in dust and fluff at the bottom of my bag. They confirm that the tiny little shoots are very difficult to find and though it grows up in the Bhutanese mountains, there is often a fight with Tibetans from across the border to get to it first.

Our hosts line up to bid us goodbye. The idea that these grave and courteous men in matching *khos* might be onto a world-beating sex aid seems as unlikely as it would be desirable.

Early lunch with Khendum at a trendy new restaurant called the Bhutan Kitchen, opened two days ago and alarmingly empty. I meet two of her international friends. Linda, a buxom American, is married to a Bhutanese *thangka* painter and has lived here for seven years.

'I love Bhutan. Bhutan is so relaxed and peaceful.'

'Everyone says that.'

She nods and shrugs.

'But there's nothing else to say about Bhutan.'

Françoise, a lively, funny French lady, who I feel I know already, as she's written the guide book that's become my Bhutanese bible, is a touch more analytical.

'I won't call it Shangri-la but there is a certain magic here, which isn't about wealth,' she says. 'Once you're trapped in, you can't get out. It's a magic trap.'

Khendum has lined up some local gastronomic specialities. As a sharpener, I take rice wine with an egg in it and, noticing the ubiquitous betel nut on the table, I decide that the moment has come for me to sample the Himalayan lorry-driver's staple diet. Khendum prepares it carefully, wrapping the hard nut in its own leaf with a smear of lime paste. The sharp bitterness of the leaf is an ugly taste, but it wears off and after a few minutes of chewing my head begins to heat up as if from deep inside. I feel my eyes water and my cheeks redden as the betel rushes my body onto full alert and soon, like everyone else who chews it, my teeth are stained red and I'm looking for somewhere to spit it out.

The main dishes are challenging. A long, stringy vegetable of some kind seems determined to strangle me from within, smashed chicken and red rice is dotted with small bone fragments and the cow-hide is, well, an acquired taste. One which, I fear, would take armed men with rifles at my head to acquire.

Our time among the flesh-pots of Thimpu is distressingly brief. Tomorrow we head north to Jomolhari mountain to begin a valedictory trek, a farewell to the high Himalaya.

By way of preparation, I plan a short training climb with my guide who, almost unbelievably, is *not* called Dorje. He's called Doje.

In the foothills near Paro is a complex of holy buildings that draws pilgrims from all over the Himalaya. Takstang, meaning 'Tiger's Lair', is built on precipitous rock ledges and, though it remains almost impossibly difficult to get to, there is now a well-trodden tourist trail up to the crags opposite.

We pass a farmhouse, whose walls are painted with motifs of tigers, devils and the curious symbol of a weasel disgorging pearls. Doje explains. The Guardian King of the North Direction traditionally holds a weasel, so anything emanating from a weasel's mouth denotes good fortune. Obvious really.

The clouds pile up as our trail climbs through oak and pine forest. Souvenirs are laid out for sale at every other corner. After an hour and a half's walking, the track levels out at a *chorten* with prayer wheels inside, from which a wide path leads to a log-cabin tea house with wood-burning stove and good local food. Outside is a terrace with fine views of the temple. It is believed to have been founded by the saint Padmasambhava, also know as Guru Rinpoche, who rode here on a tigress in the 8th century and took on terrifying form to chase away the evil spirits and convert the valley to Buddhism.

In 1998 a fire gutted the main sanctuary. Its restoration proved a formidable technological challenge, but it's almost completely rebuilt. Newly carved sections were hauled up from workshops 1000 feet below by a system of ropes and pulleys.

From across the valley, the white walls with the maroon band gleam from the top of the sheer tongue of rock that marks Takstang out as one of the most spectacular holy places anywhere in the world.

Day One Hundred and Eight: Jangothang

Just short of 24,000 feet (7315 m), Jomolhari is one of the highest mountains in Bhutan. Seen from our tiny, fragile campsite, it fills the northwestern horizon, an immense hemispherical slab, hung with mighty crusts of snow and ice save where the rock flanks of the mountain, too steep to hold anything, stand out raw and sheer.

Unlike Everest, which kept a majestic distance, Jomolhari looms very close, a presence so powerful and all-pervasive that at times it seems to be growing before our eyes. Unsurprisingly, this is a sacred mountain and no-one has ever stood on its summit.

The far side of Jomolhari is in Tibet and around it wind narrow passes that have long been used for trans-Himalayan trade. Proof of this lies in the half-collapsed dry-stone walls of a castle, built to control this meeting of two valleys. A track continues up beyond our camp and we follow it

towards Ngile La, a pass at 15,700 feet (4785 m). Another mighty mountain rises close to us. Jichu Drake, at 22,300 feet (6795 m), is a classic Paramount peak, more shapely than Jomolhari, from which a beautiful glacier trails, covering the rocks in gleaming, blue-tinted ice sheets. A milky-green stream leaks from beneath it. We're above the tree line here, but there are yaks and the odd farm, on one of which lives a national character whom Doje is keen for me to meet.

The farmhouse is of the traditional manorial style, surrounded by a compound protected by a five-foot-high wall made from stone and topped with birch twigs and dried yak dung.

Inside the compound is a solar panel unit and a number of archery targets. Archery is the national sport of Bhutan.

We climb an outside staircase, at the top of which waits the bony figure of Choni Dorje. He's 82, and has lived here all his life. He's that happy combination, a yak herder and poet, and a few years back wrote a song extolling the virtues of his favourite yak, called something like 'Jewel of the Mountains'. Describing the beast from horn to tail in loving terms, it struck a national chord and he was asked to Thimpu to sing his song to the King. He doesn't look strong. He has a cataract in one eye, turning it milky blue, white hair tight around a prominent skull, sunken cheeks and a wispy Fu-Manchu beard.

But he seems cheered to see us and happy to give us a tear-jerking rendition of his big hit. Just to bring the tone down, I reply with a verse of the Lumberjack Song, which, sadly, I can never fully remember.

The extraordinary precipice on which Takstang is perched. An ultimate test for any postman.

OPPOSITE
The Himalayas close in again. Jomolhari, nearly 24,000 feet (7300 m) high, stands astride the Tibet-Bhutan border. Ruins in the foreground show that cross-Himalaya trade was once so common, a fort had to be built to protect mountain routes.

ABOVE

Doje and I visit Choni Dorje, poet and yak farmer, who has lived up here for 82 years. He sings me his ode to the yak, which made him a national celebrity. His granddaughter is in the doorway.

Choni Dorje's granddaughter invites us inside to the big, open, timber-floored room, where four generations live together. Bed-rolls are neatly stowed at one side of the room, along with the woven rugs and blankets to keep out what must be bitter cold. A little marmalade cat peers at us from a dark corner. As befits the house of a man who wrote a love song to the animal, there are bits of yak all over the place; haunches of dried yak meat and coiled entrails hang from roof beams and a pile of yak dung is stacked by the cast-iron stove. A small shrine with a Buddha lies behind a curtain off to one side.

As we drink our butter tea, I have to remind myself that Choni Dorje, his family, his yaks and his marmalade cat have lived their entire lives higher than the summit of the Eiger.

Day One Hundred and Nine : Jangothang to Takengthanka

One by one we stumble out onto the frosty grass after a bitterly cold night. The tents are comfortable enough when you're inside, but squeezing through that tight-zippered door is like coming out of the womb. Doje tells me that Jangothang means 'land of ruins' and looking at the state of us, it seems appropriate. I think we've been in the mountains too long. Last night was a sharp reminder of the high-altitude conditions that we thought we'd left behind.

Of course, the payback for the pain is tremendous scenery, unpolluted air, brilliant light and utter silence. And once I'm up and dressed and have splashed some water on my face, I know I shall miss all these things. By tonight the majestic peaks of the Himalaya will be behind us for the last time, so, while the tents are being struck and our ponies loaded up for the journey, I pick my way up past the monolithic boulders rolled down by the glaciers and through the birch scrub and the tough little juniper trees towards Jomolhari. It's a final act of homage to the high mountains and, as Jomolhari fills the sky, I feel a bit like one of the characters in *Close Encounters of the Third Kind* when the spaceship has landed.

The Himalayan peaks are seen by the people who live among them as awful places, abodes of jealous gods and places where the dead are gathered, and I have the feeling they've got it right. What do we know, we who romanticize them? We who fly in and use them to prove something to ourselves, to plant our flags, talk of 'conquest' and then go home. I can almost feel the shoulders of Jomolhari heaving with laughter.

I find a mossy rock and just sit for a while. I look down at our camp, with flocks of alpine choughs swooping noisily in to look for morsels of food, and feel my own personal pangs of regret at leaving all this behind. There are few places outside the Himalaya where the relation of man to nature can be experienced on such a gigantic scale, and something like that may not change your life, but it does stretch it a bit.

Jomolhari is draped in cloud as we set off across the stream and down along the broad, treeless meadow of grass and stones that leads down the valley. Within minutes the mountain is out of sight.

A yak caravan sways up towards us. Doje says he prefers to use horses and donkeys for carrying. He says they're much brighter than yaks and look where they're going.

Jomolhari is 11 miles (18 km) behind us by the time we reach our next campsite. It's in a tight neck of the mountains, where the valley becomes a gorge. Thickly wooded slopes of cedar, blue pine, maple and larch rise behind us and the stream we've followed since it left the glacier is now a river, some 30 feet wide and running fast and clear. A fire has been lit and internal warmth is taken care of by a slug or two of Special Courier Bhutanese Whisky. The description on the bottle, 'brewed at Gelephu Distillery (a unit of Army Welfare Project)', suggests that we are not only warming ourselves but helping the Bhutanese military at the same time. Very odd. Food is served early and I'm one of the last to bed. It's a quarter to nine and snowing.

Day One Hundred and Ten: Takengthanka to Sharna Zampa

My tent flap is heavier when I push it aside this morning. A layer of rime has built up overnight and, as I squeeze out into the world, it brushes across my back, propelling me forwards with a shock.

The sun will take some time to penetrate this steeply enclosed ravine, so breakfast is eaten with gloves, hats and scarves on. Our horse drivers are tucking into mounds of red rice and chillies.

'They can't move without rice and chilli,' says Doje. 'Each man eats a kilo of rice a day.'

I ask him what they eat on special occasions.

'Rice,' he says, predictably. 'Rice with green chilli. Pork slices, dried spinach.'

The horses, meanwhile, nuzzle dried corn from what I've come to call Himalayan nose-bags: plastic footballs sliced in half.

The business of reducing our travelling village to whatever fits on a horse's back is elaborate and time-consuming. Homes are demolished, restaurants closed and packed into boxes, kitchens disappear into bamboo baskets. This morning the horses haul their loads up and over a series of switchbacks, some steep and slippery, before the path begins to flatten out. Very occasionally, we meet people coming the other way. Locals carrying supplies up to the nomads in the higher valleys and, at one point, out of the woods ahead, a party of immaculately dressed Japanese. We descend from the conifer forests and into richer temperate woodlands with flowering laurel and luxuriant rhododendron swelling on either side, and strips of meadow thick with edelweiss and gentian.

But it is a long way and by the time we reach the patch of grassy riverbank near the bridge of Sharma Zampa we've covered another 12 miles (19 km). Nigel is limping from a blistered toe

and Basil is appalled at what he's just done.

'No Pao has *ever* walked as far as this.' He shakes his head in disbelief. 'Never in the entire *history* of Paos has anyone walked 23 miles!' And there's more to go.

But we're down below 10,000 feet (3050 m). The valley is wider and more inviting, the river has broadened to 100 yards wide, and there are some substantial farmhouses on the far bank, where the forest has been cleared and the land terraced for cultivation. Though there is a bridge a mile upstream, most of the traffic from the other bank comes through the river. We watch a packhorse, fully loaded, followed by two women and half a dozen children, pick its way through the shallow but fast-flowing waters, and later two cows and a calf, almost submerged as it struggles desperately to get a grip on the wet rocks, make their way across.

Day One Hundred and Eleven : Sharma Zampa to Paro

I must really have been walked out yesterday, the result being a long, deep, wonderfully restorative night's sleep. Trekking beats any sleeping pill. Doje is tall, good-looking and, until he's had a drop of Special Courier in the evening, quite a serious young man. His mother was the Queen Mother's equerry and maybe that's where his rather dignified correctness comes from. So it's all the more gratifying to hear him getting quite worked up at the breakfast table. Admittedly, it's only about Bhutanese history, but there's a yelp of unalloyed chauvinism as he talks of the Tibetan invaders who used to come down trails like this.

'16th century, 17th century. I think there were nine invasions. And we trashed them!'

Doje shakes his head with relish, as if it had all happened yesterday.

'We sent them back. We sent them back!'

A herd of cows is crossing the river towards us. I think this verdant bank where we camped must be their grazing ground, for, once here, they tuck into whatever doesn't have a tent on top of it, including my jacket. The women who keep an eye on them are a feisty pair. While one looks through Nigel's camera in wonderment, another attacks one of our horsemen after he's made a joke about her, grabbing at his crutch, shrieking with laughter and revealing a perfect set of totally black teeth.

Doje keeps well out of it. He says the ladies up here are tough and can out-wrestle any of the men.

We move on. A magnificent landscape of interlocking, conifer-clad spurs stretches way above us to a mountain with a little tongue of snow and ice still clinging to its north-facing summit. On either side of us are meadows and the widening waters of the River Paro.

Civilization is gradually stretching its fingers up the valley. We pass a large army camp, more and more farms, emerald green paddy fields, orchards ripe with plum blossom. Pigs scuttling about. After five hours of walking, we cross the river on a steel-slung suspension bridge (financed by the Swiss, I notice) and at last onto a paved road. An hour and a half later, we reach the famous Drukgyel *dzong*. This fortress, raised around the time that England was fighting its only Civil War, commemorated one of Bhutan's rousing victories over the Tibetans. Reduced now to little more than a circular keep after a fire started by a butter-lamp in 1951, Drukgyel *dzong* must once have seemed impregnable, standing as it does on a strategically commanding crag overlooking the valley, with Paro on one side and Jomolhari and the Tibetan border, 35 miles (56 km) away, on the other. Now it's a little forlorn.

At its foot is a small, picturesque, alpine village, with two huge cypresses looming above it. The very first house we come to has a fine selection of wall paintings, including a chubby pink penis with wings attached. But best of all, the village contains a bus that will take us the rest of the way into Paro, and the bus contains cold beers.

I pull off my boots and peel down the socks with wondrous relief. One of my toes is bloody but otherwise no ill-effects of the longest, if not quite the most arduous, of our treks so far.

Day One Hundred and Twelve : Paro

The great religious festivals of Bhutan are known as *tsechus* and commemorate the deeds of Padmasambhava, aka Guru Rinpoche, the saint whose rocky perch in Takstang I climbed up to a few days ago. *Tsechu* means 'tenth', which was the day of the month when, by tradition, these deeds took place. Today is the start of the annual five-day *tsechu* in Paro. Primarily a religious event, it's also a big social occasion, with people taking time off from work to dress up in their best outfits and watch dancing, have picnics, attend archery contests, and generally let their hair down. Opening and closing days are the most important and the crowds will be the biggest, so we're up at 5.30 to make sure of a good position. This is also a big draw for tourists and, though only a few thousand come in every year, the hotel accommodation is easily overrun and we're staying in a rented bungalow a half-hour out of town.

We drive in past the airport, so neat, tidy and largely uncontaminated by aircraft that it looks like a toy lay-out. Northeast of the airport and commanding the valley are the imposing white

OPPOSITE

Recording a breakfast interview with Doje at our camp at Sharma Zampa. The local cows can't wait to get rid of us so they can carry on grazing.

OPPOSITE

The pageantry of the
Paro tsechu. *Opening*
day dances in the
courtyard of the
dzong.

walls of the Paro *dzong*. Like the fortress at Drukyel, where we ended our trek from Jomolhari, it was built in the 1640s, in the flush of national victory over the Tibetans. By coincidence, it also suffered a serious fire, being virtually razed to the ground in 1915. Unlike the Drukyel *dzong*, it was restored to its former glory after a special tax was levied throughout the country. Its two longest walls extend for some 500 feet (150 m) and taper gracefully upwards in the Tibetan style. The uppermost of its five storeys have long windows, the main ones projecting out from the wall, and all surrounded by finely carved frames and lintels. A band of ochre paint connects them all up and marks it out as a religious as well as administrative building.

At the main gate stalls are already set up and at one of them a bearded old lay monk, or *gomchen*, stands beside a small table, on which is a brass and silver miniature temple, with drawers that open to reveal various gilt figures of the gods. As people go by, they tuck the odd *ngultrum* note into his temple. He makes no acknowledgement of the contribution, but stares ahead, keeping up a low, monotonous, gurgling chant. He's not the slightest bit fazed when a sudden yowling and barking breaks out beside him, as two packs of Bhutan's ubiquitous stray dogs (which, of course, no-one is allowed to cull) fight for territory at the bottom of the entrance steps. After some vicious teeth baring, they're seen off and we climb up to the grand, carved doorway. The *dzong* is as impressive inside as out. There are two main stone-flagged courtyards on either side of a massive central tower. Timber-frame galleries run above the squares, connecting up the accommodation.

The opening ceremony takes place in the smaller, lower courtyard, which is hung with swathes of yellow silk, billowing out from a beamed loggia.

Out of 6000 monks supported by the government of Bhutan (there are 3000 others who live off private patronage), 200 live and work in this *dzong*, and before the crowds gather, I take a peek inside their rooms. The atmosphere seems very much like that of a Victorian public school. There are wood-panelled partitions, pegs on walls, dormitories with bare wood floors and rows of shoes at one end. I almost expect to see Dr Arnold striding round the corner of one of the dim and dusty corridors, heels clicking on the stone floor.

The courtyard is filling up. In the buildings on the far side boys faces peep out and figures in maroon robes flit across the windows, their shaved heads catching the sunbeams.

There are a few tourists, but they're heavily outnumbered by local people, and heavily out-dressed as well. Not for the Bhutanese the polyester or the Gore-Tex. For them it's fine cotton and silk brocade, or hand-woven wool, individually patterned. Colours and designs are bold but never brash. I've rarely seen showing-off done with such subtlety.

There are no rows of seats, no tickets, no security staff bristling with head-sets. Spectators are left to sort themselves out, though there is a jolly, smiling actor brandishing what looks like a cat o'nine tails, who occasionally intervenes to help little children and performers get to the front.

First in the arena are the *atsaras*, clowns with bright red costumes and face masks dominated by exaggerated, beaky noses. They look like Mr Punch. Some carry painted wooden phalluses, which they use for crowd control. In their half-frightening, half-funny masks they are extremely effective at everything, from keeping the crowd back to chasing off stray dogs who want to take part. They also keep the crowd's spirits up with slapstick routines. Doje tells me that the *atsaras*, like court jesters, have licence to mock anyone involved in the *tsechu*, including the monks. This is quite necessary, as the long dances can become a bit tedious and are notably short on laughs.

They are, however, astonishingly rich in costume. From the very first number, described in the programme as Dance of the Lord of Death and His Consort, the profusion of colour and design, the sheer quantity of brocaded silk on display, the exuberance of the ankle-length robes with their wide, swirling sleeves, is marvellous to behold.

Big, expressive, brilliantly coloured masks complement the sumptuous costumes. If the deities are to be portrayed then they must be portrayed in all their terrible, magnificent glory. The music that accompanies the dance is played on eye-catching instruments ranging from the seven-foot-long Tibetan trumpets they call *dungchen* to painted and tasselled double-sided drums that look like cushions. Oboes, bells, cymbals, conch shells and a small horn made from a shin bone contribute to the clashing, tinkling, plangent sound.

As the morning goes on, the crowd swells, more and more people squeezing into the limited space around the perimeter until it's barely possible to avoid being pushed forward. It gets hotter, the high bright sun slicing the courtyard in two, reminding me of the *sol y sombra* of a Spanish bullring.

The Dance of the Lord of the Cremation Grounds is followed by the Dance of the Black Hats. I don't know the significance of these dances and the English translations are not always enlightening: 'on the external edges of a symbolic mandala where the assembly of the secret tantric deities are residing.' What is impressive is the poise of the dancers, often carrying enormously heavy costumes and headdresses, as they trip, turn, whirl and pirouette on the hard stone flags. In the last dance I see, The Dance of the Drum From Dramitse, the Black Demons are vanquished by the splendour of the White Gods, who swirl round in golden silk skirts hung with precious jewels. It is outlandish, frequently inexplicable and very wonderful.

Day One Hundred and Fourteen : Paro

After two days at the *tsechu* I take back all I said about Bhutan being an empty country. It feels as if, apart from two or three people left up in the mountains to look after the yaks, the entire nation is here in Paro. At certain times of the day, it's queuing only on the elegant covered footbridge leading across the river and up to the *dzong*. I've heard rumours of over-booked hotels with tourists having to camp out in the grounds.

Dust rises from the crowds wandering through the temporary market, which has spread between the *dzong* itself and the out-buildings nearby, where much of the dancing now takes place. There are makeshift cinemas and fairground games like hoop-la and even bingo. I pass a packed tent where a Bhutanese man calls the numbers in a remarkably plummy English accent.

'How do you do? Three and Two.'

Nearer the dancing, every inch of grass is taken up by picnicking families, many of whom look as if they have come down from the mountains. They unroll portions of seasoned pork and chilli, mushrooms and eggs and drink butter tea from thermoses. For them, *tsechu* is both pilgrimage and party.

Having devoted most of this morning to the Dance of the Judgement of the Dead, I feel in urgent need of some light relief and take up Khendum's invitation to join her for an archery match.

For her, this means watching only. In one of the rare examples of sex discrimination in Bhutan, women are not allowed to take part in traditional archery competitions. Two other reasons why I'm relieved to be, like her, a spectator, are that it looks pretty difficult and most of the participants are roaring drunk.

The hospitality tent, set on a pretty, willow-strewn meadow, is full of bonhomie. Long, rambling stories are told, one man sings 'Waltzing Matilda' at full volume, another lurches by with a whisky and loud yell, another becomes droolingly amorous. Khendum introduces me to them.

One is the Secretary of Employment, another the Managing Director of the National Bank. Others are chairmen of this and that. I realize this is no ordinary hospitality tent. These are the

movers and shakers of Bhutan, letting their hair down. And why not?

Well, I suppose one reason why not is that they will shortly be loosing off arrows at enormous speed in a field that contains not just the target but also women, dogs and small children.

The national game, they keep trying to tell me, is taken extremely seriously and any young Bhutanese boy, in a village or a palace, learns the skills early on. However, it's clearly not a solemn sport. Though women are not allowed to play, they have an important role as vocal supporters.

Khendum tells me, with much amusement, that the night before a match the men sleep together in a dormitory with the door locked, as sex before a big game is considered bad luck.

She shakes her head in some disbelief.

'So the women are integral to the game, but the night before they don't want anything to do with them.'

Taunting is also an integral part of the game. Before a man shoots, it is the duty of his opponents to put him off by any means short of physical contact. Personal comments demeaning his appearance, physical irregularities, masculinity and the disloyalty of his wife are not only permitted but encouraged.

When the time comes, the team stagger out of the tent, exchange their drinks for huge, deadly, metal alloy bows, do a little dance, then line up to fire at a target 30 inches high, and 150 yards away. The extraordinary thing is that most of them either hit it or come damn close. I suppose that's the ultimate macho achievement. To be able to drink yourself silly and deliver a bull's eye while being told by your opponents that they've been shagging your wife for the last three weeks.

ABOVE

A rare quiet moment during the festival, on the old footbridge at Paro.

End up the day on a very different note. In the Queen Mother's Temple, a ceremony has been laid on to wish us good fortune for the rest of the journey. In a room, covered in beautifully detailed paintings of the various stages of the Buddha's life and incarnations, a group of eight monks has assembled for music and prayers. The chantmaster, or *udze,* sits on a dais and leads a chant in Cholkay, a variation of the Sanskrit in which Buddha himself wrote. The other monks chant with him or play oboes, drums, cymbals and the *dungchen,* the long trumpet that rests on the floor and makes a deeply mournful sound.

It's a serene and rather moving ceremony, quite unexpectedly interrupted by the sound of a mobile phone. An elderly monk, next to the chantmaster, fishes around inside his habit and switches it off.

Day One Hundred and Fifteen : Paro

The highlight of the last day of *tsechu,* and, indeed, the highlight of the festival itself, is the unfurling of the greatest treasure of the Paro *dzong.* It's a *thangka* measuring almost 100 feet (30 m) by 150 feet (45 m), and is known as a *thongdrol.* The survival of this huge tapestry when the *dzong* burnt down in 1915 only added to its reputation and merely to look on it conveys the very highest merit. *Thongdrol* means 'liberation by sight'.

To avoid such a precious object being damaged by the direct sunlight, it is unrolled at dawn, so our last full day in the Kingdom of the Thunder Dragon begins at 3 am.

When our bus pulls out onto the main Thimpu to Paro road, the valley seems to be already awake, if indeed it ever slept. Lights are on in the houses, buses and taxis are picking up people along the roadside. To add to the sense of great events, a full moon stares down from a cloudless sky.

Pilgrims are pouring over the covered bridge, fingers telling prayer beads and lips moving as they join a candle-lit procession winding its way up the hill. It's a quiet crowd. Buddhism is celebrated in song and chanting, but prayers are never shouted or hymns bellowed, and this morning the great throng, which must number several thousand, is almost silent.

In front of the five-storey building that will be completely covered when the *thongdrol* is unfurled, a line of butter lamps is lit. The men wear *khos,* of course, but today they also have white scarves across their shoulders and some wear them over their heads, lending an incongruous touch of the mosque.

To the sound of drum and bell, monks in procession emerge onto the forecourt and, dividing into two lines at right angles to the building, sit on the ground while the abbot, in a gold silk robe, takes his place on a raised dais between them.

Once this glittering scene is settled, the *thangka* is rolled out, up from the ground to the roof. At its centre is the figure of Padmasambhava, 20 feet high, flanked by his two consorts. In a circle around him are depictions of his eight manifestations.

The pilgrims press forward and, one after the other, pass along the base of the *thangka,* touching it, saying a prayer, and, in some cases, covering their heads with it.

Dancers come out now and some particularly intrusive, flash-popping tourists meet their match. As they push forward for their trophy close-ups, a couple of them are sent flying by a whirling dancer.

The dawn light slowly fills the sky, and as the time draws near for the *thongdrol* to be put away for another year, the line of pilgrims wanting to touch it surges forward. Not for the first time at *tsechu* I fear for the children and the frail older people who get caught up in this religious fervour. I count only six police at the front to deal with any emergency. But somehow, it never gets nasty or aggressive. The joy on the faces of those close to the *thongdrol* speaks of fulfilment not frustration.

The chill of the night softens and the sun begins to climb, revealing the full glory of this immense tapestry and the size of the crowd, banked right up the hill on both sides, that has been drawn here to see it. I turn away and look out over the shining walls and towers of the fortress to the mountains rolling away towards the looming Himalaya. This is a ceremony to match the landscape. A collective act of belief, bringing together the mountains and the faith that people need to survive them.

BELOW

The climax of tsechu *is the unfurling of an enormous* thangka *that envelops an entire five-storey building. It is brought out once a year and always at dawn to avoid damage from direct sunlight.*

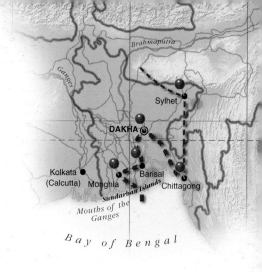

Brahmaputra

Ganges

Sylhet

DAKHA

Kolkata
(Calcutta) Monghla Barisal
Sundarban Islands Chittagong

*Mouths of the
Ganges*

Bay of Bengal

Bangladesh

Day One Hundred and Seventeen: Near Sylhet, Bangladesh

AT THEIR CLOSEST point Bhutan and Bangladesh are some 25 miles (40 km) apart, yet they could scarcely be more different. One is entirely composed of mountains, the other flat as a pancake. One is among the least crowded countries in the world, the other the most densely packed. One is an absolute monarchy with a stable government, the other a people's republic that has just topped the list of the world's most corrupt countries. But there is something that unites them: the Himalaya.

Bhutan's seclusion and stability is due largely to the physical inaccessibility of the Himalayan mountains. Bangladesh's survival is due to the water that pours off them.

Bangladesh, three times as big as Bhutan, with 75 times the number of people, has a population of around 135 million, and the only reason it can support so many is because two of the greatest mountain rivers, the Ganges and the Brahmaputra, funnel down through the country on their way to the sea, depositing billions of tonnes of rich, recycled Himalaya.

Combined with the heavy monsoons that are the blessing and the bane of Bangladesh, this gives the country some of the most productive land in Asia. The price they pay is frequent and frighteningly destructive. The most recent serious flood, in 1998, inundated two-thirds of the country and left 22 million people homeless.

The River Pijain, in the northeast of the country, falls, not strictly from the Himalaya, but from that older rock on which Nagaland and much of western Myanmar rests. As soon as it enters Bangladesh it is harvested. Not so much for fish or crop cultivation but for stones. The country is strong on mud but very short on stone and the river bed at Jaflang, just across the border from India, is like an open-cast quarry, combed by several hundred freelance quarriers. Men, women and children, in narrow flat-bottomed skiffs, put out onto the lazy, meandering waters and dredge for stones and gravel, which they take ashore to be carried by trucks to the crushing plants that line the road for many miles.

In the West all this would be done by machines and conveyor belts: in Bangladesh, human labour is abundant and cheap. For a day's work collecting stones, unskilled workers earn the equivalent of 70 pence.

To survive in such unregulated conditions you need an eye for the main chance and while the

OPPOSITE

By the shores of the Bay of Bengal. Avenue of palms at Katka in the Sundarbans National Park.

boatmen are arguing over who gets the BBC's custom, a bright-eyed, obliging young man seizes his opportunity and offers me a ride out onto the river. It's only after the smoke-belching little outboard has kicked in and we're heading towards a very low, makeshift bridge with ten-tonne trucks rolling across it that I first take a good look at my crew. The captain is probably no more than 14 and his first officer 8 at the most.

None of the boats on the river look like the sort you'd find at Henley Regatta, but ours is easily the scruffiest tub on the Pijain. The metal hull is leaking quite spectacularly. A series of small fountains erupt from the bottom of the boat as if it had been raked by tracer fire. The eight-year-old picks up a plastic bottle and bails out enthusiastically, stopping every now and then to flash me a big, reassuring smile.

By the time we reach the furthest of a succession of gravel bars I've developed considerable respect for my under-age crew.

All around us there are people sieving, sorting and sifting alluvia. Pencil-thin wooden punts are packed with boulders and gravel until they are so low in the water that it seems one extra pebble might be enough to sink them. This low-tech quarrying looks to be a family activity largely undertaken by the very poor. Out in mid-stream young boys dive for stones. From the bank a line of elderly men toss roped buckets into the water and slowly draw them in. Wives and sisters are sizing the stones and putting them in piles.

Wandering in the middle of all this are relatively affluent day-trippers, who obviously see this stretch of the Pijain as something of a beauty spot. They sit in chairs, buy soft drinks off the heads of itinerant salesmen and have their photos taken. A group of boys and girls walk arm in arm, suddenly breaking apart to splash water at each other. Bearing in mind that Bangladesh is 90 per cent Muslim, it's interesting to see girls, unveiled, hand in hand with boys in public. It's a reminder that, unlike Pakistan, Bangladesh is not an Islamic republic, it's a secular democracy.

As I scramble off the cheerfully leaky boat back onto the shore, thinking what an odd and unfamiliar world this is, where holidaymakers mingle with crushers, trucks and small hills of gravel, I hear my name called in a Bangladeshi-Cockney accent.

'Michael!'

A man detaches himself from a family group and bounds up to me.

'I'm from Milton Keynes.'

He's a chef in a restaurant there, coming back to visit his home country, a rich man by Bangladeshi standards. He says there are many like him from this part of the country.

On our way to Sylhet, we see the other side of the coin. The roadside is lined with piles of stones, carefully sifted and laid out to be crushed, either in machines or by roadside gangs, very often female. Many of these stoneworkers have come across the border from Myanmar and are not welcome. The Burmese immigrants in Bangladesh are as much of a sore point here as the Bangladeshi immigrants are in India.

Near Sylhet, the stone industry is replaced by undulating tea gardens, and we spend the night at a plantation home turned into a guesthouse called The White House and run by a slow-moving, chain-smoking, very bright, very laid-back man called Kais Chowdhury.

This was his family house. It was burnt down in the vicious war of 1971, when this country was called East Pakistan and the Pakistan army came in very hard to quash any hopes of secession. They lost and, helped by the Indians army, Bangladesh came into being at the end of that year. But it left behind scars and a lot of people who claim to have been 'freedom fighters' at that time. This substantial, spacious and attractive house, with its deep verandahs, is, sadly, in slow decline. Water squeezes arthritically from the taps and disappears even more slowly down the plugholes; the wiring is eccentric and some switches require considerable effort just to find them. The White House has some grace and charm but it also has a fatal inertia, as if it's being slowly strangled by the rich profusion of tropical flowers and shrubs that spill over onto it, mounting the walls and climbing over the balustrades.

BELOW

(left) A woman sorts out her day's catch of stones. (right) With my schoolboy crew.

All evening and long into the night, trucks from the stoneworks thunder along the road close by. Kais says that the opposition party has called a *hartal*, a protest strike against the government, for tomorrow, and the truck-drivers are hurrying to get their work done before the morning.

It's apparently the second *hartal* this week. After the steely discipline of Bhutan, my first day in Bangladesh has been, well, different.

Day One Hundred and Eighteen : Sylhet

'The Londonis' is the local name for those Bangladeshis who have made a lot of money from running restaurants and allied businesses in places like Brick Lane in East London and brought the money back to build opulent houses in their home country. Sylhetis, more Assamese than Bengali, have a reputation for being clannish, for sticking together and helping each other, and have done particularly well in England. The evidence is all over the town, in row after row of fresh-built mansions in the International Rich Style. The paint is hardly dry on some of these urban palaces, stacked with a riot of cornices, columns, pediments, balconies and burglar-proof fences. They should, one feels, all be set in ten-acre compounds, but there's no room here, so they jostle together in streets that have not yet been paved.

Abdul Rahman was one of the first successful Sylheti emigrants to Britain. He meets me outside a multistorey block of apartments he's just had built. He's dressed simply in a lungi (a

long white cloth worn round the waist and legs) and a hand-embroidered white shirt. He is carrying a hookah and puffing at it nervously. His wife died five days ago and he's not sure whether he should be talking to us at all. But in the courtyard back at his house, with various members of his family watching from the doorways, he proves to be engaging company. Mr Rahman has had three nationalities thrust upon him in his lifetime. Born an Indian in 1929, he became briefly Pakistani, when Muslim East Bengal was hived off at Independence in 1947, and finally Bangladeshi in 1971.

Despite being in his late seventies, he's an energetic, impulsive and tactile storyteller, all eyes and teeth.

'When I went to England first,' he turns towards me, wide-eyed, as if about to divulge an enormous secret. 'There was not any motorway *at all*. Wasn't *any* motorway in England.'

The conversation veers from the Pinteresque, 'Do you know Bewdley?' to the Pythonic, 'The only word I knew was "garlic".'

This didn't help when he got his first job, in a steelworks. When a workmate asked him how old he was, he had to guess at what he meant.

'I gave him my tongs.'

The man asked him again how old he was.

'Then I give him my overalls.'

Eventually, Abdul Rahman learnt English well enough to attempt his first, and perhaps most important, deal. He sold a chicken he'd bought for two shillings and sixpence to someone for ten shillings. By the end of the next year he was a poultry magnate, selling 12,000 birds a week, and, in the process, becoming the first official halal butcher in England.

With colourful hand gestures he illustrates why he considers halal killing to be superior.

He mimes a man holding a chicken.

'English way, squeeze and pull. We think this is a cruel way.' He pauses again, mouth open wide.

'Muslim way, you cut like this. Very sharp knife, quick throat, let the blood out, and she very nicely sleep. This is halal way.'

He maintains that the houses he's put up in Sylhet are for his extended family and not for profit.

'That is our tradition here.'

In any case, it cost him a lot of money. Land is expensive here, he says, more expensive than London or New York.

'Because the people who run my country, they always want money for this and that.' Bribes, he alleges darkly, are an essential part of any transaction. His hand is on my arm again and his eyes bore into mine.

'I speak true. I always speak true.'

There is a pause, and then a last big, toothy laugh.

ABOVE

The engaging Abdul Rahman, who became a poultry magnate in the Midlands before returning to Bangladesh to build homes for his family.

Day One Hundred and Nineteen: Chittagong

Have a lie-in this morning. Unfortunately, it's at the Harbour View Hotel in Chittagong. I have a distinct feeling that they are demolishing the room above me. Roars, thumps and metallic crashes above my head mingle with a tumult of car horns in the street below and ear-splitting bursts of pneumatic drilling from a building site opposite.

I pull back the curtains for a view of the harbour, but can't see it anywhere, and I'm on the tenth floor. Instead, there is a wall of concrete right opposite me, smeared grey-black as if it had been in a fire. Dozens of slight, spindly figures are at work on top of it, either demolishing it or building it. It's hard to tell.

I fear this unpromising start to the day is not entirely fair on Chittagong. We've come here, after all, in search of industrial destruction and dereliction, at the legendary ship-breaking yards further down the coast, and have no time to investigate the old bazaar or the wooded hills that rise out of the heart of Bangladesh's busy second city.

We drive out to the south, past the port that stretches along the banks of the River Karnaphuli, with its armada of mixed traffic, from break-bulk freighters to sailboats that look like sampans, waiting out in the roads. We follow the coast road through straggling suburbs and villages. Our driver hurtles along, firing off blasts of the horn at anyone and anything that moves. Basil notices that the driver's thumb is in such continuous use that it's worn a hole through the plastic on the steering column.

With some relief, we pull off the main road and up a narrow dirt lane to the ship-breaking yard, one of several along this coast that have taken advantage of a plentiful cheap labour force to grab a lion's share of what was once a lucrative market. We're welcomed by the manager of the yard, a bearded, thoughtful man with dark glasses and a wide, embroidered shirt, not the sort you'd expect to be running such a rough and ready business. He leads us up a concrete stairwell and out across a patio, past serried ranks of toilets and washbasins that have been stripped off the ships. He shows us into a room where refreshments have been prepared and we take coffee and biscuits looking out over a panorama of sanitary fittings and hear about the state of the industry. It's not good. A quarter of a century since ship-breaking businesses first sprang up on this stretch of coast only two or three remain. The privately owned Bangladeshi yards are finding it very hard to compete with their state-financed Chinese rivals.

We walk outside and up onto the level above for a view of the yard. It is an extraordinary sight. Dismembered sections of once-mighty ships are scattered across a blackened, oily beach, like the remains of some disastrous invasion. Two ships stand off-shore, awaiting their fate. Furthest away is the *Ocean Breeze*, a sizeable cruise liner. With her trim white superstructure and matching navy-blue hull and funnel, she looks more like she's on a maiden voyage than in her death throes. Nearby is a supertanker, the *Luccott*. Every now and then, a shower of sparks spills down her hull as the oxy-acetylene torches begin eating her away from inside.

I hardly notice the Bay of Bengal. It's grey and neutral here, like a workshop floor, and it comes as something of a jolt to realize that this is my first sight of the sea in six months of travelling.

Above the shoreline, slices of ships sit marooned in the sand like giant sculptures. The further they are from the sea, the less recognizable they become, until great leviathans are finally reduced to their component parts, piles of pipes, cylinders, air vents, staircases, propellers, lamps, doors and portholes, stacked neatly next to each other.

The manager, who says it takes six to seven months to break down a big ship, tells me that the money is not made from spare parts but from the bulk steel. There is enough in each supertanker to build two skyscraper blocks.

I walk down onto the beach. The stranded sections, an entire boiler room, a beehive of exposed cabins, pipe systems like prehistoric animals, have a mournful beauty, but otherwise it's like Dante's inferno. The once golden sand is in a chronic state, pock-marked with grease, oil, human and animal excreta, sinister patches of blue asbestos and scarred by trenches gouged by steel cables dragging heavy metal up the shore. The workforce, supplied by private contractors and brought in from other parts of the country, swarm like ants over corpses. Surrounded by jutting, often jagged, edges of solid steel, flying sparks, falling metal and billows of evil-smelling black smoke, they seem desperately short of protective clothing. Headscarves, oil-stained trousers and T-shirts, baseball caps and sandals seem to be the order of the day for labourers, but even skilled men like welders can be seen operating without goggles or workboots. Tools are basic. Apart from the oxy-acetylene torches, most of the demolition work is done with hammer and crowbars. I see a cylinder block being carried away by two boys of school age.

It's not only ships that are on the scrap heap here.

On the main road outside, almost every shop is selling some kind of marine salvage, from taps and towel rails to crockery and capstans. One salesman stands proudly in front of a pond full of orange lifeboats.

Later, as our Biman flight from Chittagong descends into Dhaka, the Bangladeshi capital, I can see for the first time the full extent of the watery plain created by the great rivers. From up here I can easily believe the astonishing statistic that Bangladesh has 5000 miles (8000 km) of navigable waterways. Sometimes it's hard to see where earth and water separate, as the coiling river courses twist and turn and tangle with each other. Villages, marked out by clumps of trees, cling to raised mud banks like vessels adrift in a flat green sea.

Nearer Dhaka the riverbank is lined with brick kilns, all built on the same pattern, symmetrically laid out around a single towering chimney, looking like ancient temples.

Apparently, there are 2000 of them around the capital, and though they look rose-red and eye-catching in the evening sun, every one belches out clouds of unfiltered smoke particles that drift across what they say is already the most polluted big city on earth. Well, whatever it is, we're in it.

Day One Hundred and Twenty One : Dhaka

You need help to enjoy Dhaka. You certainly need help to understand Dhaka. Otherwise, you might easily be scared off. In 1971 the population was one million. Even conservative estimates believe that number to have grown to 15 million, and with 80 per cent of the country's jobs

LEFT

Toilets that have travelled the world. Nothing is wasted at the ship-breaking yards near Chittagong.

FOLLOWING PAGES

Sculpture park or knacker's yard? The Ocean Breeze (in the background, out at sea) awaits its turn to be disembowelled.

located here, there's little sign of this headlong growth rate slowing down. I've been warned that getting around can be slow and uncomfortable, but I have great faith in my companion Ishraq Ahmed, a short, canny man with a trim beard and an immense list of contacts.

This morning's *Bangladesh Observer* carries front-page reports of the second *hartal* this week. Both leading parties use these one-day strikes as political weapons and there are reports of marches, arrests, accusations, counter-accusations and several deaths in violent clashes with the police. The paper's mailbag seems united in condemning yesterday's action. Today, Dhaka is back to normal. This means unmoving lines of cars, trucks, buses, and over-revving, smoke-belching tuk-tuks, interwoven with any number of the estimated 700,000 bicycle rickshaws that offer a sporting alternative to the traffic jam.

There seem to be very few rules of the road. Road sense, in Dhaka, is knowing how to get to your destination by any means possible.

'It's the only country in the world where every one has right of way,' says Ishraq, with, I detect, a certain quiet pride.

There's a bracing, nerve-shredding excitement to Dhaka's street life, especially as we near the river, at the heart of the old city, where the traffic is infiltrated by hundreds of people weaving in and out of the crush, dodging from warehouses to shops to dealers with heads and shoulders full of anything from fish to electric fans and company ledgers to car parts.

There are women in black burkhas and women in riotously coloured saris, men in white skull caps and long robes, men in dark glasses with two-piece suits. Ishraq is emphatic that Bangladesh is ideologically tolerant and politically diverse. This may be part of its problem but it also explains the relative absence of the religious fundamentalism we saw in Pakistan.

We emerge from the press of markets and wharves and out onto the wide open spaces of Friendship Bridge Number 2, a graceful, grey curve slung across the River Buriganga by gift of the Chinese government. Adverts for 'Green Love' condoms have been slapped onto its concrete columns and beneath it is surely one of the most tumultuous stretches of river on earth. It

reminds me of those paintings of the lagoon in Venice or the Pool of London in their heyday, before there was any other way of shifting goods and people en masse. The parallel is relevant. Only a few miles upstream from downtown Dhaka, the Ganges (known here as the Padma) meets the Brahmaputra (re-christened the Jamuna) and a combined total of 3357 miles (5730 km) of water sweeps on down to the sea. The only form of transport that can adequately deal with the delta is waterborne. Hence the ranks of multistoreyed ferries, drawn up off-shore like floating new towns, the broad-bottomed junks fat with sacks of rice, the smeared and shabby freighters carrying steel rods twisted like barley sugar, the barges almost invisible beneath cones of sand and, everywhere, the slim, low-slung, cigar-shaped water taxis waiting to launch out into the middle of this mayhem.

I walk down to the shore below the bridge. A line of men, teeth clenched and bow-legged with the weight, scuttle up the riverbank with blocks of ice on their heads. Others emerge, like a line of ants, from within the dark hold of a barge, balancing wide baskets full of sand ballast as they negotiate a wobbling gangplank. A pye dog, all sores and clouded eyes, collapses in the shade of a van. When I get out my notebook, a curious crowd presses against me. The *Lonely Planet Guide* devotes a whole column to 'Staring': 'The Western concept of privacy is not a part of the culture in Bangladesh,' it warns, and I can see what they mean. I find it as much comical as threatening, as 20 or more people all peer over my shoulder to try and see what I'm writing in a very small book. When I stop writing, all eyes turn to my face, watching expectantly. When I resume, they go back to the book, following every line and curve with the utmost concentration.

Just when I think they may be with me till the end of the series, they're distracted by shouts of indignation from the film crew, who, it appears, have been peed on from the bridge above. Whether intentionally or not, no-one seems to know. I try to console Nigel by telling him there's a first time for everything, but he's not in a humorous mood.

Despite the oil, the grime, the smell and the procession of unspeakable things flowing along it, the River Buriganga is lined with impromptu laundries. The crew of a timber barge wash their

ABOVE

A very few of the estimated 700,000 bicycle rickshaws in Dhaka, Bangladesh's capital. Individually decorated in bright, bold patterns, they can often move faster than the city's grid-locked motor traffic.

clothes by treading them inside old oil drums, before taking them out and beating them hard on wooden planks and tossing them onto a pile, from which they're picked up and laid out to dry on the sand. The odd thing is that they do look sparkling clean.

I am intrigued, and impressed, by the number of women in high positions in Bangladesh. The two main parties, the Bangladesh National Party and the Awami League (the ones responsible for the current wave of *hartals*) are both led by women. One of the most successful groups of garment factories, employing 7000 people and exporting 68 per cent of their output to the USA alone, is run by the highly charming Rubana Huq and her husband, but she is the one who travels the world and brings in the orders.

In early afternoon Ishraq takes me to meet Naila Chowdhury, a director of Grameen Phone, one of the great success stories to come out of Bangladesh. Naila, impressively built, with a strong handsome face, is, like Rubana, charming, accommodating and, I suspect, pretty ruthless when necessary.

'Grameen' means village and the villages of Bangladesh are poor. To try and help break the spiral of poverty, a man by the name of Muhammad Yunus came up with the idea of micro-loans aimed at the rural poor, who maybe need a few extra *taka* to buy a cow or a plot of land or a sewing machine. He set up the Grameen Bank 25 years ago and now it has over three and a half million borrowers, 95 per cent of whom are women. (Grameen prefer to lend to women, as they're less likely to run off with the money.) The Grameen Phone project is an extension of the idea. A woman in the village takes out a loan to buy a mobile telephone and a solar panel with which to recharge it. She earns money to pay back the loan by charging local people for calls, both within the country and internationally. A lot of Bangladeshis are migrant workers in places like Saudi Arabia and the Gulf.

The women have three years to pay back the loan, and to prevent the whole scheme suffering the fate of well-intentioned causes in a cruelly commercial world, the interest is a hefty 20 per cent.

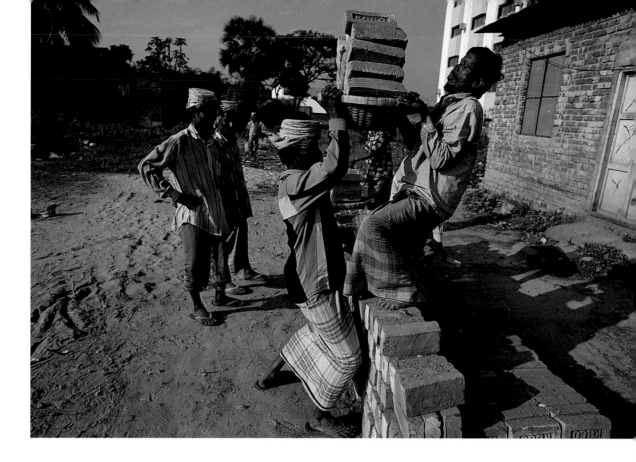

The results, as Naila explains to me, as we drive out to the countryside some 25 miles (40 km) from Dhaka, have been impressive. Grameen Phone has led to the empowerment of women and the empowerment of local village communities.

Not only are villagers able to talk with family members abroad, but villages themselves are able to talk to each other. They can compare prices of basic goods like seed and fertilizer and avoid being ripped off by unscrupulous suppliers.

'They can't be hoodwinked,' as Naila puts it.

Watched by a small caravan of Grameen advisers and feeling rather like a royal visitor, I'm led by Naila, wearing a smart orange and yellow *shalwar*, black, medium-heeled, leather shoes and rolled umbrella, along a narrow mud path between the fields. Pumps chug away, irrigating the rice paddies, and families of ducks are scudding about among the young shoots. Naila finishes a call and snaps her mobile shut.

'I love my work,' she says, steadying herself to cross an unsympathetic patch of wet, sticky mud, 'I love it so much.'

She apologizes for her executive outfit, but she has a big business meeting later. I ask her if the endemic corruption everyone talks about here hinders her work. She shakes her head. Bribes are a commonly accepted part of the system, if you want things to get done fast.

'They call it speed money,' she says. 'It's not always such a bad thing.'

Passing by a field of lentils, with fragrant blue flowers and clumps of bamboo with bee-eaters darting in and out of them, we reach Athalia village. In a month's time, when the monsoon starts, we could not have walked here, for the surrounding fields become a lake and stay that way for half the year.

A reception committee is waiting to meet us as we scramble up the bank, and we're led into the village, composed of around 30 huts of palm thatch and corrugated iron. The huts are built on hard, smoothed mud, freshly treated with liquefied cow dung, which seals the clay and keeps it waterproof. There is no electricity here. The village phone has been held for the last four years

OPPOSITE

*In downtown Dhaka
it's quicker to deliver
by hand, or shoulder,
or head.*

by Mrs Abida Sultan, a short, middle-aged woman with prominent, gold-rimmed glasses and matching gold watch. She is shy and rather quiet today, continually readjusting her pale pink sari modestly over her head, in a way that makes me think she wouldn't wear it like this if we weren't here. Her phone is in a plastic cover with a purple trim, and she grips it tight as she answers Naila's questions.

Being the only phone-lady for miles around means Mrs Abida Sultan is in demand. She must be available 24 hours a day, 7 days a week. She is making between 7000 and 10,000 *taka* profit every month, about £70 to £100. A rural family needs about 5000 *taka* a month to survive, so, unlike most of those who live in Athalia, Mrs Abida Sultan can comfortably break out of the life of subsistence. Grameen Phone has enabled her to send her 19-year-old daughter to university, something she could previously never have dreamt of.

Naila says that, despite Grameen's success, the potential has barely been tapped. Only one million of the 140 million in Bangladesh have been connected through the mobile system, and Grameen Phone, half owned by the Norwegians, is now the biggest single investor in the country. The concept has been exported to poorer rural communities in places like Malaysia, Thailand and Ukraine.

The pace at which Naila and her PR team work is very different from the leisurely diurnal rhythms of this soft, warm, inviting countryside and once away from the village her mobile starts up again and doesn't stop until we're back in Dhaka.

For those able to survive the sound and fury of the capital there is a reward. Ishraq puts it simply.

'The best international cooking in Southeast Asia.'

And he's determined to prove it. Last night we ate some fine Chinese, surpassed tonight by a wonderfully authentic Lebanese dinner. And tomorrow, yet another strike day has been called, so we can stay in bed and sleep it off.

Day One Hundred and Twenty Three : Dhaka to the Delta

Life down in the delta rarely makes the news. Goings on in Dhaka, Chittagong and Sylhet hog the headlines. But today is different. In between all the *hartal* horror stories, the *New Nation* has a mention of the Sundarban Islands, my final destination. Apparently, the decomposed remains of six villagers, killed by man-eating Royal Bengal tigers, have been discovered deep in the mangrove forest. I sort of wish I hadn't read that.

On the way to the boat terminal, through lanes crowded with commerce and alleyways of go-downs where old men, still calculating by abacus, sit cross-legged beside sacks of rice or swat flies away from fruit stalls with feather dusters, we pass an incongruous set of cast-iron railings. Behind them rises the Ahsan Manzil, a wedding-cake pink building that was the palace of the Nawab Abdul Ghani, a Muslim and the largest landowner in East Bengal at the time of the Raj. By all accounts, this influential man was also a man of learning and culture, and his son Salimullah founded the Dhaka Medical School. The Pink Palace, as it's known, has been restored to its former glories and is a reminder of the beauty that lurks beneath the surface of this scuffed and overworked city, and makes me wish I'd had more time to explore.

The Sadarghat boat terminal is Dhaka at its most exasperating and exhilarating. Everyone fights for everything: parking and unloading space, space at the ticket counter, space on the long pontoons, space on the boats that moor up against them. No-one is actively hostile, they're just there. There where you want to be, and in huge numbers.

BELOW

Looking for the
Ostrich *at the*
Sadarghat boat
terminal, Dhaka.

After many wrong directions, I eventually find our boat and can't understand why I hadn't seen it earlier. With an ochre-painted superstructure and massive paddle wheels, the PS *Ostrich* is an old-fashioned, pleasing shape, like a great nautical sausage. It is part of the Rocket Service, pride of the succinctly named Bangladesh Inland Waterway Transport Corporation. The identification plaque records that its Year of Built (sic) was 1929 and that it was 'Renovated and Dieselized' in Narayagonj (just outside Dhaka) in 1996. It accommodates a total of 700 people on two decks and has 24 places in First Class.

I step onto the gangplank. Below me, the water is thundercloud grey. An evil-smelling, viscous grease-slick covers the surface of the Buriganga like lacquer. Then I'm shown to a flight of steps with a banister rail in polished wood, which leads up to the first class accommodation. Here, the world is transformed. The cabins, their numbers in polished brass, lead off a long and gracefully proportioned state room, down the centre of which runs an elegant mahogany table. The wood panelling on the walls is painted a subtle combination of light and dark grey, and interspersed at intervals with fluted bas-relief columns picked out in gold leaf. Outside, a covered deck set with tables and chairs offers the enticing prospect of cocktails at sunset. Sadly, this being a Muslim country, there is no bar on board, but Ishraq, ever ingenious, has access to supplies of his own.

Five minutes before our scheduled departure time the *Ostrich* emits two sonorous blasts from its horn, warning late-arriving passengers and waterborne tradesmen selling hard to the

open decks below us that departure is imminent. We cast off and pull away from the seething Sadarghat dead on time, narrowly avoiding collision with one of the many ferries fighting for our place at the pontoon.

Ishraq has invited a friend of his along, a delightful lady called Mahjabeen Khan, but known to all as Moni. She is probably not far from my own age, but is blessed with a good head of glossy dark hair and intensely dark eyes. She was born in Guwahati, Assam, but at Partition in 1947, her family, being Muslim, moved from there to Sylhet in what had become East Pakistan. Looking back now, she can see that trying to turn East Bengal into a part of Pakistan was a terrible mistake.

'They wanted us to behave differently, look differently, eat differently, dress differently. We were always a secular country.'

She and her seven siblings, six sisters and one brother, were sent to high school in Dhaka and encouraged to study a musical instrument. Moni discovered a talent for singing as well as playing and turned professional, until she married an ambassador and spent 15 years in Washington and Bangkok. Her husband, Abu Zafir Obaidullah Khan, was not just a diplomat and scholar but one of Bangladesh's leading poets. Her story seems to paint a portrait of a charmed life and it's quite a shock when Moni reveals that before she met Abu Zafir she had spent 12 largely unhappy years in an arranged marriage.

But before all that, when she was 13 or 14, she and her family took the Rocket Service when they went on holidays down south. She remembers its formality: the crisp linen tablecloth and gloved waiters in white uniforms with braided epaulettes, brass buttons and matching white turbans.

Tonight, there's less ceremony. People eat at different times. A tasty, fleshy local fish called *bekti* is served, but not with white gloves.

A thin, bespectacled man introduces himself after supper. He spent several years at the Botany Department at Sheffield University and, in one of those serendipitous moments that give travel a good name, I find myself on both the Ganges and the Brahmaputra swapping stories with a Bangladeshi botanist about the church I used to go to when I was nine.

The waterways of Bangladesh seem to operate on the same philosophy as the roads of Dhaka, an improbable synergy that, by the most dangerous means possible, successfully accommodates every kind of river user. None of them seem to have lights or horns. And as we don't have radar, Captain Mohammed Rahman has to rely on instinctive judgement.

I'm in bed in my cabin reading Patrick O'Brian when we make our first stop at Chandpur.

There is a lot of noise and light and the sound of shouts and the slap of sandals, and the loading and unloading is still going on when I put down my book about Napoleonic sea battles, feeling that, perhaps, past and present aren't so far apart.

Day One Hundred and Twenty Four : Chandpur to Mongla

Up at six. It's a soft, drowsy morning. The banks are shrouded in mist, from which fields and trees occasionally emerge, tinged with diffused morning sunlight. The mist and the water mingle, giving the impression that everything, on water and land, is floating.

From a map on the wall of the state room and a few enquiries to the waiters, I work out that we are west of the main river channel and south of Barisal, heading slowly through a maze of curling rivers in the rough direction of the Sundarbans National Park. Breakfast is a disappointingly routine affair, enlivened only by discovering that my bottle of 'Mum' mineral water is proudly labelled 'Official Drink For the 10th Asian Conference on Diarrhoeal Diseases'.

At half-past seven we reach a place called Jahlokati. An archetypal scene of passengers waiting beneath a spreading neem tree, a few thatched buildings and a tin-roofed warehouse, its walls stuck with political posters and daubed with slogans. The signs are only in Bangla, reminding us that we are well away from the cosmopolitan world of Dhaka. Well away from the hustle and bustle too. Though a lot of people are getting on and off here, the noise is as muted as the morning light.

As the gangplank goes down, the line of disembarking passengers begins to move, most of them balancing their possessions in bundles or cardboard boxes on their heads. Then the porters come aboard and take off the big stuff: massive, tight-strapped, white bundles that are manoeuvred slowly up the gangplank to the accompaniment of a chant.

The river is low and the root systems of the mangrove trees run along the banks like exposed wiring. A slew of fresh-cut logs is floating up against the shore and a man, balancing on one of them, dips his hand in the water and cleans his teeth with his finger.

The timeless rural peace is shattered by the warning sound of the ship's horn, which reverberates around this quiet little place like the roar of a bull elephant. After ten minutes or so, the gangplanks are raised, provoking the usual last-minute rush, as people leap out of the bushes and race aboard.

Our kitchen staff have secured a sackful of green coconuts, which they split open for us, and we drink the sweet but cool milk as we pull out onto the stream again.

A few minutes later, a modern concrete bridge materializes, silently, shockingly, out of the mist, then slips away behind us and we're back into the past again. Spreading rain trees, rubber trees and date palms cluster tight along the bank. A white-robed figure strides dramatically among them. Deep-hulled, tall-prowed boats, like Chinese sampans, bob up and down in our wake. I watch an immensely distinguished-looking man with a bushy, grey beard carefully prepare his fishing net. He tosses it into the water and slowly pulls it in and examines it. There is nothing there but mud. With infinite patience, he gathers the line, tosses it out and draws it in again. Nothing.

There is something about the dignity both of the man and his slow work that leaves an impression. And the fact that he never once looks up as a yellow 1920s paddle steamer with 700 people on board goes by.

The morning wears on. The sun grows stronger, but I find it hard to tear myself away from the deck rail. The dancing silver patterns of light reflected on the water, the gradual release of the countryside from the mist, the sound of a flute drifting across, all create a feeling of the world slowed down, a seductive and fragile sense of peace.

Moni and I are talking about this, about how the world's most crowded country can offer such a sense of calm, and she asks if I've read any of Tagore's work. I'm ashamed to say I haven't. Rabandranath Tagore was the Shakespeare of Bengal. A crude metaphor, perhaps, but it reflects his status here. He was a poet and playwright and, though he was a Hindu, he wrote of the universal preoccupations of Bengalis and particularly of the countryside, which, Moni thinks, has changed not at all since he died over 60 years ago. He had an international reputation, winning the Nobel Prize for Literature in 1913, and being awarded a knighthood by the British, which he returned in protest at the massacre in Amritsar in 1919. (Evidence of which I saw on Day 30.)

A lot of Moni's favourite songs are Tagore's poems set to music and she sings some to me as the countryside he celebrated slips past. As Moni points out, he was sympathetic but never sentimental about the rural life. We are in what they call 'cyclone alley', and in Tagore's time, just like now, this golden panorama of huge skies and wide water, of rice paddies and thatched houses, bordered by the long, dark outline of the mangrove forest, could be transformed overnight into a killing field by the storms that brew up over the Bay of Bengal.

One of the songs Moni sings tells of the bruised Bengali people standing in a line, crying, and asking their god to 'speak into our ears and into our hearts and tell us there is good news'.

We stop more frequently now and in the middle of the afternoon pull up at the jetty of a small settlement rejoicing in the name of Moralgunj. Big crows eye us from the bare branches of a dying mangrove tree.

I've worked out that the relative importance of our ports of call can be determined by the number of gangplanks the ship puts out. Chandpur was a four-plank stop, but Moralgunj is only a two-plank stop. Mongla, where we arrive after 13 hours, is Bangladesh's second port after Chittagong. It's also where we bid goodbye to the *Ostrich*, and disembark down five planks, with a security rail on either side.

Day One Hundred and Twenty Five: Mongla to the Bay of Bengal

There is one task we have to complete today and that is to cover the remaining 90 miles (144 km) between here and the Bay of Bengal, and rendezvous with a forestry department launch, which will take me out onto the ocean and off into the sunset for the final shot of the series.

I'm up before five. Shower, pack my things together, grab a basic breakfast at the Hotel Pashur, then walk out past the bus station and down to the jetty, where two of the three boats on which our day depends are bobbing up and down on the water. They don't inspire confidence. Named *Feni 1* and *Feni 3*, after a frontier town north of Chittagong, they're ex-lifeboats with a Do-It-Yourself viewing platform built on top and furnished with plastic chairs. The boat is steered from the top deck by a Heath Robinson rudder extension made from various pieces of scrap metal, into which is fitted a handle made from a tree branch. Well, not made from it exactly. It *is* a tree branch.

This whole unsteady collation is topped with a few lengths of domestic, wrought-iron railing and a sun canopy suspended from four sticks.

The crew is lively and enthusiastic. Unlike the engine.

We cast off at dawn and, as the light slowly improves, we can see our surroundings are as magical as yesterday. We chug through a clinging mist, past the temporarily exposed mudflats they call *chars*, islands that appear briefly after the flood waters recede and are instantly planted so that at least one crop can be harvested before the next monsoon washes the island away.

About an hour south of Mongla, the cultivated land comes to an abrupt end and we are

hemmed in by the dark, impenetrable walls of the largest coastal mangrove belt in the world. There are few settlements down here, and the short, steep, slimy banks offer no landing opportunities. If one needed any further reason for staying away, the forest is also the habitat of the much feared Royal Bengal tiger, whom the people of the forest refer to as 'uncle'. It's considered bad luck to utter its real name.

Occasionally, we come across some fishing boats, at which, oblivious to our deadline, the cooks insist on stopping so they can investigate luncheon ingredients. They eventually settle on crab, sweet-water lobster and some of the largest prawns I've ever seen. Ishraq says these are of such quality that these small fishermen sell them on to bigger trawlers, which take them up to freezer plants at Mongla, from where they will be sent to the dining tables of the USA and Europe. It's a business worth $100 million a year.

I watch kingfishers skimming along the shoreline and a fish-eagle with bold, rufous wings hunting in our wake, snapping up tiny fish and eating them on the wing. After a while, I drift into a deep sleep in which I dream someone shouts.

'Michael! Crocodile!'

I wake up to hear someone shouting.

'Michael! Crocodile! Look!'

And I do, just in time to catch sight of a grey metallic shape the size of a small submarine turn its panto-villain face towards me and slide into the river, sending out waves of repulsion and muddy brown water. I feel sorry for crocodiles. Just because God gave them teeth too big for their mouths and yellow eyes that open and shut like Porsche headlights you can't imagine them ever having a single decent thought. But for all I know, they might be quite lovable, salt-of-the-earth reptiles who, given half a chance, might well help an old lady across the road and surprise us all by not eating her.

Worn out by all this mental exercise, I go back to sleep until lunch. And what a lunch. The cooks have achieved a minor miracle. In a tiny space beside the toilet they have cooked up the crab, prawn and lobster with turmeric, quince, chilli, coriander, onions and ginger into a perfectly balanced and gorgeously fresh-tasting stew, which must rate as one of the best meals on the entire journey.

After this celebration, sober reality intrudes. Time is no longer on our side. One of the boats is not even making nine knots and, in a last hope of reaching our rendezvous, we lash the two

ABOVE

The end of the journey. Ishraq, with baseball cap and radio, gets our accidental actors organized.

Fenis together and use the power of the better performing engine.

From here on, it's all anxiety. Looking at watches and trying not to look at them at the same time. Watching the sky, cursing the slightest headwind, fearing the worst at every change in engine tone.

With less than an hour to go until sunset, the waterway opens out into a wider bay and suddenly we are at the sea. Not far ahead, with huge relief, we catch sight of the jetty at Katka, where we have arranged to meet up with our forestry launch. The only thing missing is the forestry launch.

By the time we reach the tall, mud-encrusted pier and the launch still isn't there, we have resigned ourselves to the fact that it's never going to be there in time. We look around helplessly.

The place is silent and empty apart from the curved ribcages of boats long-since abandoned to the mud.

Then into the bay comes another boat, a plain but picturesque small trawler with pointed prow, central cabin and some heavy structure at the stern. It's moving steadily towards the jetty. Ishraq issues orders. As soon as the fishing boat reaches the shore, the bemused crew find themselves, literally, roped into the final sequence of a BBC television series.

Feni 3, acting as camera boat, is roped up to the trawler and a complicated procedure worked out, in which, having delivered my last piece to camera from the fishing boat, the ropes will be loosened and I and the plucky little trawler will drift off into the sunset.

It is a crazy, impossibly risky idea, depending on split-second timing, but, with total credit to everyone concerned, we complete a successful take minutes before the sun and the Bay of Bengal merge.

In the last words of this last shot, I say that, despite all the wonders I have seen, the majestic scenery of a half-dozen countries, the power and majesty of the highest mountain range on earth, it is the people I've met that will stick in my mind.

The enjoyment of the world is immeasurably enhanced not just by meeting people who think, look, talk and dress differently from yourself, but by having to depend on them. The trio of Bangladeshi fishermen who learnt the arcane art of television filming in a little less than half an hour are only the last of a long list of those who had every reason to think that we were completely mad, but who decided, against all the odds, to be our friends instead.

In the heady rush of our emergency ending, I almost forgot why we were here. Only after the camera's turned off for the last time and we're heading for the muddy shores of the Sundarban Islands do I have time to feel that umbilical connection between the water I'm on now and the remote mountains where it all began for us, many months and several thousand miles ago.

Acknowledgements

At four o'clock on the morning of 25 September 2003, in a cheerless hotel foyer in Delhi, Roger, cameraman Nigel Meakin and I celebrated, as best we could, an anniversary of sorts. It was 15 years ago to the day that, at the Reform Club in London, Roger had called 'Action!' and set *Around the World in Eighty Days* in motion. One thing we all agreed on that morning in Delhi is that not for one minute had any of us imagined we'd still be travelling together five series and a decade and a half later.

I owe Roger a great debt of thanks for being patient and tolerant, careful, critical and above all wonderful company. As series producer, he took the lion's share of responsibility for *Himalaya* and, as co-director, led Saga Platoon through Pakistan, India and Bangladesh.

John-Paul Davidson, who directed us in Nepal, Tibet and Yunnan in China, Nagaland, Assam and Bhutan, is a veteran of the Himalaya and his unflagging mix of energy, enthusiasm and invention was only matched by his empathy with the people, his love of the countries and his ability to produce fresh-brewed ground coffee at any altitude. Nigel Meakin made a mockery of the passing years by producing superb work in often awful and uncomfortable circumstances. Peter Meakin, his son and heir, is not only a credit to the family filming business, but also a dab hand with the sound recorder who got us out of a hole or two when altitude sickness struck. For a few weeks we were sadly deprived of John Pritchard's affable company, as it was he who the altitude struck. His replacement, Chris Joyce, came out from England at very short notice, and ably picked up the baton (or whatever it is that sound recordists hold).

Vanessa Courtney, iron fist in velvet glove, negotiated us brilliantly through the choppy waters of security-ridden Pakistan and India, and the manic delights of Bangladesh. Claire Houdret soothed frayed nerves in Nepal, Nina Huang Fan was a tower of strength in China and Havana Marking and Natalia Fernandez kept morale up in the rarely trodden pathways of Nagaland and Assam. No-one could have looked after us better in the high Himalaya than Wongchuk Sherpa, Mingmar Dorji Sherpa (who reached the top of Everest on 17 May 2004) and Nawang Dorjee Sherpa. Migma was both on-screen and off-screen star in Tibet.

Life on the road would not be complete without Basil Pao, gastronomic adviser, menu translator, peerless photographer and, I suspect, closet trekker.

RIGHT

Saga Platoon (with apologies to young Peter Meakin) meets the Dalai Lama. (left to right) Roger Mills, Thingy, DL, Nigel Meakin, Peter Meakin, Vanessa Courtney, Basil Pao, John Pritchard.

VANESSA COURTNEY

In the front office, the experienced hands and cool heads of Anne James and Mirabel Brook once again set our journey up with speed and great efficiency. Anne watched us through to the end, whilst Sue Grant stepped into Mirabel's shoes with aplomb. Natalia Fernandez worked tirelessly throughout the series, counting us out and counting us back. Lyn Dougherty and Steve Abbott took on the care of finances, and kept us both above the law and in the black. Paul Bird has done just about everything for us, short of coming on the journey, and Alison Davies has been wonderfully encouraging, as ever, as well as uncomplainingly taking on perhaps the worst job in the world – deciphering my sound tapes.

Special thanks to the sage of Harlesden, Alex Richardson, who should by now have been made the first saint of the editing world. Thanks too to Saska Simpson for taking on Alex's role on one of the shows. And to Lorraine Heggessey, Nicola Moody and Tom Archer at the BBC for their continuous and constructive support.

Apart from those mentioned in my text I would like to thank others without whom Himalaya would have remained just another mountain range: Jonny Bealby, Abdul Kadur Jaffer, General Rashid Quereshi, Anuraag Jacob, Onkar Singh, Holly Williams. Mr Yang Le, Sun Shuyun, Mr. Ding Duzhang, Yatish Bahuguna, Fazal Kamal, Doug Scott. We would have got nowhere without Maqsood Ul-Mulk and Hindukush Trails in Pakistan, Royal Expeditions in New Delhi, Peak Promotions in Nepal, Chhundu Travel in Bhutan and Purvi Discovery in Assam. Special thanks to all at Whitehouse Cox who made me two shoulder bags that went with me everywhere, and to Mike Griffin for all those farewells and welcomes.

Enormous thanks, too, to all those at Weidenfeld & Nicolson who have worked wonders to produce a complex book in such a short time, Michael Dover, my editor, whose unflappable and generous support was never more necessary, David Rowley, my art director and designer, who has done a fine job at a furious pace, ably assisted by Austin Taylor and Justin Hunt.

To Claire Marsden for making sure I spelt her name right, as well as about 4000 others. Thank you also to Tara Redmond and Angela Martin for making sure the world knows we exist and, finally, special thanks to Richard Hussey, who rejected a life of ease to stay on and see this book through production.

JOHN PRITCHARD

LEFT

With (right to left) John-Paul Davidson, Nawang Dorjee Sherpa and son, and Wongchu Sherpa, at the Yak and Yeti Hotel, Kathmandu.

Reading matter

Footprint, *Lonely Planet* and *Rough Guides* were never far from my side, but Isobel Shaw's *Pakistan Handbook*, Michael Buckley's *Bradt Guide to Tibet* and Francoise Pommaret's *Odyssey Guide to Bhutan* were outstanding. The beautifully illustrated *Insight Guides* add a touch of local colour. I eagerly devoured Patrick French's three books on the history of the region: *Younghusband*, *Tibet Tibet* and *Liberty or Death*, whilst among other favourites were Kathleen Jamie's *Among Muslims*, Peter Matthiessen's *The Snow Leopard*, Geoffrey Moorhouse's *To The Frontier*, Peter Hopkins' *Trespassers on the Roof of the World*, Sun Shuyun's *Ten Thousand Miles Without a Cloud*, Namu's enchanting *Leaving Mother Lake* and Romesh Bhattacharji's travels in Assam, *Lands of Early Dawn*.

First published in the United Kingdom in 2004 by Weidenfeld & Nicolson

THOMAS DUNNE BOOKS.
An imprint of St. Martin's Press.

www.stmartins.com

Library of Congress Cataloging Information Available upon Request

ISBN 0-312-34162-8
EAN 978-0312-34162-6

First published in Great Britain by Weidenfeld & Nicolson
First U.S. Edition

10 9 8 7 6 5 4 3 2 1

Design and art direction by David Rowley
Editor Claire Marsden
Design assistance by Austin Taylor and Justin Hunt
Maps by Maps Ink

Visit *www.palinstravels.co.uk*

PAGE 1

Tickling the ivories, Kaziranga National Park, Assam.

PAGE 2

On the footplate, Khyber Railway.

LEFT

Making notes at the shipbreakers yard, Chittagong.